Building Bridges Through FAITH:
The Journey Continues Journal

SUNDAY SCHOOL

FAITH
ADVANCED
™

EVANGELISM STRATEGY

Bobby H. Welch and Doug Williams

as developed with David Apple

LifeWay™

ISBN: 0-7673-9443-7
This book is a resource in the Leadership and Skill Development Category of the
Christian Growth Study Plan for course numbers
LS-0037, LS-0050, and LS-0054 (Sunday School).

Dewey Decimal Classification: 269.2
Subject Heading: EVANGELISTIC WORK IN THE SUNDAY SCHOOL

Printed in the United States of America

Sunday School Group
LifeWay Christian Resources of the Southern Baptist Convention
127 Ninth Avenue, North
Nashville, Tennessee 37234

As God works through us . . .
We will help people and churches know Jesus Christ and seek His Kingdom
by providing biblical solutions that spiritually transform
individuals and cultures.

Acknowledgements:
Scripture quotations marked NIV are from the Holy Bible, *New International
Version* © copyright 1973, 1978, 1984 by International Bible Society.

The *New King James Version* is the text for Scripture memory in the FAITH
gospel presentation. Scripture quotations marked NKJV are from *New King James
Version,* © 1979, 1980, 1982, Thomas Nelson, Inc. Publishers. Used by permission.

*The FAITH Sunday School Evangelism Strategy® is an evangelistic venture of
LifeWay Christian Resources of the Southern Baptist Convention and is endorsed
by the North American Mission Board.*

Expression of Commitment

Dedicated to all FAITH participants who are continuing their journeys of faith through Building Bridges training

Building Bridges Through FAITH:
The Journey Continues

I commit myself to continue **FAITH** Sunday School evangelism training in my church. I recognize **FAITH** training as a way to help my church and Sunday School, to continue to grow as a Great Commission Christian, to be obedient to God's command to be an active witness, and to equip others to share their faith.

_____
(SIGNATURE)

Address: _____

Phone Number: _____

My Role in Building Bridges: ❏ Team Leader

❏ Assistant Team Leader　❏ Other_____

My Sunday School Class/Department:

_____

Dates of My FAITH Advanced (Building Bridges) Training:

_____

Contents

Foreword

The FAITH Sunday School Evangelism Strategy was born out of a desire to see churches become involved in a process that would lead the church member to become a Great Commission Christian. This process begins with the teaching and modeling of Jesus and of His disciples. In 2 Timothy 2:1-2 Paul exhorts Timothy to be strong in the grace of Christ Jesus and to go and teach others.

First Baptist Church, Daytona Beach, Florida—the birthplace of the FAITH Sunday School Evangelism Strategy—sought to train 28 churches in this process. After implementing FAITH for themselves, those churches (under the direction of LifeWay Christian Resources) began holding training clinics to train other churches in this process.

By the time you receive the material for FAITH Advanced training, entitled *Building Bridges Through FAITH: The Journey Continues*, more than 3,000 churches will have been trained in FAITH Basic, the first semester of FAITH (A Journey in FAITH).

The FAITH Sunday School Evangelism Strategy is a process through the Sunday School of a local church. It is not a program in a box, but a process in a big picture, in which the church functions as a Great Commission church.

FAITH Advanced will lead FAITH members to help those they reach for Christ to follow up in baptism and to enroll in and become active in a Sunday School class. Building Bridges will help the FAITH Team members be sensitive to how God works ahead of them and wants them to depend daily on the Holy Spirit.

I want to encourage you as a FAITH church to build a bridge for those new people coming into your church. I also want to thank you for being faithful to the cause of Christ.

It is my prayer that, as a FAITH Team member, you remain faithful to the teaching of our Lord Jesus and that, as you serve Him through the FAITH process, God may be honored and glorified. Thank you for building bridges to people.

With a Grateful Heart,

Jay Johnston, Director
Sunday School/FAITH Ministry Department

How Can You Build Bridges?

According to *Merriam Webster's Collegiate Dictionary, Tenth Edition*, one definition of bridge is "a time, place, or means of connection or transition."[1] Other synonyms for this meaning of *bridge* might be *relationships, personal connections, or rapport* that establishes trust. Everyone has experienced this kind of significant connection with another person.

As a Great Commission Christian who is experiencing the dynamics of FAITH, you are part of a "construction" process. You not only are consciously "constructing" means and opportunities to connect with people, you also are allowing God to strengthen your foundations of faith in Him and trust in His leadership throughout all of life.

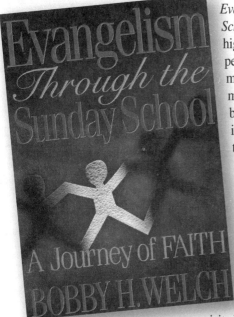

Look again at the art on *Evangelism Through the Sunday School: A Journey of FAITH*. The highlighted person is linked personally to two other people— much like you will be to your Team members. The next 16 weeks will bond the three of you in inexplicable ways, as you work together toward common goals.

This art also can represent a Great Commission Christian, who links his church and Sunday School to the community. Those linkages occur in daily life; in intentional visits; in ministry actions; and in other ways.

One of the privileges you have is to continue to make visits into the community and to "connect" someone, perhaps for the first time, to Christ and to the church. You will learn how to help a new believer cross a bridge into obedience, discipleship, and growth.

In another sense, the highlighted person in this cover art could represent a group—your Sunday School class/department. FAITH can help strengthen that linkage to members who need to grow in their faith through the experiences of the Sunday School class/department.

If these examples do not describe bridge building, then read "Tony Remembers" (viii-ix), the basis of our theme interpretation on video (Part 1, Session 1). It is a poignant reminder of what can happen when one Team or one person is obedient. Refer to it throughout training for encouragement.

Ask (and answer) a question that is the basis for this semester of training: *Can I build a bridge to someone today?*

Think about some meanings and implications of bridges:

"To bridge" means 1: to make a bridge over or across (to join by a bridge) 2: to provide with a bridge.[2]

Other synonyms of the verb are to join, connect, link, span ("Oh, the mighty gulf that God did *span* at Calvary")

Definitions of the verb "connect" include to have or establish rapport; to place or establish in relationship.

---

[1] *Merriam Webster's Collegiate Dictionary, Tenth Edition*, "bridge," 142.
[2] Ibid., 142.

Tony Remembers

I never knew the spiritual shape I was in. I hoped everything was alright between me and God . . . I tried hard to do what was right . . . to be a good father and husband . . . a good neighbor. So I just kept on working hard to be good, hoping it would be enough. But I remember thinking "there's gotta be more." I didn't know God wanted a personal relationship with me.

I didn't realize then that there was this huge gulf between me and God.

Then three people came to my door, and nothing has been the same since.

They told me about Jesus. They told me about abundant life. They told me about heaven. And for the first time in my life I spoke to God, actually believing that He heard me. And I gave my life to Jesus.

Those three people became a bridge for me. A bridge to walk from my life across that huge gulf to the abundant life God wants for me.

Those people became a bridge for me to walk into a world where I was not ashamed of Jesus, . . .

. . . where the love and friendship of a Sunday School class helped my faith and love grow;

. . . where my commitment to my new church family was publicly proclaimed;

Now every time I cross a bridge I am reminded of where I used to be and where I am now and I remember those three people. And then I stop and think . . . I can help build a bridge for someone on the other side, too.

My friend Andrew talks a lot about divine appointments. Would I have come to know Jesus without those three people? Would I have known the joy of His church? Would I have experienced the thrill of sharing my faith? Maybe . . . maybe not. Would that have been my last chance to respond to the gospel? I don't know.

But God knew that night what I needed and He knew what Andrew, George, and Myra needed. And He brought us together. God was there, and none of us have been the same since.

Now I see people every day and I wonder if they know what I know . . . if they know Jesus the way I know Him. Does God have an appointment with us?

FAITH VISIT OUTLINE

Preparation

INTRODUCTION

INTERESTS

INVOLVEMENT

    Church Experience/Background

        Ask about the person's church background.

        Listen for clues about the person's spiritual involvement.

    Sunday School Testimony

        Tell general benefits of Sunday School.

        Tell a current personal experience.

    Evangelistic Testimony

        Tell a little of your pre-conversion experience.

        Say: "I had a life-changing experience."

        Tell recent benefits of your conversion.

INQUIRE

Key Question: In your personal opinion, what do you understand it takes for a person to go to heaven?

    Possible answers: Faith, works, unclear, no opinion

Transition Statement: I'd like to share with you how the Bible answers this question, if it is all right. There is a word that can be used to answer this question: *FAITH (spell out on fingers).*

Presentation

F is for FORGIVENESS.

We cannot have eternal life and heaven without God's forgiveness.

    "In Him [meaning Jesus] we have redemption through His blood, the forgiveness of sins"—Ephesians 1:7a, NKJV.

A is for AVAILABLE.

Forgiveness is available. It is—

AVAILABLE FOR ALL

    "For God so loved the world that He gave His only begotten Son, that whoever believes in Him should not perish but have everlasting life"— John 3:16, NKJV.

BUT NOT AUTOMATIC

    "Not everyone who says to Me, 'Lord, Lord,' shall enter the kingdom of heaven"—Matthew 7:21a, NKJV.

I is for IMPOSSIBLE.

It is impossible for God to allow sin into heaven.

GOD IS—

    • **LOVE**

        John 3:16, NKJV

    • **JUST**

        "For judgment is without mercy"—James 2:13a, NKJV.

MAN IS SINFUL

> *"For all have sinned and fall short of the glory of God"—Romans 3:23, NKJV.*

Question: But how can a sinful person enter heaven, where God allows no sin?

T is for TURN.

Question: If you were driving down the road and someone asked you to turn, what would he or she be asking you to do? (change direction)

Turn means repent.

TURN from something—sin and self

> *"But unless you repent you will all likewise perish"—Luke 13:3b, NKJV.*

TURN to Someone; trust Christ only

> (The Bible tells us that) *"Christ died for our sins according to the Scriptures, and that He was buried, and that He rose again the third day according to the Scriptures"—1 Corinthians 15:3b-4, NKJV.*
>
> *"If you confess with your mouth the Lord Jesus and believe in your heart that God has raised Him from the dead, you will be saved"—Romans 10:9, NKJV.*

H is for HEAVEN.

Heaven is eternal life.

HERE

> *"I have come that they may have life, and that they may have it more abundantly"—John 10:10b, NKJV.*

HEREAFTER

> *"And if I go and prepare a place for you, I will come again and receive you to Myself; that where I am, there you may be also"—John 14:3, NKJV.*

HOW

> How can a person have God's forgiveness, heaven and eternal life, and Jesus as personal Savior and Lord?
>
> Explain based on leaflet picture, F.A.I.T.H. (Forsaking All I Trust Him), Romans 10:9.

Invitation

INQUIRE

Understanding what we have shared, would you like to receive this forgiveness by trusting in Christ as your personal Savior and Lord?

INVITE

> Pray to accept Christ.
>
> Pray for commitment/recommitment.
>
> Invite to join Sunday School.

INSURE

Use *A Step of Faith* to insure decision.

> **Personal Acceptance**
>
> **Sunday School Enrollment**
>
> **Public Confession**

What's Ahead
in Building Bridges

Date, _____ **Session 1: Building Bridges—an Orientation**
  Purposes/outcomes: To overview goals and content for the next 16 weeks; to equip Team Leaders to lead their Teams in FAITH; to emphasize Sunday School as a visible, vital bridge between saved/unsaved people and the church

Date, _____ **Session 2: Building Bridges of Growth and Commitment**
  Purposes/outcomes: To review growth commitments a new believer might make during a FAITH visit and the Team's use of *A Step of Faith*; to reinforce the responsibility of the FAITH Team to follow up; to emphasize Sunday School's role in building bridges between the new believer/family and the church

Date, _____ **Session 3: Building Bridges to Baptism Using** *My Next*
                       Step of Faith
  Purposes/outcomes: To enable Team members to participate effectively in a FAITH follow-up visit to discuss baptism and to use the leaflet *My Next Step of Faith* as a tool for encouraging a new believer to take that step of obedience

Date, _____ **Session 4: Building Bridges Through Follow-up Visits**
  Purposes/outcomes: To review principles and processes for making other kinds of follow-up visits

Date, _____ **Session 5: Building Bridges to People with the**
                       Opinion Poll
  Purposes/outcomes: To enable Team members to use the Opinion Poll as a tool to discover prospects, to engage in nonthreatening conversation with the unchurched/unsaved, and to share the gospel as opportunities allow

Date, _____ **Session 6: Building Bridges with the FAITH Visit**
                       Outline: FORGIVENESS and AVAILABLE
  Purposes/outcomes: To review FORGIVENESS and AVAILABLE in the FAITH Visit Outline, adding some verses and illustrations to increase understanding

Date, _____ **Session 7: Building Bridges with the FAITH Visit**
                       Outline: IMPOSSIBLE and TURN
  Purposes/outcomes: To review IMPOSSIBLE and TURN in the FAITH Visit Outline, adding some verses and illustrations to increase understanding

Date, _____   **Session 8: Building Bridges with the FAITH Visit**
                        Outline: HEAVEN and the *Invitation*
  Purposes/outcomes: To review HEAVEN and the *Invitation* in the FAITH Visit
Outline; to equip Team Leaders to lead their Teams effectively through these points
in a visit

Date, _____   **Session 9: Building Bridges to People Through**
                        Sunday School
  Purposes/outcomes: To reinforce the importance of the various kinds of Sunday
School ministry visits; to explain the Sunday School's role in assimilating new
believers; to suggest ways classes/departments might be more effective in
assimilation actions

Date, _____   **Session 10: Building Bridges to the Entire Family**
  Purposes/outcomes: To remind participants to consider the potential of reaching
an entire family for Christ, especially after one member has made a decision; to
point out approaches for follow-up, cultivation, or conversation according to the
age group being addressed; to emphasize enrolling family members in appropriate
classes and departments

Date, _____   **Session 11: Building Bridges for Divine Appointments**
  Purposes/outcomes: To remind participants how God works ahead of them to
prepare hearts for the gospel; to encourage dependence on the Holy Spirit

Date, _____   **Session 12: Building Bridges Through Practicing FAITH**
  Purposes/outcomes: To devote time to practice by Teams

Date, _____   **Session 13: Building Bridges in Daily Life**
  Purposes/outcomes: To remind participants to be sensitive to daily-life
witnessing opportunities and to be intentional in sharing FAITH in such settings

Date, _____   **Session 14: Building Bridges to People During**
                        Difficult Visits
  Purposes/outcomes: To provide FAITH participants with specific approaches for
handling situations they may encounter

Date, _____   **Session 15: Building Bridges for a Stronger**
                        FAITH Strategy
  Purposes/outcomes: To emphasize the importance of continuing in FAITH; to
build bridges to potential Learners, encouraging them to be part of FAITH

Date, _____   **Session 16: Celebrating Building Bridges: Final Checkup**
  Purposes/outcomes: To assess, through a written review, how much participants
have learned during Building Bridges; to provide a time of celebration and
recognition (if a FAITH Festival is not scheduled later).

A Look at Your Resources

Your journey of faith continues. *Building Bridges Through FAITH: The Journey Continues* will enhance and reinforce earlier FAITH training experiences. There is no new memory work; you already have learned the **FAITH Visit Outline.** You will continue using it in visits and will learn to share it with greater confidence.

Building Bridges can help you continue to grow as a Great Commission Christian. During the next 16 weeks, expect God to work in your life, in your Sunday School/church, in the lives of people you meet, and in your Team.

As was true in FAITH Basic, you have a **Journal** as your main resource. You can expect similar training times each week—**Team Time** (15 min.), in which you debrief and work together as a Team; **Teaching Time** (45 min.), in which you and Learners go separate directions for a focused time to learn appropriate new information; **Visitation Time** (110+ min. depending on your church's schedule), that vital time when, as a Team, you put feet to prayers and training; and **Celebration Time** (30 min.), a time to report Team and FAITH strategy victories.

Each week commit to be on time; to listen attentively during Teaching Time; and to ask questions. After you have filled in the blanks for each session, it can be helpful during home study to re-read that session for the big picture.

If you are a Team Leader, the "Leading Team Time" suggestions each week will help you debrief, practice, and review with your Team. Suggestions are based on Learners' *A Journey in FAITH: Journal* Team Time agendas for each week.

Home Study Assignments continue to be important. They provide ways to reflect on your personal growth ("Your Journey Continues") and tools to help do your work as Team Leader ("An Important Bridge: the Weekly Sunday School Leadership Team Meeting," "For the Team Leader"). Occasional "FAITH at Work" testimonies provide examples of how God is at work in other churches, too.

You will grow in faith as you put into practice 2 Timothy 2:1-2. You may have taken on the privilege of mentoring two new Learners. They will be uncertain, concerned, excited—just as you once were. Keep in touch during the week. Explain why you handled a visit a particular way. Pray for Learners and seek to help them.

In addition, you will learn to use a **new leaflet:** *My Next Step of Faith— Baptism.* This resource may be used in follow-up visits when baptism is discussed.

Your Facilitator is using these resources to help you enjoy training and learn: **video,** in which different visits are modeled, the FAITH Visit Outline is reviewed, and evidence of changed lives becomes apparent; **cels or PowerPoint® computer slides** to help you fill in the blanks and understand that session's teaching.

Your Sunday School class and department is one of your "main resources." It is the unique dynamic of FAITH. Your class/department can be where names become people, needs become visible, and assimilation become more than a term. Attending the weekly Sunday School leadership team meeting creates this bridge.

Prayer is your most important and most powerful resource. The Lord has promised to hear us when we call on Him. Call on Him throughout FAITH.

FAITH PARTICIPATION CARD

Name _____   Semester Dates _____

Address _____   Phone _____

Sunday School Dept. _____Teacher _____

Other Team Members: _____

Circle One:　　　　FAITH Team Leader　　　　FAITH Learner　　　　Assistant Team Leader

	1	2	3	4	5	6	7	8	9	10	11	12	13	14	15	16	Totals
CLASS PARTICIPATION *Place a check to indicate completion for appropriate session.*																	
Present																	
Home study done																	
Outline recited																	
VISITATION *Indicate a number for following areas.*																	
No. of Tries																	
No. Visits																	
No. People Talked with																	
TYPE OF VISIT (Assignments)																	
Evangelistic																	
Ministry																	
Follow-up																	
Opinion Poll																	
GOSPEL PRESENTED																	
Profession																	
Assurance																	
No Decision																	
For Practice																	
GOSPEL NOT PRESENTED																	
Already Christian																	
No Admission																	
SS ENROLLMENT																	
Attempted																	
Enrolled																	
LIFE WITNESS																	
Profession																	
Assurance																	
No Decision																	

SESSION 1

Building Bridges— an Orientation

I n this session you will

HEAR IT: be introduced to "The Person God Uses" devotional segment that is a feature in every session—and to the importance of allowing God to use you; overview ways, through FAITH Advanced, to build bridges to your FAITH Team, to the Sunday School, and to unchurched people;

SEE IT: see video on the impact of building bridges and on ways to build bridges through FAITH;

STUDY IT: overview Home Study Assignments for Session 1.

The Journey Continues

Welcome to the second course in FAITH training, *Building Bridges Through FAITH: The Journey Continues.* Your journey in faith indeed will continue as you participate in this vital second semester of FAITH training.

If you are like most FAITH participants, you can recall some wonderful spiritual experiences and insights from A Journey in FAITH—and some challenges to your faith. Know that God will keep on honoring your commitment and desire to grow as a Great Commission Christian. Know also that you are helping our church in many ways.

Everyone receiving this training has learned the FAITH Visit Outline; you have participated as a FAITH Team Learner. *Many* have agreed to serve as Team Leaders; know that God will honor that desire to equip others from your Sunday School class or department. *All* will be assisting individuals who are learning to share their faith; we will be encouraging them as, through FAITH training, they take steps of obedience as Great Commission Christians.

Although there is no additional memory work in Building Bridges, this training will provide information and experiences to supplement your role in assisting Team members to share their faith. This course also will help you focus on being a person God uses.

The Person God Uses
The person God uses is saved and secure.

On page 126 of *Evangelism Through the Sunday School: A Journey of FAITH*, Bobby Welch lists a number of characteristics of a person God uses. As you consider four very important ones now, place a check mark in each box that reflects your response.

1. I know that I am saved.   Yes ____   No ____
2. I have assurance of my salvation.   Yes ____   No ____
3. I have followed Christ in scriptural baptism.   Yes ____   No ____
4. I am active in Sunday School and church.   Yes ____   No ____

"The person God uses to do soul winning is to be a saved person, a born-again soul with a personal relationship to Jesus Christ as Savior and Lord" (p. 120). Welch continues, "The saved person needs to be assured of his or her own salvation. If you are in doubt about your salvation, . . . stop

. . . and thank Jesus . . . for keeping you alive to this moment. . . .

"State your belief in His death, burial, and resurrection. You are turning from yourself and your sin to accept His forgiveness. You trust in Jesus and Him alone for your salvation" (rephrase, p. 121). As you are saved and secure in your salvation, both your life and your words will draw people to Him.

Also consider the importance of praying for God to use you. How serious are you about being used by God? Do you know what you are asking when you tell God you want to be used by Him?

Are you certain you want to be stretched as well as blessed? Are you ready to be sent across the street or across other barriers? Are you ready for the kinds of experiences that are ahead, experiences that both strengthen and purify the believer?

Understand that growing as a Christian means growing in your willingness to do whatever God wants. You are placing yourself in His hands. Your commitment will be tested and your persistence will be tried. Pray that God will make you into the servant who is available to Him.

God may choose to do several things with you as you make yourself available to Him. He may use you to plant seeds. Sometimes He will use you to cultivate seeds planted by others. On still other occasions God will use you to harvest fruit planted or cultivated by someone else.

God will show you miracles. He also will let you see ways He chooses to answer prayers in His own time. No matter what the circumstance, He wants you to "Be still, and know that I am God" (Ps. 46:10, NIV).

God Uses Christians to Build Bridges

Do you remember Tony from our video visits in FAITH Basic, *A Journey in FAITH?* Tony was visited by a FAITH Team (Myra, George, and Andrew), and he gave his life to Christ. During the weeks that followed, the FAITH Team continued to build bridges to Tony and his family. Tony was embraced by his new Sunday School class. Tony also accepted the opportunity to receive training in FAITH so he could build bridges to others.

The Tonys you encounter in FAITH will motivate you to continue and to train others, as Christ commanded (Matt. 28:19-20). And don't forget that the members of his FAITH Team—George, Myra, and Andrew—were changed, too!

Notes

FAITH: Building Bridges to People

By virtue of having completed the first semester of training, you have experienced all of the basic ingredients of the FAITH Sunday School Evangelism Strategy®.[1] Building Bridges brings to completion what was begun in A Journey in FAITH. This course will help you refine what you have learned and become more confident in sharing your faith. Building Bridges will enable you to increase your skills, knowledge, and participation in FAITH.

This study emphasizes opportunities for _building bridges_, or establishing vital relationships and connections, between yourself and _those who are learning faith_ for the first time. Since evangelistic prospect visits will continue to be a major focus, you will learn to build bridges between your FAITH Team and _persons who make decisions_ in a visit. You will learn how to build bridges between our church and _our community_, often to people who have never heard about Jesus. You will receive help in handling new and sometimes difficult situations.

You will learn to build bridges between the persons your FAITH Team visits and your _Sunday School class or department_ as we continue to make ministry visits. You can see how to better build bridges of faith in the different settings of your _Daily life_.

During Building Bridges you will discover how to—

• *Better understand your role in training and in encouraging others in FAITH*

• *Strengthen ministry visit opportunities*

• *Lead and train Team members to use the Opinion Poll*

• *Strengthen opportunities for follow-up, such as to help someone who trusts Christ to follow Him in baptism*

• *Effectively deal with difficulties that may arise when a FAITH Team makes evangelistic and ministry visits.*
(Although there is no new memory work, you will learn supportive material such as illustrations and other verses to give you more confidence at any point of sharing the FAITH Visit Outline. As a result you will be better able to answer a question or challenge posed in a visit.)

Understand Your Roles

Building Bridges training is intentionally designed for the person who already has learned the FAITH Visit Outline. Everything is planned to help you encourage and train individuals who are learning the FAITH Visit Outline for the first time. Although not every participant is a Team Leader, the importance of this role will be evident in this course.

If you are in this training as a Team Leader, you will be learning specific ways to lead your Team through training. If you are participating in some other way, you still will be focusing on actions you can take to enhance your skills in leading persons to faith in Christ. God may be preparing you for the time when you will lead a Team of Learners through FAITH.

- First and foremost, you are a _Role model_.

You already have memorized the FAITH Visit Outline and have shared it during visits. Now you are being looked to as one who will _Demonstrate how to make a Faith visit_. Your Team members will be watching you. They will be learning from you what to say.

It is very important that you follow the FAITH Visit Outline in leading a visit. You will be showing others what to do and what to say in a visit. This modeling role is significant.

You know from experience the importance of FAITH leaders being a positive role model _in Faith Training_. By example, you model—

being on time for Team Time;
learning and demonstrating what you have learned in FAITH Basic and FAITH Advanced;
keeping up with all Home Study Assignments;
making sure the Team has positive Visitation Time experiences; and
participating in Celebration Time.

You know the importance of FAITH leaders being positive role models _In Sunday School_. You know by now that FAITH cannot be separated from effective Sunday School work. Many who are participating in FAITH training are declaring that FAITH teaches us how to do Sunday School as it was intended to be.

People will look to you to be a positive example of—
taking leadership roles in Sunday School;
participating in weekly Sunday School leadership team meetings; and
assimilating people, especially new members, into Sunday School.

Notes

WHAT LEARNERS NEED

Learners need a Team Leader who will—

• Hear them recite the FAITH Visit Outline every week during Team Time

• Contact and pray for them during the week

• Gently persuade them to share what they have learned in actual visits

• Motivate and encourage them

• Check off memory work every week

• Model the outline in visits

• Use the Opinion Poll correctly in visits

• Knows how to adjust the pace of training to meet Learner needs/abilities

• Be with them and encourage them to attend Celebration Time.

Your example may be more important to Team members than the training sessions themselves. Team members will be looking to you to set a good example.

• You are needed as an *Encourager and motivator*, one who recognizes and responds to Learner needs.

Do you remember times of discouragement while in FAITH training? Did you ever consider dropping out? Just as you may have needed encouragement when you began FAITH training, your Team members may need you to be an encourager and motivator. You can be an encourager by—

recognizing Learner needs;

helping class and department members know about and want to be a part of the FAITH strategy;

letting Learners know you are praying for them;

getting to know Learners and helping them feel comfortable with you during training sessions and throughout the week;

assisting Learners as they memorize various parts of the FAITH Visit Outline during the week;

encouraging Team members in things they are doing well leading up to, during, and after visits;

helping Learners during Team Time to recite memory work and to share experiences from home study;

celebrating what Learners have memorized and completed by signing off on their assignments during Team Time; and

(at the appropriate times and with sensitivity) *gently persuading Learners to take the lead in specific parts of the visit for which they have received training.*

Because you have been where Learners now are, you can respond appropriately to their needs. Someone learning the FAITH Visit Outline for the first time needs a Team Leader who will work with him or her during training sessions and during the week; one who will gently correct in words and model appropriately in visits; one who knows how to make adjustments and then explains why changes were made.

Learners need to be a part of actual visits. They need to experience the satisfaction of finishing the course. As you are aware of these and other uniquely personal needs, you become an encourager and a motivator in every sense of these words.

Be aware that Learners will face " *Pressure   Points* " at specific times throughout training. Be sensitive as Learners are called on to—

write and share their evangelistic testimonies (Sessions 4 and 5);

(at the Team Leader's cue and with his/her help) *present appropriate parts of* **Preparation** *and the gospel presentation in an actual visit* (Session 6);

memorize and recite a maximum amount of information related to the FAITH Visit Outline (Session 10);

take leadership in an entire visit (after Session 11); *and*

complete a final written review (Session 16).

For some Learners, such pressures can result in dropout if care is not taken. So as Team Leader, be especially sensitive to _dropout_ _signals_ . Some symptoms include—

failure to attend a session without calling in with an excused absence;

getting behind in memory assignments;

expressions of dissatisfaction with some aspect of FAITH training;

resistance to reciting the FAITH Visit Outline;

arriving too late to participate in Team Time or some part of Teaching Time;

not having a prayer partner within the Sunday School class or department;

experiencing learning difficulties or challenges;

disinterest in regularly attending Celebration Time; and

expressing fear about the final written review.

• You are expected to be one who is _Growing in your Faith_ .

FAITH training brings together many ingredients that help a Christian grow in maturity. Other experiences also help us grow as Great Commission Christians. It will become obvious personally and to other people if you are not "prayed up" and "powered up" from studying and applying God's Word. Making yourself available to be used of God is essential.

FAITH participants, as well as other church members, will be watching to see ways you are being challenged and blessed through FAITH training experiences. They will be particularly interested to see how you grow through the challenges and valleys of life. Your Journey Continues journaling pages, part of each session's Home Study Assignments, are designed to help you focus on ways God is helping you grow throughout your training experiences.

At the same time, realize that Satan seems to assert himself with great intensity against Christians who commit themselves to obey and follow God. Not only are you on the defense against Satan, you also are bringing other believers along with you in assault on the Evil One.

This is no game. You must be obedient, pure, available—in Jesus' name!

Notes

Building Bridges with the FAITH Visit Outline

God is using the FAITH Visit Outline in significant ways. For example, in our FAITH video visit, did you observe—

• the Team connecting to Tony in various ways (Sunday School testimony, Key Question, and so forth)?

    • some initial relationships established that made follow-up easy?

    • Tony being enrolled in his adult Sunday School class?

    • discussion about family members?

These will be important points of emphasis—bridges for relationship— in your Building Bridges Through FAITH: The Journey Continues training.

Overview What Happens During Team Time

Team Time is a very important part of the schedule for FAITH Learners. During these 15 minutes, Learners practice and recite the portion of the FAITH Visit Outline they have been assigned to learn up to that point. Since learning the entire FAITH Visit Outline is such a significant part of FAITH training, Team Time becomes a time of accountability.

If You're a Team Leader:

Your job is to help Learners rehearse the outline so they feel more comfortable and natural in making a visit. Although Team Time is only 15 minutes during most sessions, Learners will increasingly see it as a much appreciated checkup and time of practice.

This resource provides some help each session in getting ready for and leading Team Time. Although Team Leaders are responsible for conducting Team Time each week, everyone who has completed FAITH Basic will have an important role. Let's review what is to take place during Team Time.

Team Time begins with the first 15 minutes of Session 2. Since good use of time is extremely important throughout training, it is vital that you model by beginning and concluding on time each week. (Session 12 is an extended Team Time, in which Learners spend the entire session practicing material they have learned.)

Each week, ask Learners to _Recite_ the assigned portion of the FAITH Visit Outline as designated in the Team Time portion of *A Journey in FAITH: Journal.* Take the Learner's FAITH Journal and follow the

outline as each person recites it.

Notice that these same assignments are capsuled in your resource in the section, "Leading Team Time," which begins each session. This feature will help you be aware of what Learners are expected to know. Your copy of the FAITH Visit Outline is on pages x-xi of this resource.

During the first few sessions, you likely will have adequate time for both Team members to recite. Be aware that the longer the recitation, the greater the likelihood that only one person will be able to complete the outline during the 15 minutes before the session. Some of this work can continue in the car, as the Team goes to and from visits.

In early sessions, ask the person who feels most comfortable reciting to share first. Try not to put a Team member on the spot.

As a general rule and especially in later sessions, try to call on the person who most needs practice to share first. Do so with sensitivity and gentleness.

As a Team member correctly recites each line or phrase of the outline, _place   a   check   mark_ in the box beside the phrase. If the Learner has difficulty or does not recite it appropriately or overlooks any portions, write notes in his copy of the FAITH Journal for his review. Be prepared to answer any questions the Learner might have regarding the outline, and suggest ways to strengthen sharing the outline. When a Team member has successfully recited the assigned portion of the outline, sign off by writing your name or initials in the space provided.

Overview the Learner's _Home Study Assignments_ from the previous week. Feel free to raise questions and to discuss any aspect of the assignments. Doing so can help reinforce many of the important concepts taught through these assignments—concepts that only may have been introduced during the session. Once again, sign off in the Learner's Journal any assignments that have been completed and that call for your approval.

As you debrief assignments or answer questions related to the previous session, highlight ones that will appear on the final written review. On a weekly basis, help Learners reduce their concern about the final review.

Although you will not read the Learner's Your Journey in Faith pages, it will be significant to check to see that the Learner is keeping a _written   journal_ of his experiences throughout FAITH. It is easy to overlook this important aspect of home study.

However, journaling brings an enriching dimension to FAITH training. Suggest that Team members record their experiences and reflections on the Bible study. Encourage Learners to read back through previous journaling pages, particularly during times of discouragement. At the end of this semester, both you and your Learners will be asked to write testimonies of what FAITH has meant personally, so your Journal is a wonderful record.

Notes

Notes

If You're Not a Team Leader:

You still need to participate in Team Time by being prepared to recite the FAITH Visit Outline, review the Home Study Assignments, and discuss ways to strengthen a visit. You may be asked to ___*assist*___ the Team Leader by working with a Team member who needs help and encouragement in learning and reciting the FAITH Visit Outline.

Remember, as Team members ride together to and from the visits, Learners can continue to practice sharing the outline and to discuss ways to strengthen a visit.

Review Ingredients of FAITH Training

While we are meeting, Team Learners are assembled for their Orientation to A Journey in FAITH. They are overviewing many of the important ingredients of FAITH. They will learn to depend on you to interpret and reinforce many of the things they are discovering for the first time.

- *Faith Teams*

Three people are on every FAITH Team. In addition to the Team Leader who has been trained in the FAITH strategy, two Team Learners have been enlisted to be trained and to visit together. Each Team represents a designated Sunday School division, department, or class.

Write the names of your Team members in the space provided. If a Team member already has received training but is not participating as a Team Leader, write that member's name and role on the Team (Assistant Team Leader, for example).

_____

_____

_____,

Team Leader

• Faith Participation Card

One of the first things Team members are doing is preparing their FAITH Participation Cards. You will remember that this card is used each week as a name placard and to record numbers and types of visits attempted and made by the Team. If you have not already completed the top portion of your Participation Card, do so now. Make sure your name is printed in large letters on the reverse side for your name placard.

Take a few minutes to review the categories of the Participation Card. You will be responsible for helping your Team members understand the categories identified on the card. You also will be responsible for helping them to complete their cards following visits that begin with Session 2.

The Participation Card is the basis for information on the FAITH Report Board. Remember that reports from the visits are summarized here. Continue to be familiar with the categories and with recording responses on the board. Your job is to orient your Team members to this process so they can eventually report during Celebration Time.

• Types of visits

Each Team will be prepared to make several types of visits. In all visits you should be ready to share the message of the gospel, as well as to invite unsaved people to saving faith in Christ. You will look for opportunities to represent Christ by ministering to individuals in need, by enrolling some people in Bible study, and by helping others grow in their journey of faith.

Teams will make visits to prospects, some of whom have had contact with our church as visitors to Bible study, worship, or a special event. Some have been referred by a member, and others were discovered through some People Search opportunity. Generally, prospects are those who are open to a contact from or a relationship with our church.

Teams also will be prepared to make ministry visits to class members. Teams will learn to make visits using the Opinion Poll. Additionally, Teams will be equipped to make follow-up visits to persons who have made a significant decision (to trust Christ, join the church, enroll in the appropriate Sunday School class/department).

Although you will discover many new experiences when you make visits, Learners will be interested in knowing about each of these types of visits when they receive their assignments. Your experience, as well as what is taught during Teaching Time, will be particularly helpful as Learners determine ways to participate in each type of visit.

• Visitation folder

Each Team will have a visitation folder that has been prepared for that week's visits. Be prepared to explain the significance and use of each item before, during, and after visits.

Notes

Notes

Contents of the visitation folder may include these and other items designated by the church:

• *Visitation assignment forms*—Each week you should have several forms. Some assignments will be to a specific person or family indicated to be a prospect. Other forms might be for visits to members. Some forms will indicate the assignment as a follow-up visit. Each form should indicate the general nature of the assigned visit.

If the card does not indicate that the person is enrolled in Sunday School, then assume you are visiting to cultivate a relationship on behalf of the church and Sunday School. Approach the visit assuming you may have an opportunity to share the gospel.

Lead your Team to make as many visits as are feasible during the designated time. If you are unable to make assigned visits and/or have extra time, use the Opinion Poll to identify opportunities for evangelism and ministry.

• *Information about our church and our Sunday School ministry.*—A diagram, list, or information sheet can help family members identify with and know where Sunday School classes/departments meet.

• *A Step of Faith*—Use this leaflet when sharing the gospel with a person and issuing an **Invitation**. Also use to enroll a person in Sunday School and to record decisions made during a visit.

• *My Next Step of Faith*—In Session 3 you will receive detailed help in using this leaflet to help a new believer take a next step of obedience, through believer's baptism.

• *Opinion Poll cards*—Use these forms to ask and to record responses when making Opinion Poll visits.

• *Bible study material used by your class*—Give a copy of current material to new enrollees and to nonattending members during a visit.

• *Church promotional information about upcoming special events and opportunities.*

You will be responsible for demonstrating how to use each item in the visitation folder. Until Learners overview how to use these items and complete the forms, you will be responsible for training them in how to use. Briefly review what is expected in completing the visitation forms.

No matter what type of record form is used by the church, you need to take the following actions:

1. _Fill_ _in_ _every_ applicable _blank_ in which information is requested.

2. If an assigned person is not at home or is not willing to respond to selected questions for information, _initial_ the card (or blanks left incomplete), and _indicate_ the date of the attempted visit and the reason information was not recorded.

3. ~~Initial~~ *Print* information *legibly*.

4. Write information discovered from the visit that will help in making any *Follow-up* *Contact*.

5. Record information about all other *prospects* *discovered* in the home.

6. Turn in the detachable *Response card* portion of *A Step of Faith*.

• *Prayer and practice*

As we have a sufficient number of Teams participating in FAITH visits, one group of Teams will be assigned to Prayer and Practice each week. These Teams remain in the Teaching Time room while other Teams make visits. This process will begin no earlier than Session 3. Assignments for Prayer and Practice are made on a rotating basis and are communicated each week.

As soon as visiting Teams depart to make visits, the assigned Group Leader assembles his or her Teams for prayer. Teams pray throughout Visitation Time specifically for the Team members visiting and for the individuals to be visited. They pray for divine appointments. The Group Leader might call the names of people visiting and being visited.

During Prayer and Practice, the Group Leader also can lead Teams to practice reciting the FAITH Visit Outline with each other. Team members also can spend time writing notes to prospects and members. When Prayer and Practice is over, the Group Leader leads participants to complete their session Participation and Evaluation Cards.

Your Building Bridges Journal

As a review, your Journal is designed to help you—

• lead Team Time activities (**CHECK IT**, "Leading Team Time");

• participate in Building Bridges Teaching Time content: Each week's Teaching Time includes an accountability check of the previous week's session, new content and important fill-in-the-blank concepts, video viewing (unless otherwise indicated), a brief time of practice with a partner, and an overview of Home Study Assignments. As part of home study, try to reread the session after fill-ins have been added.

• make visits (**DO IT** through Visitation Time) and reports (**SHARE IT** during Celebration Time).

Home Study Assignments facilitate journaling, recording of prayer concerns/answers, additional readings, reporting in weekly Sunday School leadership team meetings, and (for the Team Leader) relating to the FAITH Team during the week.

Notes

Your Responsibilities During Celebration Time

During each week's Celebration Time, you are responsible for leading your Team to report about visits attempted and visits made. This can become a very meaningful and motivational time. In addition to helping Team members update and submit their Participation Cards, Evaluation Cards, and visitation assignment cards, help them know how to complete the Report Board.

Particularly during the first few weeks of training, Team members will be looking to you to share verbal reports during the report time. Even if a Team seemingly has not had a productive visit, Team members share in the ministry's victories during this time segment. Keep these guidelines in mind as you lead and help your Team members to verbally report.

1. *Be brief.* The amount of time needed will be determined by the number of Teams reporting.

2. *Be precise.* Do not give unnecessary details.

3. *Be positive.* Discuss problems or negatives in another setting, such as with your Group Leader.

4. *Be enthusiastic.* Remember, you and your Team have been attempting the greatest opportunity in the world!

5. *Be accurate.* Do not embellish what really happened.

6. *Be careful.* Do not report anything of a confidential nature that was shared with your Team. Use first names only of the people you visited.

7. *Be thankful.* Even if no decision was made or no one allowed you to share, be grateful for the opportunity to dialogue.

8. *Be affirming.* If Joe shared a Sunday School testimony for the first time in a visit and did a great job, tell the entire group. You not only encourage Joe, you also motivate other Teams, too!

Ask God to Use You

Think back on your own journey in faith. Reflect on how one or more people built bridges to you. Who was most influential in leading you to Christ? Thank God for saving you, and thank Him for using these people to build that bridge to you.

Were specific individuals influential in your growth as a Christian? In your ministry and life calling? In reaching family members for Christ?

Pray that God will use you in significant ways throughout FAITH Advanced to build bridges of faith and hope.

Home Study Assignments

Home Study Assignments reinforce this session and prepare you for the next session. "Journaling" experiences in Your Journey Continues are an important part of your development as a Great Commission Christian through FAITH training. Other assignments may include additional reading that enhances your experience.

Selected features in this section highlight opportunities the Team Leader has to build bridges to his or her Team, class/department (especially through weekly Sunday School leadership team meetings) and church, and community. They can assist you in accomplishing your important responsibilities.

Your Journey Continues

What factors motivated you to participate in FAITH?

_____

_____

_____

_____

What advice would you give to your Team members, knowing they are excited yet uncertain about being used of God?

_____

_____

_____

_____

_____

_____

Read 1 Peter 1:3-9. In what ways has the FAITH strategy help you prove your faith genuine?

_____

_____

_____

_____

Notes

Read 1 Peter 1:10-12. What are some things you have learned about salvation by participating in FAITH?

_____

_____

_____

_____

_____

Read 1 Peter 1:13-25. In what areas of your life do you understand God to be calling you to "be holy, because I am holy" (v. 16, NIV)?

_____

_____

_____

_____

_____

Prayer Concerns   Answers to Prayer

_____   _____

_____   _____

_____   _____

_____   _____

_____   _____

_____   _____

_____   _____

_____   _____

_____   _____

_____   _____

An Important Bridge:
Your Weekly Sunday School Leadership Team Meeting

Use this space to record ways your FAITH Team impacts the work of your Sunday School department or class. Use the information to report during weekly Sunday School leadership team meetings. Identify actions that need to be taken through Sunday School as a result of prayer concerns, needs identified, visits made by the Team, and decisions made by the persons being visited.

Highlight needs/reports affecting your class/department or age group.

_____

_____

_____

Pray now for this important meeting.

How does preparation for Sunday need to consider needs of individuals or families visited through FAITH?

_____

_____

_____

How will Team members receiving training be recognized and prayed for?

_____

_____

_____

Indicate ways your Sunday School leaders can help you and Team members in FAITH.

_____

_____

_____

For Further Reading

Read pages 120-26 of *Evangelism Through the Sunday School: A Journey of FAITH* by Bobby Welch.

Notes

For the Team Leader

This weekly feature suggests actions the Team Leader can take to support Team members, prepare for Team Time, and consider ways to improve visits. This work becomes part of the Team Leader's Home Study Assignments. Add any actions suggested by your church's FAITH strategy.

Team Leader, you are the most vital link in FAITH training. God bless you as you faithfully discharge your responsibilities as a FAITH Team Leader.

Support Team Members

❏ Contact Team members during the week. Remind them you are praying for them. Discuss their orientation to FAITH. Remind each person of the importance of being present and on time for Team Time. Briefly remind members of their role during Team Time.

❏ As you talk with Learners this week—

• find out whether they understood their Home Study Assignments, especially that of writing their Sunday School testimonies;

• ask whether they have a prayer partner from their class;

• suggest they preview a FAITH Tip for Session 2, "Helpful Visitation Tips."

❏ Remind members to bring a small Bible with them to take along on visits. Teams will make visits after Session 2 and return for Celebration Time.

❏ Record specific needs and concerns of Team members in the margin to the left.

Prepare to Lead Team Time

❏ Review Home Study Assignments of Team members.

❏ Review "Leading Team Time" for Session 2.

Prepare to Lead Visits

❏ Review the FAITH Visit Outline.

❏ Be prepared to explain the contents of the visitation folder.

❏ Be ready to model a visit in which Team members are asked to share their Sunday School testimonies.

❏ Be prepared to lead the Team to participate during Celebration Time.

Build Bridges to Sunday School

❏ Participate in your weekly Sunday School leadership team meeting. Share pertinent information in this meeting using the feature on page 17 and FAITH visit results.

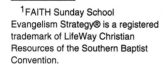

[1]FAITH Sunday School Evangelism Strategy® is a registered trademark of LifeWay Christian Resources of the Southern Baptist Convention.

SESSION 2

Building Bridges of Growth and Commitment

In this session you will

CHECK IT: engage in Team Time for the first time;

KNOW IT: review selected principles from Session 1;

SEE IT: review the *Invitation* portion of the FAITH Visit Outline;

HEAR IT: learn how to build follow-up bridges with persons who make a commitment to Christ and/or enroll in Sunday School during a FAITH visit;

SAY IT: practice sharing the FAITH Visit Outline with another participant;

STUDY IT: overview Home Study Assignments for Session 2;

DO IT: lead Learners in their first visits as a Team, being prepared to lead the entire visit;

SHARE IT: celebrate.

Leading Team Time

All Team members participate in Team Time. They are primarily responsible for reciting the assigned portion of the FAITH Visit Outline and for discussing other Home Study Assignments.

As you direct this important time of CHECK IT activities with your Team, keep in mind how Learners also look to you as role model; motivator; mentor; and friend. Team Time activities can continue in the car, as the Team travels to and from visits.

Lead CHECK IT Activities

Since this is the first time for Team Time activities, provide any additional explanation that is needed. Make good use of the 15 minutes that begin each session.

✓ FAITH Visit Outline

❑ Team members should be ready to recite all aspects of *Preparation* up to INQUIRY and the key words in *Presentation* (FORGIVENESS, AVAILABLE, IMPOSSIBLE, TURN, HEAVEN) and *Invitation* (INQUIRE, INVITE, INSURE).

❑ Indicate your approval by signing or initialing Journals. Encourage Learners.

✓ Sunday School testimonies due

❑ Ask Team members for their written Sunday School testimonies, due this session. Help evaluate each testimony to make sure it includes one or two of the following aspects: friendship/support received; assistance received during some crisis; personal benefits of Bible study through the class; or ways they have grown as a Christian through experiences in or through the Sunday School class. Discuss how benefits can and do change, reflecting different experiences.

If the written testimony is acceptable, make sure each Team member understands the importance of learning to share it naturally, in his or her own words. Ask for permission to print the testimony in any church materials that publicize FAITH and/or that encourage persons to share their testimony.

✓ Other Home Study Assignments

❑ Are Learners on track with Home Study Assignments? Provide any feedback or help they may need.

✓ Session 1 (Orientation to FAITH Training) debriefing

❑ Make sure major concepts from Session 1 are understood, since this is such a key session.

✓ Help for strengthening a visit

❑ This is the first session in which Teams will make home visits. Encourage members and try to allay any concerns. Explain that the Team Leader will take the lead in the INTRODUCTION portion of the visit(s) following this session.

❑ Identify a Team member(s) who would be prepared to share a Sunday School testimony at the Team Leader's prompting during a visit. Be sensitive to persons who are ready to share.

Notes

_____

_____

_____

_____

_____

_____

Actions I Need to Take with Learners During the Week

_____

_____

_____

_____

_____

Notes

Notes

A Quick Review

If you were to define the nature and number of your relationships each day or week, you would find yourself interacting with many different people in a variety of roles and settings. In an intentional way, Building Bridges will help you become aware of these and other opportunities as means of building bridges to people through Sunday School.

This second course (FAITH Advanced), which brings your foundational FAITH training to completion, provides additional intentional visitation opportunities. For an unsaved person, you and your Team may be that individual's first contact with someone who tells them about God. Your Team may help an inactive member/family become involved again. You can help new believers begin their journey of faith in an easy and natural way. Our visitation assignments each week indicate the nature of the visit and previous contacts that have been made.

As you grow in your commitment as a Great Commission Christian, you will find yourself becoming a person God can use in great and mighty ways.

The Person God Uses
The person God uses is growing as a Christian.

In *Evangelism Through the Sunday School: A Journey of FAITH* (pp. 120-26) Bobby Welch highlights indicators or characteristics of personal spiritual growth. These disciplines must be part of the lifestyle of a growing Christian:
- prayer;
- Bible study;
- corporate and private worship;
- fellowship with other Christians;
- caring for others; and
- sharing with other people what Jesus is doing in your life.

It is unlikely that a farmer would say a plant is growing unless some roots, stems, and leaves were apparent. Similarly, it is unlikely that someone would declare a Christian to be growing unless he or she could see evidences of spiritual growth. Other people should be able to see differences in your life as you walk in a close, growing relationship with God.

Do you find yourself characterized by these descriptions? Are you someone who is—

- Saved
- Selected
- Separated
- Sound in doctrine
- Spiritual
- Sensitive to God's leading
- Steadfast
- Characterized by a servant heart?

As you begin a new commitment to share your faith and to equip others to do so, reexamine your own life. Will you commit yourself now to God, that He might strengthen these characteristics in your life? As you do, you will find yourself growing as a person God uses.

Lead Your Team to Build Bridges for Growth

One of the greatest joys a Christian can have is to share the gospel with another individual and to lead that person to a saving relationship with Jesus Christ. Your FAITH Team will be making visits to several people who are assigned to your Sunday School class or department and whom you discover to be unsaved.

The next three sessions will help you focus on ways to make follow-up visits to people who make a commitment, particularly to accept Jesus as Savior, during a visit. You will review some ways to use *A Step of Faith* to begin the follow-up process. You also will be introduced to other resources designed to help you follow up with persons who make decisions of commitment.

As your Team provides reports during Celebration Time, be certain to identify specific opportunities for follow-up. You can help suggest ways your Team and others from your church can be involved in building bridges to and helping the person follow up on any decision that was made.

It is possible that your FAITH Team will visit someone after this session who hears the gospel and _accepts Jesus_ as his or her Savior. Your Team might be involved in leading a person to decide to _enroll_ in Sunday School. Your Team likely could identify specific _ministry_ or _evangelistic_ _opportunities_ that need attention during the upcoming days.

COMMITMENT

☐ I am not ashamed and have personally
accepted Jesus as my Savior and Lord.
*Date/Place of Decision:*_____

☐ I am not ashamed and want to grow in
Christ through a Sunday School class.
*Class:*_____
*Room/Location:*_____

☐ I am not ashamed and want to
acknowledge my new faith in Jesus by
standing with other believers.
_____ will stand with me.

Commitment Prayer
*"Dear Jesus, thank You for saving my soul.
I do not want to be ashamed of You. Instead, I want to
publicly stand for You before my family,
my friends, and my coworkers. I also want to stand
_____ with other Christians,*

and desire is for each Christian to
grow. Ways to grow in your journey of
faith are to—

• READ THE BIBLE,
• PRAY,
• FELLOWSHIP with other Christians.

for doing these important things is His
church and the Sunday School. Here you
will make friends, enjoy fellowship, and
grow in your faith. You will learn more
about how God wants you to live each day.

*Our church and Sunday School
want to offer you the warmest and friendliest
invitation to join us.*

Come

GROW

"What about baptism?"

*If you have accepted Jesus as Savior, baptism
is your next step in following Him.*

*Jesus set the example for us when He was
baptized (Matt. 3:13–17). We please God
when we obey Jesus' command and follow His
example in every area of life, including
baptism.*

Baptism—

■ Is an outward picture of what Christ has
done inside of you.

■ Does not save a person.

■ Is an act of obedience.

■ Is your privilege as a new believer.

(7)

It is important to be ready, from the very beginning, to help your Team know how to begin building bridges. You will need to be prepared to identify ways to follow up. You have some resources to help.

Tools for Effective Follow-up

• *A Step of Faith*

You were introduced to this useful leaflet during FAITH Basic, A Journey in FAITH. The picture of people looking at the cross generates many emotions, and it has been used by God in eliciting decisions of commitment. It will always be helpful to refer to *A Step of Faith* when you follow up with someone who has made a decision.

"*I am not ashamed*" is a theme that runs throughout *A Step of Faith*; as such, it can help you in follow-up discussions. You remind yourself, as well as the person who made the decision, that Jesus was not ashamed to die for you. You also remind yourself and the other person(s) that further steps of faith come because we are not ashamed to follow Him.

The Commitment panel *(5)* of the leaflet reminds the individual of the decision(s) made during a previous visit with the FAITH Team. By showing or referring to this panel, you remind a person of the exciting and important decisions already made and identify the next steps he or she can and should take.

Highlighting the "Come Grow with Us!" panel *(6)* gives you opportunity to reintroduce, in a follow-up visit, the *importance of Bible Study, prayer,* and *fellowship* through the ministry of a Sunday School class and the church.

Finally, the "What about baptism?" panel *(7)* gives you opportunity to talk with someone about the opportunity and questions they may have about baptism. It also sets the stage for sharing, as needed, the presentation of *My Next Step of Faith—Baptism.*

• *My Next Step of Faith—Baptism*

The entire third session of Building Bridges will help you focus on using this new resource to interpret and emphasize the importance of _Baptism_ for a new believer. One of the important bridges your Team is to help build is between the new believer and the church.

Since many people your Team will visit likely have never been to church, you can understand the apprehension and anxiety they might feel when asked to go somewhere new or to do something new. Your Team has a wonderful and important opportunity to be among those who explain the importance of baptism in a believer's life. Team members can dialogue about what a person should expect during a worship experience that includes baptism.

It is so important to remember: Your Team now has the responsibility to lead in building the bridge so a new believer will follow up his or her commitment to Christ by being baptized.

• *Other visitation assignment follow-up information*

Any other contact than that made by the FAITH Team is indicated on your visitation assignment card. Since the follow-up visit should promptly follow the person's initial decision, your FAITH Team may have much of the available information.

However, in some cases, there also has been a staff contact, a contact to reach out to other members of the family, or some other initiative. Much of that information should be _summarized_ for you, so your Team can make an effective follow-up visit. Bible study material or other items provided from the church also may be in your folder for such a visit.

Some Bridge-Building Information to Share

You have heard throughout FAITH the importance of Sunday School in ministering to and teaching believers as well as nonbelievers. One of the vital responsibilities of the FAITH Team is to help build bridges of relationship between a person and a caring Bible study group. This is one reason FAITH Teams are all from the same department or class and are assigned to visit persons who would be assigned to that department or class. It is important that the person being visited already knows at least one person who would be in the class he or she would be attending.

Notes

Your Team can take several actions during a follow-up visit to build bridges through Sunday School:

Share a _Sunday   School   Testimony_. One of the first things learned during FAITH training is to share a testimony that identifies examples of support and friendship, assistance received during crisis, benefits of Bible study through the class, and/or examples of ways a person has grown through Sunday School.

A Sunday School testimony is usually shared during the first part of the initial visit. However, it is important to be prepared to share additional testimony about the Sunday School class during a follow-up visit.

Share information about Sunday School. Often, during an initial visit with a person, your Team provides basic information about the class or Sunday School. On many occasions, the initial FAITH visit may be the first time the person has heard about the ministry opportunities through the specific class.

During a follow-up visit, be prepared to share _additional information about the class_. This might include (but is not limited to) such things as providing a directory of members or a calendar of upcoming fellowship events and indicating ministries provided through the class or department.

It also may be important to provide specific information regarding other classes or departments if the person does not seem comfortable relating to the ministries or target groups of your class. The important concept is to help the person find an entry point into the church through a specific class or department.

Also appropriate in a follow-up visit is to invite the person to meet at a specified place to sit with you during Bible study and worship.

Take   specific   actions *to build bridges of ministry and relationship with the person.* FAITH Team members can identify specific follow-up actions they can take to build a relationship with someone they have visited. Team members do not have to wait until another visit to initiate actions such as to—

• *share about their personal journeys of faith and experiences in the church;*

• *make a phone call to respond to ministry needs;*

• *meet the person for a meal, at a recreation site, or some other place of common interest;*

Do not overlook the importance of building bridges to people at every opportunity.

Engage other members of Sunday School in building *bridges.* The FAITH Team is very important in initiating relationships with many unrelated persons. In many instances, the FAITH Team will be the first persons from your class who make contact and share about Sunday School ministries and/or the gospel.

However, there likely will be several other persons in the class who will share a common interest or will be able to identify with the person. *Activate* class members who will take such actions as—

• *praying for the person who received a visit;*

• *writing a card or letter;*

• *making a phone call;*

• *providing specific ministry (child care, transportation, or other assistance or encouragement).*

Involve professional ministerial staff *in responding to specific needs or concerns.* There will be times when the pastor or other staff member may be the best person to be involved in building bridges with a person who makes a decision during a FAITH visit. Make sure you are sensitive to the person(s) God would involve.

The primary objective of follow-up visits is to build bridges between the person and the church so the person can take the actions needed to grow in his or her new faith. Even though the FAITH Team becomes "the first line of offense" in making contact with a person who makes a decision during a FAITH visit, your job is to begin identifying those who can strengthen possibilities for relationship.

Disciplines Are Brand New

A new Christian likely will have questions about his or her new daily walk. A new member class, plus Sunday School, can help answer them.

POSSIBLE QUESTIONS FROM A NEW BELIEVER	
Why is the Bible important?	Share—reasons/help to be gained; idea to begin with John's Gospel; role of Sunday School; suggestion to write down questions and to talk with other Christians about them
Why should I pray?	Suggest—words that communicate certain thoughts; specific time/place to pray can help; can talk to God but need to listen as well; prayer can occur anytime
Can I not worship God alone?	Describe—reasons fellowship/worship with other Christians are important; plans for class social functions; meaning of different parts of the worship service; new member class schedule

Notes

Notes

Visitation Time
DO IT

As you go . . .

Keep in mind—
• the Team Leader guides preparation for all visits;
• a "game plan" should be in place *before* visits. This means alerting Team members in advance if they are to do Sunday School/evangelistic testimonies;
• the Team Leader always has the option to change the game plan but the responsibility to say why changes were made;
• the visitation tips Learners have been asked to review (p. 35, *A Journey in FAITH: Journal*). Highlight any you feel are especially helpful or needed.

Most of all, encourage Team members as they make their first home visits. Be prepared to take the lead in all visits. Model a visit and debrief what happened so Team members can learn.

Celebration Time
SHARE IT

As you return to share . . .

Encourage Team members to listen carefully as reports are shared, especially about decisions made in visits; the information can be helpful in follow-up. Take the lead in sharing reports. Help Learners complete the necessary forms.
• Reports and testimonies
• Session 2 Evaluation Card
• Participation Card
• Visitation forms updated with results of visits

Home Study Assignments

Home Study Assignments reinforce this session and prepare you for the next session. "Journaling" experiences in Your Journey Continues are an important part of your development as a Great Commission Christian through FAITH training. Other assignments may include additional reading that enhances your experience.

Selected features in this section highlight opportunities the Team Leader has to build bridges to his or her Team, class/department (especially through weekly Sunday School leadership team meetings) and church, and community. They can assist you in accomplishing your important responsibilities.

Your Journey Continues

Read Luke 19:2-10.

We learn many things from Jesus about ministering to and reaching people. We can learn very important and practical ways to help a person move beyond the initial decision he or she has made. This familiar passage, about Jesus' meeting Zacchaeus, gives us a glimpse of ways we can take time to work with individuals. Make a list of actions you see Jesus taking in this passage.

From the same passage find an example in which Jesus does these action(s) as part of follow-up. Write the appropriate verse or verses in the blank. Sometimes follow-up—

• begins immediately after meeting a person who is seeking spiritual things (v. _____);

• involves asking the person to do something with you (even eating is appropriate, (v. _____);

• references appropriate biblical teaching (vv. _____);

• involves leading the person to make a decision or commitment (v. _____);

• includes celebrating with a person about the decisions he is making (v. _____).

Notes

Read Luke 3:21-23. Why do you think God was pleased with Jesus? Why is He pleased when we follow Him in believer's baptism?

Think about your own baptism experience. If it has been some time since that experience, think about what it means to you now to see other people baptized. Which of those impressions or emotions would be meaningful to share with a new believer?

What does baptism do for a new believer? What did baptism do for you?

_____

_____

_____

_____

_____

Prayer Concerns   ## Answers to Prayer

_____   _____

_____   _____

_____   _____

_____   _____

_____   _____

_____   _____

_____   _____

_____   _____

_____   _____

_____   _____

_____   _____

An Important Bridge:
Your Weekly Sunday School Leadership Team Meeting

Use this space to record ways your FAITH Team impacts the work of your Sunday School department or class. Use the information to report during weekly Sunday School leadership team meetings. Identify actions that need to be taken through Sunday School as a result of prayer concerns, needs identified, visits made by the Team, and decisions made by the persons being visited.

Highlight needs/reports affecting your class/department or age group.

_____

_____

_____

Pray now for teachers and department directors.

How does preparation for Sunday need to consider needs of individuals or families visited through FAITH?

_____

_____

How can Sunday School leaders and members pray for and encourage Team members?

_____

_____

What are ways our Sunday School ministry can be prepared to include people who are being discovered and reached through FAITH Team visits?

_____

_____

For Further Reading

Read pages 113-14—"Visitation: the Way It Usually Is" and "Visitation: the Way It Could Be"—in *Evangelism Through the Sunday School: A Journey of FAITH* by Bobby Welch. Begin your FAITH visits expecting God to make visitation all that it can be for your church!

Notes

For the Team Leader

This weekly feature suggests actions the Team Leader can take to support Team members, prepare for Team Time, and consider ways to improve visits. This work becomes part of the Team Leader's Home Study Assignments. Add any actions suggested by your church's FAITH strategy.

Support Team Members
 ❑ Call Team members and encourage them regarding their participation during the first home visits.

Prepare to Lead Team Time
 ❑ Overview "Leading Team Time" at the beginning of Session 3.

Prepare to Lead Visits
 ❑ Review the FAITH Visit Outline to be able to model the entire process for Team members.
 ❑ Be prepared to explain the procedures in the car, going to and from the church, as well as the role of the Team Leader in making visits.
 ❑ Be prepared to model a visit in which Team member(s) are asked to lead in sharing a Sunday School testimony.
 ❑ Be prepared to model the use of the Opinion Poll in making visits.
 ❑ Be prepared to lead the Team to participate during Celebration Time.

Build Bridges to Sunday School
 ❑ Participate in your weekly Sunday School leadership team meeting. Share pertinent information in this meeting using the feature on page 31 and other FAITH visit results.
 ❑ Describe response to your FAITH Team's first home visits.

SESSION 3

Building Bridges to Baptism Using My Next Step of Faith

Ⅰn this session you will

CHECK IT: engage in Team Time activities;

KNOW IT: review selected principles from Session 2;

SEE IT: view a video segment in which Myra, George, and Andrew follow up on Tony's decision and talk with him about believer's baptism;

HEAR IT: learn how to make an initial follow-up visit to a new believer using *My Next Step of Faith;*

STUDY IT: overview Home Study Assignments for Session 3;

DO IT: participate in visits as a Team (Team members are available to share their Sunday School testimony; a Learner may be ready to share his or her evangelistic testimony; but the Team Leader leads in the entire visit);

SHARE IT: celebrate.

Leading Team Time

All Team members participate in Team Time. They are primarily responsible for reciting the assigned portion of the FAITH Visit Outline and for discussing other Home Study Assignments.

As you direct this important time of CHECK IT activities with your Team, keep in mind how Learners also look to you as role model; motivator; mentor; and friend. Team Time activities can continue in the car, as the Team travels to and from visits.

Lead CHECK IT Activities

✓ FAITH Visit Outline

❏ Be prepared to check off each Learner's memorization of all of *Preparation* (through Transition Statement) and the key words in *Presentation* and *Invitation.* Indicate your approval by signing or initialing each Learner's Journal. Encourage Learners as you do, and indicate any notes you have jotted down that might be helpful.

✓ Other Home Study Assignments

❏ Give as much time as needed to helping Learners understand different responses people might make to the Key Question and ways to answer those responses in love. Indicate that such answers will become clearer throughout FAITH training/visits.

❏ Discuss how FAITH Tip and/or other readings can provide specific help or answer some questions from sessions.

✓ Session 2 (Preparing for a Meaningful Visit) debriefing

❏ Answer any questions that remain from Session 2. Emphasize the importance of a good beginning in building trust that ultimately can result in the gospel being shared. Highlight ways the Sunday School testimony helps build bridges to people.

❏ Review Learners' written Sunday School testimonies.

❏ Indicate specific content areas that may appear again on the Session 16 written review.

✓ Help for strengthening a visit

❑ Answer any questions that emerged from home visits following Session 2.

❑ Review ways to begin a visit.

❑ Identify actions Team members took during last week's visits that were particularly good and others that might need to be changed.

❑ Suggest ways Team members can improve sharing their Sunday School testimonies.

❑ Call attention to the evangelistic testimony you shared during last week's visit(s); mention that Team Learners will be introduced during this session to ways to share their testimony during a visit.

Notes

_____

_____

_____

_____

_____

_____

Actions I Need to Take with Learners During the Week

_____

_____

_____

_____

_____

_____

Notes

A Quick Review

A FAITH visit in which someone makes a profession of faith is only the beginning. The FAITH Team also is privileged to be a part of follow-up to this new believer.

With an official visit assignment in their visitation folders, the FAITH Team returns within two weeks to dialogue further with the person. This is a time to answer any questions the person may have about the decision, to discuss baptism, and to talk about opportunities for growth through involvement in a Sunday School class and in the church.

Additional information can be shared about the class/department at this time. Other members can become involved in reaching out to and involving the new believer in Bible study. Opportunities to reach out to the entire family may become most apparent during times of follow-up. In some instances, a staff member may make a specific follow-up contact.

The Person God Uses
The person God uses spends time in His Word.

The source of strength for any believer is the power of God. The Bible is not just words about God that inspire and encourage; the Bible is God's Word. Many verses identify the specific benefit of God's Word. Psalm 119:105; Isaiah 55:11; and Hebrews 4:12 are examples.

Imagine the waste for a beautiful automobile to be confined to a garage because there is no gas. Imagine a beautiful chandelier hanging in the dark because there is no power. Even more tragic is to imagine a believer who does not hear, study, and meditate on God's Word.

Deuteronomy 31:12-13 is a wonderful passage that identifies specific actions we are to take regarding God's Word. Underline key words that relate to those actions: "Assemble the people—men, women and children, and the aliens living in your towns—so they can listen and learn to fear the Lord your God and follow carefully all the words of this law" (NIV).

Notice we are to *listen, learn to fear,* and *follow carefully* God's Word. God uses persons who know His heart and seek to obey His desire.

As you continue in your journey of faith, remember the importance of receiving strength and direction from God's Word. Remember the blessings of reading, hearing, memorizing, meditating on, and investigating personal truths for life from God's Word.

Also, remember God says we are to study His Word so we can do what it says. God will use you as you spend time each day letting His Word pierce, dissect, and heal you.

Pray for a growing reliance on God's Word and the discernment to follow God's leadership in your life, as revealed through His Word.

Transformation Begins at Conversion

The decision to accept Jesus Christ as Savior is unquestionably the most significant action a person can ever take. You know as a believer that the Holy Spirit enters the life of a person at the moment of salvation. Eternal life begins at that moment for the believer! Indeed, this is a time of celebration and life transformation.

You know that a new believer needs to go ahead and take the next steps designed to help him or her grow as a Christian. Baptism is one of those extremely important next steps. For many new believers, the longer they wait to be baptized, the more difficult it will be to take this next step. This session will help you focus on how to use another simple leaflet, *My Next Step of Faith*, to build bridges for baptism.

Many people with a church background have been taught that a person is baptized into the church as an infant; that the person has no decision to make but is "born" into the church. Others have seen baptism in a form other than immersion. One of the important bridges to be built is to help a person understand and follow his or her commitment to Christ with believer's baptism.

Your FAITH Team will be assigned to make a follow-up visit to people who commit their lives to Christ. Since this is such a significant opportunity for your Team, let's take time to overview ways to build bridges to the next step of faith.

Notes

Baptism: a Next Step
of Obedience

After your Team has become reacquainted with the person you visited previously, there are several steps to take in dealing with baptism. If, by the time you visit again, someone has not followed up his commitment to Christ by being baptized, then take time to explain each of the following steps. If the person has been baptized since his/her recent commitment, take time to discuss the significance of the issues reflected in the following steps.

1. <u>Remind the person of the Significance of his decision</u> to trust Christ. Use appropriate panels of *A Step of Faith* to recall and celebrate the decision(s) made during the previous visit to follow Christ. Help the new believer recall how Jesus was not ashamed to die for him.

Panel 5 of *A Step of Faith,* where the person checked his decisions and commitments, is a good one to highlight. Call attention to *panel 7,* about baptism. Ask whether he or she has had a chance to read that information.

2. <u>Call attention To the importance of baptism</u> as a next step in being obedient to Christ after salvation. Share a brief testimony about the significance of baptism.

Such a testimony could have three short parts. Perhaps you can remember the parts with these words: <u>After</u> , <u>next</u> , <u>although</u> . The following example uses this format:

AFTER I prayed and trusted Jesus and Him only as my Savior, I was so thankful that He was not ashamed of me and had died for me. I was not ashamed to obey and follow Jesus in scriptural baptism.

NEXT, I was baptized by the pastor.

ALTHOUGH I knew baptism did not save me, I understood that it showed a symbol of what had happened to me—dying to my sins, burying my former rebellious life, and being raised to a new life in following Jesus.

You might choose to give a <u>personal illustration</u> to validate how baptism strengthens and encourages you as a believer. For example, one person might recall, "I knew I was being obedient to Jesus. I also knew baptism was a great way for me to share with my friends and family what Jesus had done for me."

Continue by saying something like: "I'd like to explain the next step to take in your new journey of following Jesus."

3. Put away *A Step of Faith*. Now bring out *My Next Step of Faith—Baptism*. (As you did with *A Step of Faith*, show and dialogue about each panel of this leaflet; but do not give it to the person at this time.)

Briefly call attention to the title now. Share that you will use this leaflet to help show the significance of baptism as being obedient to Jesus.

4. Open the leaflet to *panel 2*. Call attention to the reminder that Jesus was not ashamed of us and does not want us to be ashamed of Him. Comment that not only does baptism show we are not ashamed of Jesus, it also motivates and encourages us to confess Him publicly.

Introduce the significance of believer's baptism as an act of obedience. Emphasize that __*individuals*__ ___*to be baptized*___ are those who—

• *already have trusted Jesus as Savior;*

• *understand that baptism does not bring salvation but is a symbol of what Jesus already has done for them, and thus is an expression of obedience;*

• *are not ashamed to follow Christ's example.*

In nearly every case, new believers also are joining the church.

5. Point out *panel 3: Why be baptized?* Although you do not need to read the following information from the leaflet, be familiar enough with the reasons to be able to overview them clearly, referring to the leaflet for supporting Scriptures:

• *Jesus commanded it;*

• *Baptism is an act of obedience for which Jesus Himself, as well as His followers, set the example;*

• *Baptism is a picture of breaking from the past and beginning a new life with Christ;*

• *In the New Testament baptism is a public testimony of faith.*

6. Open *My Next Step of Faith* to *panel 4*; point out major concepts visualized on the front cover and in pictures inside the leaflet. Help the person realize that baptism is a picture of what Jesus has done for the believer; by pointing out elements of baptism in the leaflet pictures, you clarify the beauty, symbolism, and significance of baptism.

Call attention to the fact that baptism is __*by immeRSion*__ in water. The best way to understand the scriptural example (Matt. 3:5-17) and command (Matt. 28:19) is to understand the basis of the word *baptizo* (**baptisma**) which means to immerse in water.

Baptism is __*in front of witnesses*__, not a private ceremony. Because it is a picture of what already has happened in the

believer's life, baptism is a public expression of faith. Both Christians—who share baptism as a common experience—and nonbelievers—who have yet to turn from sin to Christ—are encouraged to watch, as the convert gives testimony of his new relationship with Jesus.

Most churches baptize new believers and new members in their baptismal pool as part of their worship service, _with worshipers looking on_. Some congregations do not have facilities to accommodate baptism by immersion and so will baptize new members in a pool or a river.

Baptism is an _ordinance_ of the church. Usually the pastor or another minister conducts the baptism while the congregation looks on. Some churches, however, may invite other people into the water with the one who is being baptized. Either way, baptism is a meaningful experience.

7. Refer now to *panel 5*. Emphasize the importance of being baptized _As soon as possible_. Churches that follow the scriptural example emphasize the importance of being baptized only after a person has willfully accepted Jesus as Savior. Churches also emphasize the importance of persons who have experienced believer's baptism by immersion as those who can be accepted into their full membership.

This stresses the importance of baptism as something every church member has in common. Some churches require that, before a person can be baptized into their membership, he or she complete a new member training class. Other churches encourage new believers to participate in this kind of new member orientation during the weeks after baptism.

No matter the polity of the church, it is important for a new believer to begin his next steps as a Christian as soon as possible.

Will you now follow Jesus by being baptized?

8. One of the most important reasons for a follow-up visit to someone who recently has accepted Jesus is to encourage the person to decide to be baptized into the membership of the local church.

Call attention at this point of the visit to the question at the bottom of this panel (5): _Will you now follow Jesus by being baptized_? Use the person's name when asking the question; for example, "Tony, will you now follow Jesus by being baptized?"

9. Many people likely will have some ___*questions*___ about the reasons for and logistics of baptism in a church. As needed, use *panel 6* to answer their questions. They likely will want to know such details as—

When and with whom am I to meet before the baptismal service?
What am I to wear during the baptism service?
Where and when will I change clothes after being immersed?
Will I be asked to say anything during the worship service?
How will I keep from falling while in the baptismal pool?

If the person does not have significant questions, refer to the information as something he or she may wish to overview privately. Otherwise, explain the logistics of how baptism is done in your church.

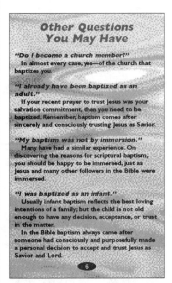

10. ___*Invite the person To Record his Commitment*___ to be baptized on the appropriate part of *panel 7*. Point out the place for the person to sign and to date the occasion of his commitment to be baptized. Affirm the new believer for being willing to take this next step of obedience. Indicate whether your church provides a baptism certificate or other special memento. Explain that *My Next Step of Faith—Baptism* will be a significant memento as well.

Now ask ___*Another Significant question*___, "Would you allow us (referring to the FAITH Team) the honor and privilege of accompanying in this wonderful next step of faith—baptism?" Point out the spaces for the members of the FAITH Team to sign their names and to indicate their phone numbers. Indicate how, not only through support for baptism but also in many other ways, your Team wants to build bridges so the new believer can grow through the ministries of a local church.

> ## Would you allow us the honor and privilege of accompanying you in this wonderful next step of faith—baptism?

If the person answers yes to this question, ask for a ___*preferred date*___ for the baptismal service; indicate that this request will be shared, followed up on, and confirmed in a few days by a minister of the church. Also record that information on the Appointment for Baptism panel, which the Team takes back to the church. Indicate the ___*Location and time*___ to meet prior to baptism; also indicate that information on the Appointment for Baptism card. Write down the pastor's name as well. Even though he may not be the minister who does the baptismal service, the new believer needs to know his name.

Appointment for Baptism

Name of person to be baptized

Preferred date of baptismal service

Time of baptismal service

Meeting place

Team Leader signature

Although most FAITH Teams cannot determine the date and time for the person to be baptized (generally this is done by the ministerial staff after a person makes a public declaration of faith and comes for church membership by baptism) requesting a preferred date and time (morning or evening worship service) helps solidify the decision and provides the church with additional information by which to follow up.

Be sure to _Record_ , on the FAITH Visit Assignment Card, appropriate information that needs to be shared with the church staff about the person's decision. Return the perforated Appointment for Baptism panel to the pastor.

With a person who has not yet made a decision for church membership by baptism:

If a new believer who has not been baptized makes the commitment for church membership, make sure one of the Team members indicates this information on the Visit Assignment Card. Explain the procedure (of most churches) for a new believer to declare his faith in Christ and his intention to join the church and be baptized by coming to the front of the congregation during the invitation part of the worship service.

Make certain the person knows Team members' willingness to stand with him or her during this time (and to support in many other ways). Explain that the minister will share specific information about time and location to meet for baptism. Make sure this information is forwarded to the pastor. Identify additional opportunities for ministry and follow-up.

11. _Give the copy_ of *My Next Step of Faith* to the individual. Encourage the person to think about inviting someone, perhaps an unsaved friend, to attend the baptismal service. _Conclude_ the visit ~~Conclude~~ _with prayer_.

If the person declines to be baptized:

It will be rare that someone your Team visits for follow-up will choose not to be baptized. If he or she does not make a baptism appointment during this visit, ask whether there are any questions the Team might answer. Explain why waiting is not an acceptable action:

• We have no record in the New Testament about anyone waiting.

• Delay is dangerous because it gives the devil a chance to create doubt or uncertainty.

• It is always best to obey the Lord as soon as He tells us what to do.

Plan for follow-up by your Sunday School/church.

The Journey Continues

"In the New Testament baptism is for believers (Acts 2:38; 8:12-13, 37-38; Eph. 4:5). Water apart from personal commitment to Christ makes no difference in the life of anyone. In the New Testament baptism occurs when a person trusts Christ as Lord and Savior and obeys the command to be submerged in water and raised from it as a picture of the salvation experience that has occurred. Baptism comes after conviction of sin, repentance of sin, confession of Christ as Lord and Savior. To be baptized is to preach a personal testimony through the symbol of baptism."[1]

Recall your own baptism experience. Think about the people who observed you "preach a personal testimony" through your baptism. How were conversion and baptism only the beginning in your journey of faith? How did obedience in baptism prepare you to be obedient to Christ in other, more challenging ways?

Notes

Visitation Time
DO IT

As you go . . .

Think about this:

"One Thursday morning, our visitation team called on a young wife. She and her husband had just been transferred to Tinker Air Force Base, which was located near our church just outside Oklahoma City. Eager to meet new people, she invited us into her home and wanted to hear all about our church and the gospel. Before we left, we had the joy of leading her to Christ. On the following Sunday, she and her husband joined our church by baptism.

While in their home, I had given her a follow-up booklet. Later her Sunday School teacher called. But those were not the reasons they joined. Actually, a lady on our visitation team told her husband, who was also in the Air Force, about the visit. As he was driving home on Friday, he went by that house and saw a man struggling to attach a camper shell to a pickup truck in the tricky Oklahoma wind. He stopped, introduced himself, and helped with the chore. They both discovered that they liked chili and a certain board game, so they made a date for the two couples to get together on Saturday evening.

Somewhere between Park Place and Boardwalk, the conversation turned to spiritual matters; the airman responded to the gospel and prayed to receive Christ. Both couples sat together in Sunday School and the worship service the next day. The instructive element of follow-up is foundational, but it usually won't happen without a relationship."[2]

Celebration Time
SHARE IT

As you return to share . . .

- Other reports and testimonies
- Session 3 Evaluation Card
- Participation Card
- Visitation forms updated with results of visits

Home Study Assignments

   Home Study Assignments reinforce this session and prepare you for the next session. "Journaling" experiences in Your Journey Continues are an important part of your development as a Great Commission Christian through FAITH training. Other assignments may include additional reading that enhances your experience.

   Selected features in this section highlight opportunities the Team Leader has to build bridges to his or her Team, class/department (especially through weekly Sunday School leadership team meetings) and church, and community. They can assist you in accomplishing your important responsibilities.

Your Journey Continues

   Read Acts 8:26-40. This is a very helpful passage regarding baptism of a new believer. Look at the passage from Philip's perspective. Answer the following questions:

   • Although Philip had been involved in Samaria where a crowd heard and received him (8:5-8), he was led by God to a desert road where few people traveled. What is your reaction when God leads you to "deserts" when you have experienced (or would rather experience) great results in the crowds?

_____

_____

_____

_____

_____

SUNDAY SCHOOL
FAITH ADVANCED™
EVANGELISM STRATEGY

Notes

• A stranger asked Philip to explain a Scripture. Write an example of a time when you were given an opportunity to share the meaning of Scripture with someone who was looking for spiritual things.

_____

_____

_____

_____

• The eunuch asked Philip, "Look, here is water. Why shouldn't I be baptized?" (NIV). What would you explain to the eunuch about the significance of and opportunity for baptism?

_____

_____

_____

_____

Write an example of an opportunity you have had to explain baptism to someone.

_____

_____

_____

_____

Practice your baptism testimony using this format:
AFTER

_____

_____

_____

_____

NEXT

_____

_____

_____

_____

ALTHOUGH

_____

_____

_____

_____

Prayer Concerns	Answers to Prayer	*Notes*
_____	_____	
_____	_____	
_____	_____	
_____	_____	
_____	_____	
_____	_____	
_____	_____	
_____	_____	
_____	_____	
_____	_____	
_____	_____	
_____	_____	
_____	_____	

Notes

An Important Bridge:
Your Weekly Sunday School Leadership Team Meeting

Use this space to record ways your FAITH Team impacts the work of your Sunday School department or class. Use the information to report during weekly Sunday School leadership team meetings. Identify actions that need to be taken through Sunday School as a result of prayer concerns, needs identified, visits made by the Team, and decisions made by the persons being visited.

Highlight needs/reports affecting your class/department or age group.

_____

_____

_____

Pray now for teachers and department directors.

How does preparation for Sunday need to consider needs of persons/families—
• who have prayed to receive Christ through FAITH but have not yet attended Sunday School? _____

_____

• who have not followed up by being baptized? _____

_____

How can Sunday School leaders and members pray for and encourage persons who have made a decision or other commitment during a FAITH visit? _____

_____

How can Sunday School leaders and members encourage new believers who recently have been baptized into the membership of the church?

_____

_____

For Further Reading

Read the FAITH Tip, "The Significance of Believer's Baptism."
Read pages 91-97 in *Evangelism Through the Sunday School: A Journey of FAITH* by Bobby Welch.

FAITH *Tip*

The Significance of Believer's Baptism

"Christian baptism is the immersion of a believer in water in the name of the Father, the Son, and the Holy Spirit. It is an act of obedience symbolizing the believer's faith in a crucified, buried, and risen Savior and the believer's death to sin, the burial of the old life, and the resurrection to walk in newness of life in Christ Jesus. It is a testimony to his faith in the final resurrection of the dead. Being a church ordinance, it is prerequisite to the privileges of church membership and to the Lord's Supper. . . ."[3]

The word for baptize in Greek is *baptizo*, which means "to dip, plunge, submerge, or immerse." "Baptism" translates *baptisma,* the meaning in the act of baptism, namely, a symbol of what Jesus did to save us—death, burial, and resurrection—and what He does in the believer—death to the old life, its burial, and resurrection to a new life in Christ.

"Baptism in the New Testament was related to the ministry of both John the Baptist and of Jesus. John's baptism was symbolic of one's repentance from sin and of willingness to participate in the kingdom of God (Matt. 3:6-8; Luke 3:3-16). Jesus submitted to John's baptism (Matt. 3:16) not to denote repentance but to authenticate John's ministry, to set an example for His followers, and to dedicate Himself publicly to His redemptive ministry. In it Jesus symbolized His death, burial, and resurrection. . . .

Keeping in mind the meaning of *baptisma,* what is the significance of Christian baptism? Is it sacramental in nature and necessary for salvation, or is it symbolic in nature? The word itself strongly suggests the latter. The idea of baptismal regeneration did not appear in Christian teachings until late in the second and early in the third centuries. . . .

However, by the late second and early third centuries, baptismal regeneration came to be accepted by the group which later evolved into the Roman Catholic Church. . . .

That immersion is the original form of baptism is generally agreed. *Baptizo* itself teaches that neither pouring nor sprinkling constitutes New Testament baptism. Because of the later belief in baptismal regeneration, the practice arose of pouring water all over a sick person. This was called clinical baptism. Later, water was poured only on the head. It should be noted that while the verbs for 'pour' and 'sprinkle' appear in the New Testament, neither is used for baptism. No usage has been found where *baptizo* means either pour or sprinkle. The practice of sprinkling for baptism gradually replaced immersion in the Catholic Church and when it divided into the Roman and Greek branches, the latter retained immersion. It was not until the thirteenth century that sprinkling became the official mode of Roman Catholic baptism."[4]

Notes

For the Team Leader

This weekly feature suggests actions the Team Leader can take to support Team members, prepare for Team Time, and consider ways to improve visits. This work becomes part of the Team Leader's Home Study Assignments. Add any actions suggested by your church's FAITH strategy.

Support Team Members

❏ Call Team members and talk with them about their participation during the class training and visits. Discuss any observations they made during the visits and particularly about sharing their Sunday School testimony.

❏ Discuss ways to prepare and share their evangelism testimonies without giving away the answer to the Key Question.

❏ Encourage them as they memorize all of ***Preparation*** in the FAITH Visit Outline.

Prepare to Lead Team Time

❏ Overview "Leading Team Time" at the beginning of Session 4.

Prepare to Lead Visits

❏ Review the FAITH Visit Outline in order to model the entire process for Team members.

❏ Be prepared to model a visit in which Team member(s) are asked to lead in sharing a Sunday School testimony and evangelistic testimony.

❏ Be prepared to model the use of the Opinion Poll in making visits.

❏ Be prepared to lead your Team to participate during Celebration Time.

Build Bridges to Sunday School

❏ Participate in your weekly Sunday School leadership team meeting. Share pertinent information in this meeting using the feature on page 48 and other FAITH visit results.

❏ Does every member of your Team (including yourself) have a prayer partner from within the Sunday School class? If not, present the need to your class on Sunday.

[1]Johnnie Godwin, "Baptism," in *Holman Bible Dictionary,* gen. ed Trent Butler (Nashville: Holman Bible Publishers, 1991), 151.

[2]David Self, *Good News for Adults: The Power to Change Lives* (Nashville: Convention Press, 1998), 52.

[3]Herschel H. Hobbs, *The Baptist Faith and Message* (Nashville: Convention Press, rev. 1996), 72.

[4]Ibid., 73-75.

SESSION 4

Building Bridges Through Follow-up Visits

In this session you will

CHECK IT: engage in Team Time activities;

KNOW IT: review principles taught in Session 3;

HEAR IT: learn how to make other follow-up visits (in addition to follow-up for baptism), to persons not participating in Sunday School and/or discipleship opportunities;

SAY IT: provide opportunities to practice the FAITH Visit Outline:

STUDY IT: overview Home Study Assignments for Session 4;

DO IT: participate in visits as a Team (Team members are available to share their Sunday School testimonies; a Learner may be ready to share his/her evangelistic testimony; but the Team Leader takes the lead.);

SHARE IT: celebrate.

Leading Team Time

All Team members participate in Team Time. They are primarily responsible for reciting the assigned portion of the FAITH Visit Outline and for discussing other Home Study Assignments.

As you direct this important time of CHECK IT activities with your Team, keep in mind how Learners also look to you as role model; motivator; mentor; and friend. Team Time activities can continue in the car, as the Team travels to and from visits.

Lead CHECK IT Activities
✓ *FAITH Visit Outline*

❏ Listen as each Learner recites the appropriate portion of the FAITH Visit Outline (all of **Preparation**, adding the Key Question and Transition Statement; plus key words for **Presentation** and **Invitation**). Indicate your approval by signing each Learner's Journal.

Involve an Assistant Team Leader in this part of Team Time, if you have this Team member.

✓ *Evangelistic testimony—first draft*

❏ Review the first draft of written evangelistic testimonies, due this session. Use the criteria from Session 3 FAITH Tip (A Journey in FAITH). Explain why you are making your suggestions. Indicate that most testimonies undergo some revisions. Be sensitive in helping Team members develop their testimony, keeping their story intact. As a reminder, these are the criteria which Learners have used to develop their testimonies:

- Define some specific event before (pre-conversion) and after your conversion (benefits).
- Do not answer the Key Question in your testimony.
- Keep your testimony brief (three minutes or less).
- Do not give unnecessary details; instead, concisely reflect your experience.
- Conclude your testimony with the assurance that you are going to heaven.

✓ *Sunday School testimony—practice*

❏ As possible, provide time for Team members to practice their Sunday School testimonies. Review of the evangelistic testimony, however, should be your priority.

✓ *Other Home Study Assignments/*
Session 3 (Developing Your Evangelistic Testimony) debriefing
❏ Answer other questions Learners may have from Session 3 or as a result of their Home Study Assignments.

✓ *Help for strengthening a visit*
❏ Identify ways Team members can improve sharing their evangelistic testimony in a visit.
❏ Help your Team, especially Learners, know how to—
- dialogue with someone who answers the Key Question with a faith answer, by discussing his or her journey of faith in Christ.
- briefly explain to a person who answers the Key Question with a works answer, that many people feel that doing good things gets them into heaven. Discuss the various ways such a response might be verbalized.
- look for opportunities to ask permission to share what the Bible says about how a person goes to heaven.
- look for ways to get clarification or explanation if someone shares an unclear response to the Key Question.
- prayerfully look for ways to talk with a person who indicates no opinion about the Key Question.

Notes

_____
_____
_____
_____
_____
_____
_____

Actions I Need to Take with Learners During the Week

_____
_____
_____
_____
_____
_____

Notes

Notes

A Quick Review

You will encounter several types of FAITH follow-up situations. One of the most important is the follow-up visit in which you discuss baptism as a next step of obedience with a new convert. Test your knowledge of key truths by choosing one or more answers, as appropriate:

___ **1. Use *My Next Step of Faith—Baptism* when—**
    a. making a follow-up visit to someone who enrolled in Sunday School during a FAITH visit;
    b. making a follow-up visit to someone who has a ministry need, as discovered during a FAITH visit;
    c. making a follow-up visit to someone who accepted Christ;
    d. a FAITH Team member has completed sharing the FAITH gospel presentation.

___ **2. Three words—*AFTER, NEXT, ALTHOUGH*—help you remember an appropriate format for—**
    a. elaborating on your evangelistic testimony;
    b. sharing your baptism testimony;
    c. remembering details of your Sunday School testimony.

___ **3. Three requirements for persons to be baptized, as identified in *My Next Step of Faith—Baptism,* are individuals who—**
    a. already have trusted Christ;
    b. understand that baptism does not bring about salvation but is a symbol of what Jesus has done for you and is an expression of obedience;
    c. are not ashamed to follow Christ's example and command and are joining the church.

The Person God Uses
The person God uses is an encourager.

One of the characteristics of a person God uses (p. 126, *Evangelism Through the Sunday School: A Journey of FAITH*) is that of encouraging others. This seems like such a simple and obvious action. On the other hand, the importance of encouragement cannot be overlooked.

Think about how God has used other people as an encouragement to you. Consider how important it is for you to have someone who encourages you, particularly when you are facing new or challenging ventures.

God has placed His hand on you to be an encouragement to other FAITH Team members, as well as to other Sunday School members. You also are building bridges to individuals visited by your FAITH Team. You now are called on to demonstrate the ministry of encouragement.

Nehemiah 4 records some simple yet profound actions Nehemiah took to overcome the discouragement of the Israelites who were rebuilding the city walls. Consider selected truths to ponder:

• You begin encouraging others when you recognize the potential they have to be discouraged.

• You encourage others when you join them in prayer.

• You can be used of God when you give people specific actions they can successfully take to improve their overall situation.

• You encourage others by your very presence and your confidence ("You can do it," "I believe in you," and other sincere expressions) in them.

• God uses you meaningfully when you help people recognize how He is at work in their midst and how He is choosing to fight on their behalf. You encourage as you remind people to "remember the Lord, who is great and awesome" (4:14).

You will be called on by God to encourage some persons as they learn to share their faith. You will be used of God to encourage others as they begin considering new directions for their lives.

Keep in mind how God has used others as a model of encouragement to you. Pray that He will use you in similar life-changing ways.

Put Yourself in Their Shoes

Put yourself in the place of someone who recently has decided to accept Jesus as Savior and Lord or to enroll in a Sunday School class. Recall your own excitement of newfound faith.

When placing yourself in this situation, think about some of the advantages of having caring people build bridges to you as you begin taking your new steps of faith. Think about some of the challenges for the new believer or new enrollee who does *not* have persons seeking to build bridges during the important initial steps of discipleship.

Notes

Take the Initiative to Build Bridges

Do you expect new Christians or new enrollees to take the initiative in building bridges to us, the church? In reality, most people who make a commitment to Christ or to enroll in a Sunday School class/department need encouragement from others. Our initiative is important in helping them take steps in building relationships and in beginning to follow Christ.

The FAITH Team is a vital link in building bridges to the church and people who make commitments to Christ and/or who enroll in Sunday School. The FAITH Sunday School Evangelism Strategy recognizes the importance of building bridges between these people and Sunday School classes/departments.

Instead of waiting for a new member to take the initiative, Team members—and the entire class—are motivated to reach out because they know this person and have been involved in what is happening in his or her life. Such bridge-building is a vital reason for a follow-up visit.

During a FAITH follow-up visit, you will lead your Team to do these and other types of actions:

- _Introduce / reintroduce_ Team members and briefly talk about interests.
- Share the _purpose_ of the visit: "We wanted to spend some time talking about your recent decision to _____ *(describe)*."
- Dialogue with the person about his _experience since_ making ____ _____. Talk about ways the Sunday School class can assist.
- Share some _actions a person can take_ in building or strengthening his journey of faith.
- Share a _Sunday School Testimony_ to indicate the benefits that are experienced by participating with a small group in Bible study.
- Ask whether a FAITH Team member can "_Practice_" the gospel presentation based on the word *FAITH*.
- _Discuss_ some _barriers or cha_____ that might confront the person in participating in discipleship actions.
- If the person has not attended worship or Bible study since making the decision, discuss _____ ____ _____ ____ _____ can take to build bridges to strong participation.
- Identify _____ _____ members of the

_____ / _____ can take to assist the person in his or
her journey of faith.
* _____ together.

Real People, Real Life: How Would **YOU** Build Bridges?

Four case studies represent real situations our church might
encounter—and about which we always should be sensitive. Now think
about *specific* actions your FAITH Team might take to build bridges before
the situation becomes discouraging for the individual who made the
significant commitment.

CASE STUDY #1

*I recently gave my life to Christ after a friend shared with me. He
encouraged me to come to Sunday School, and I really wanted to
attend. I heard so much from him about his class and the way they
help each other. But I work on Sundays, and it really is impossible
for me to come to worship and Bible study. Although my friend is
supportive and understanding, I feel like a fish out of water. It
would be good if someone could accommodate my situation.*

Bridge-Building Principles:
Follow-up seems challenging if all we are doing is seeking to get
someone to come to our class. This situation demands some creativity and
flexibility.

When the FAITH Team realizes that this person cannot come on
Sunday, they could share this concern during _____ _____
_____ _____ _____ _____.

Many churches are identifying ways to start Bible studies that meet at a
time other than Sunday morning or perhaps at a facility other than the
church.

It also is important that the Team share with the _____
_____ _____ that members need to identify specific actions
to build bridges with this person through regular ministry, fellowship, and
Bible study opportunities that meet in addition to Sunday.

Notes

CASE STUDY #2

The church conducted Vacation Bible School, and my kids went. They had a great time and met some really nice people. Afterwards, we agreed to enroll our family in their Sunday School since I figured they would keep treating us with the attention and encouragement they did when we agreed to be enrolled. Right after we signed up, my husband's father was placed in the hospital and we spent several weeks going back and forth to take care of him.

We really forgot about Sunday School. Besides, no one has checked with us. I guess it's because we did not show up in the class like we said we would.

Bridge-Building Principles:
One reason some people do not come is that they ____ _____ _____ _____ in the class. Others go through short-term experiences in which they are not able to participate. If they have little or no contact with class members, particularly during times when they are away, many times newcomers feel _____ ___ _____. Individuals may feel let down by the class they thought would care for them during difficult times.

Although it is difficult for a class to know how to care for people who do not come, it is important that _____ _____ take the initiative in leading members to discover and respond to these types of challenges. Caring class members can—
   • *initiate prayer chains to members;*
   • *make phone calls to persons with special needs;*
   • *plan to take meals or care packages; and*
   • *provide child care, transportation, or lawn-care assistance during extended absences, when there is a special need.*
FAITH Team members may be the best people to identify and begin building bridges so some initial needs can be addressed.

CASE STUDY #3

I started going to the church because a friend invited me. I had just gone through a traumatic experience with my health and realized I needed some hope. I was encouraged by the music and the preacher's messages. I decided to accept Jesus into my life. I know that He saved me.

I've been a bit disappointed with the church, though. When I hear people talk, they share about how many friends they have in the church and how friendly the church is. So far, I haven't really found it to be that way. I sit in the same place in worship nearly every Sunday I can attend. The people around me are friendly, but I just do not feel like I fit in.

Bridge-Building Principles:

A couple of clues in this case study should help us respond. First, if a FAITH Team follows up within a week or two of the person's commitment, members can begin building bridges. It sounds as if this person does not _____ about Sunday School. A FAITH Team will want to be particularly conscious about enrolling a person in a _____ Sunday School class during the first visit. Often a person is hesitant to enroll when he does not know anyone in the class. The follow-up visits give additional opportunities to emphasize enrollment and benefits of being linked to a specific class or department.

If the person already is enrolled but is not yet attending, this may give opportunity to emphasize _____ _____ _____ _____ ____ _____. It also should clue a Team about additional follow-up opportunities for other Sunday School members and leaders.

CASE STUDY #4

It hasn't been long since I prayed to receive Christ into my life. I could tell that my life had new hope and joy, which I had never before experienced. But, you know, it just hasn't lasted like I thought it would.

Maybe I've been too busy or too scared to go to church like I know I should. Maybe I feel like I'll go to church and ask a dumb question or say something really stupid to the people who have been going for a long time.

Bridge-Building Principles:

Every Christian needs to take actions that assist and enhance spiritual growth. It is nearly incomprehensible for a Christian to grow in isolation to other believers.

This believer, like every other Christian, needs to *participate in Bible study and worship*. This person needs opportunities to apply God's Word. Many people will feel intimidated by participating in a Bible study or discipleship group, where they think they will be put on the spot or be made to feel uncomfortable. It is important that persons in the class encourage new *believers and non-attenders* to participate in a variety of experiences designed to enhance Christian growth.

Many *resources* are designed to help new and young Christians develop Bible study, prayer and worship, and ministry skills. Since many newcomers initially may feel that they would not fit in to an existing *group*, starting new groups periodically—and targeting individuals who do not participate—will increase the possibility of their participation.

The FAITH Team needs to be aware of these types of needs and to *communicate* the needs and potential actions through Sunday School leadership team meetings, as well as in class gatherings.

In some cases, a person thinks he will have to do something in class, something that might embarrass him if he does it incorrectly (for example, to be called on to read Scripture when not familiar with the Bible). *Providing current Bible study materials* to the new believer ahead of time helps him know what to expect and eases his assimilation into the class. Also, sensitizing teachers to the presence of new members and to ways of involving them appropriately can help the entire class be more open to new people.

What are some additional actions that can be taken during and after a FAITH Team visit to build bridges to people who are not attending worship, Bible study, and/or discipleship opportunities?

Visitation Time
DO IT

As you go . . .

Be sensitive to opportunities to build bridges with people who already may have had some contact with your church. You may not know all the details behind their lack of response or participation. With sensitivity and without being judgmental, attempt to find out more so your church can be responsive.

Always be aware that you and your Team represent Christ and the church in someone's life. Even people with whom God is working may be unaware of their spiritual need or are reluctant to seek out someone in the church. Your FAITH Team can build the bridge that may enable someone to begin his or her journey in faith.

Are you and your Team experiencing opportunities to share FAITH in daily life?

Celebration Time
SHARE IT

As you return to share . . .

Celebrate every victory, even the "small" ones. What seems minor or insignificant at the time, may be a major inroad in the life of an individual or a family. Celebrate the faithfulness of participants to train and to visit.

- Other reports and testimonies
- Session 4 Evaluation Card
- Participation Card
- Visitation forms updated with results of visits

Notes

Notes

Home Study Assignments

Home Study Assignments reinforce this session and prepare you for the next session. "Journaling" experiences in Your Journey Continues are an important part of your development as a Great Commission Christian through FAITH training. Other assignments may include additional reading that enhances your experience.

Selected features in this section highlight opportunities the Team Leader has to build bridges to his or her Team, class/department (especially through weekly Sunday School leadership team meetings) and church, and community. They can assist you in accomplishing your important responsibilities.

Your Journey Continues

Read Matthew 5:13-14. Rewrite verse 14 in your own words here:

_____
_____
_____
_____
_____
_____

What are some experiences you have had in FAITH training that have helped you to be salt and light?

_____
_____
_____
_____
_____
_____

Notes

What are some ways you have seen your Sunday School class minister to persons visited through the FAITH Sunday School Evangelism Strategy?

_____

_____

_____

_____

_____

_____

What are some things you feel you have learned about ministering to people by participating in FAITH training?

_____

_____

_____

_____

_____

_____

Prayer Concerns

_____

_____

_____

_____

_____

_____

_____

_____

_____

Answers to Prayer

_____

_____

_____

_____

_____

_____

_____

_____

_____

Notes

An Important Bridge:
Your Weekly Sunday School Leadership Team Meeting

Use this space to record ways your FAITH Team impacts the work of your Sunday School department or class. Use the information to report during weekly Sunday School leadership team meetings. Identify actions that need to be taken through Sunday School as a result of prayer concerns, needs identified, visits made by the Team, and decisions made by the persons being visited.

Highlight needs/reports affecting your class/department or age group.

_____

_____

_____

Pray now for teachers and department directors.

How does preparation for Sunday need to consider needs of individuals or families who have agreed to enroll in Sunday School but have not yet attended Bible study and/or worship?

_____

_____

_____

How can Sunday School leaders and members follow up on people who have made a decision or commitment during a FAITH visit?

_____

_____

For Further Reading

Read pages 62-72 in *Evangelism Through the Sunday School: A Journey of FAITH* by Bobby Welch.
Are any of these results becoming apparent in your church? In your Sunday School class? Pray that God will change your Team and your church.

For the Team Leader

This weekly feature suggests actions the Team Leader can take to support Team members, prepare for Team Time, and consider ways to improve visits. This work becomes part of the Team Leader's Home Study Assignments. Add any actions suggested by your church's FAITH strategy.

Support Team Members

❏ Call Team members and dialogue with them about their participation in class training and in visits. Talk about observations they made during the visits and particularly as they shared their Sunday School testimonies. Discuss ways to prepare and share their evangelistic testimony without giving away the answer to the Key Question. Encourage them as they are memorizing all of *Preparation* of the FAITH Visit Outline.

Prepare to Lead Team Time

❏ Overview "Leading Team Time" at the beginning of Session 5.
❏ Be prepared to evaluate the written evangelistic testimonies. Use these criteria:
- • Define some specific event before (pre-conversion) and after your conversion (benefits).
- • Do not answer the Key Question.
- • Keep your testimony brief (three minutes or less).
- • Do not give unnecessary details; instead, concisely reflect your experience.
- • Conclude your testimony with the assurance that you are going to heaven.

Prepare to Lead Visits

❏ Review the FAITH Visit Outline to be able to model the entire process for Team members.
❏ Be prepared to model visits in which Team member(s) are asked to lead in sharing a Sunday School testimony and/or evangelistic testimony.
❏ Be prepared to model the use of the Opinion Poll in making visits.
❏ Be prepared to lead your Team to participate during Celebration Time.

Build Bridges to Sunday School

❏ Participate in weekly Sunday School leadership team meetings. Share pertinent information in this meeting using the feature on page 64 and FAITH visit results.

FAITH at Work

"In August 1998 we were averaging 105 in Sunday School and 150 in worship. In October (after 10 weeks of FAITH training), we averaged 131 in Sunday School and 200 in worship. We have had 7 professions of faith in the 9 weeks of visitation and countless numbers of lives touched at just the right moment as God led us to the right home at the right time, again and again. With 19 people involved, we attempted 93 visits, resulting in 76 actual visits. From these we enrolled 40 people in Sunday School.

While the numbers are amazing, the change in the lives of my people is even more amazing. I have watched people who are shy and bashful turn into warriors for Christ, sharing the gospel every chance they get. These are people who would never have considered visitation, much less evangelism.

The only way I know to accurate describe the change in these people is that they now have a new heart, a broken heart; a broken heart for people who are living and struggling without Jesus as Lord and Savior."

—Steve Jones, pastor,

First Baptist Church, Oak Hill, Florida

SESSION 5

Building Bridges to People with the Opinion Poll

In this session you will

CHECK IT: engage in Team Time activities;

KNOW IT: review principles taught in Session 4;

HEAR IT: learn how to lead in using the Opinion Poll and to discover benefits of its use;

SEE IT: see video on what can be learned by using the Opinion Poll;

SAY IT: practice the FAITH Visit Outline beginning with the Key Question;

STUDY IT: overview Home Study Assignments for Session 5;

DO IT: participate in visits in which Team members are available to share through the Key Question and/or use the Opinion Poll;

SHARE IT: celebrate.

Notes

Leading Team Time

All Team members participate in Team Time. They are primarily responsible for reciting the assigned portion of the FAITH Visit Outline and for discussing other Home Study Assignments.

As you direct this important time of CHECK IT activities with your Team, keep in mind how Learners also look to you as role model; motivator; mentor; and friend. Team Time activities can continue in the car, as the Team travels to and from visits.

Lead CHECK IT Activities

✓ FAITH Visit Outline
❑ Call on each Learner to recite the assigned portion of the FAITH Visit Outline (all of *Preparation,* plus key words in *Presentation* and *Invitation*). Indicate successful completion by signing your name or initials in each Learner's *A Journey in FAITH: Journal.* Be prepared to answer any questions Learners may have. Make suggestions for improvement.

✓ Final draft of evangelistic testimony due
❑ Call for final written copies of Learners' evangelistic testimonies. Congratulate Team members for achieving another important milestone.

Make sure any revisions include criteria discussed in Sessions 3 and 4 (not answering the Key Question with your testimony, and so forth). Ask for permission to print these testimonies in church materials that publicize the FAITH strategy or that encourage persons to share their faith.

Emphasize to Team members the importance of sharing their testimonies naturally, in their own words, in actual visits.

✓ Practice Key Question/Transition Statement
❑ Practice the Key Question/Transition Statement, helping Learners comfortably spell out the word *FAITH* on their hands.

✓ Other Home Study Assignments
❑ Look over Learners' Home Study Assignments. Are Learners on track? Clarify or emphasize key points from FAITH Tips and/or *Evangelism Through the Sunday School: A Journey of FAITH* as needed.

✓ Session 4 (Making a Ministry Visit) debriefing

❑ Review the importance of and approach for making Sunday School ministry visits. Help Team members understand how such visits "reconnect" many inactive members to church life. Highlight ministry visitation assignments and indicate why certain comments are made during different types of ministry visits (to absentees, nonattenders, members with ministry needs). As inactive members return to Sunday School, remind Team members they had a part.

Ask any questions you feel would solidify the Learners' understanding of Session 4, including questions that will appear on the final written review.

✓ Help for strengthening a visit

❑ Be prepared to discuss ways to strengthen a visit based on what has been discovered in previous sessions.

❑ Be prepared to model an Opinion Poll visit during Visitation Time.

❑ Identify which Team member(s) will take the lead in sharing a Sunday School testimony. Ask another Team member to be prepared to share his or her evangelistic testimony. With sensitivity to Learners and person(s) being visited, be prepared to resume the visit after Team members have shared.

Notes

Actions I Need to Take with Learners During the Week

Notes

Notes

A Quick Review

A new Christian needs a strong bridge into a life of discipleship and spiritual growth. *Your* Sunday School class can form a vital bridge to someone who has been reached for Christ from your age group. In some cases, your class can connect an entire family to the church.

If a follow-up visit is appropriate, that information will be on your FAITH Visit Assignment Card. You can *know* that your FAITH Team, if a part of leading a person to Christ, also will have the privilege of following up on that individual and his/her decision. You can help a person—

• clarify his or her decision;

• understand why a public profession of faith is important;

• realize how Bible study and worship experiences can start him on the right road; and

• explain baptism and discipleship as important steps of obedience.

Your Team also may uncover unique needs or situations by making a follow-up visit into the home. This information affects how you relate to the person and his/her family. Sensitive, caring follow-up can make the difference in how someone's new journey in faith begins.

The Person God Uses
The person God uses has a heart for lost people.

Jesus said, "The Son of Man came to seek and to save what was lost" (Luke 19:10, NIV). It is hard to imagine the enormous heart God has for the unredeemed masses of people in our world. It is hard to comprehend the vast love God has, that He would sacrifice His own beloved Son so that lost humanity might be saved.

The person God uses has a heart for lost people. What are some indicators of a growing Christian who has a heart for lost people? Here are a few:

• You understand that, like many people you will visit, you once were in a state of rebellion against God and were living a life of lostness.

• You have compassion and understanding for people who are running from God's love.

• You realize a sense of urgency to share God's message of redemption with the unsaved.

• You know God's grace can penetrate and change the most hardened sinner.

• You cannot wait for unsaved people to come to you or the church. Instead, you intentionally go to them where they are.

• You develop relationships with unsaved people and take advantage of opportunities provided by the Holy Spirit to share the good news of the gospel.

Dear Lord, help me to develop a caring heart for the unsaved—and to be an instrument You can use to help reach them.

Returning the Word *Go* to the Great Commission

We have been appropriately taught that, for every two unsaved people we enroll and cultivate in our Sunday School, at least one person is likely to be saved within a year. That's wonderful and encouraging, and it motivates us to continue our efforts.

However, it is obvious that on any given week many people choose not to participate in any church's worship or Bible study experiences. For every 3 people we enroll there likely are 30, 300, 3000, or even more in highly populated areas who are not interested in attending any Bible study group. How do we reach them?

Once again, the Great Commission gives us our __Focus and mandate__. Review the first part: "Therefore *go* (italics added) and make disciples of all nations, baptizing them . . . " (Matt. 28:19-20). This mandate appears in all four Gospels and in the Book of Acts, indicating its priority to our Savior.

But a strange thing has happened in many churches today: the word *come* has been substituted for the word *go*. Have you noticed this shift?

As important as it is, inviting people to *come* to church, to *come* to Sunday School, to *come* to our homes for Bible study, to *come* to special events is not sufficient. We must __go__ into our communities with the gospel, __not waiting for people__ to come to us.

Going is how __Jesus__ related to people, and it is how we are to relate. Going reflects our awareness that people are lost without Christ. It reflects our urgency and commitment to share the good news. As obedient Great Commission Christians, we must intentionally go into our communities to share the good news.

This session will help you train Team members to use the Opinion Poll—one way we have of putting the word *go* back into the Great Commission. It also will help you discover some unique opportunities to build bridges between our church and our community.

A Bridge to
Important Opportunities

When you first were asked to participate in FAITH training, you likely became excited about the possibility of sharing the gospel with and ministering to people assigned to your Sunday School department/class. You may feel more comfortable visiting your peers than you would visiting people you have never met or about whom you have no information. *Then* you heard about the Opinion Poll.

Most participants in FAITH training are apprehensive about the Opinion Poll until they see it work. Likely your FAITH Team members will feel just as uneasy until they see how God uses people to build bridges through this simple tool. The Opinion Poll gives your FAITH Team some important bridge-building experiences and opportunities.

1. Your Team can help *fulfill the Great Commission* by intentionally going to people who have not necessarily expressed interest in any church's Bible study or worship.

2. The Opinion Poll helps our FAITH Teams *go to people* who likely would not be contacted/reached by another evangelical congregation.

3. Teams potentially can *make a large number of contacts* in which people learn of our interest in them.

4. The Opinion Poll allows our Sunday School to discover and receive information, potentially on a *large number of prospects*. A growing FAITH ministry demands a large number of prospects for visitation assignments. Since it is preferable to have at least three prospects for each Team each week, it is obvious that Opinion Poll visits will be a great asset to any FAITH ministry.

5. Through Opinion Poll surveying, your FAITH Team can help us *locate ministry needs* and opportunities.

6. The Opinion Poll helps us *identify simple and natural ways* to share the gospel with people we ordinarily would never encounter.

7. Use of the Opinion Poll will help you *grow more confident* in talking about spiritual matters and in sharing the gospel with strangers.

This is another major reason we include Opinion Poll visits in FAITH training—for the benefit Team Leaders and members receive. Using the Opinion Poll builds confidence since it places you and your Team with

people you do not know and gives you a usable format to dialogue with and get information from persons.

8. The Opinion Poll gives us greater opportunity to _experience divine appointments_ with individuals who need to hear the message of the gospel.

Opinion Poll: a Team Effort

As is true with other visits, Opinion Poll visits are a _Team effort_. We pray for one another, and we take different responsibilities. In general, we follow these guidelines in making Opinion Poll visits:

When approaching different houses, encourage _all_ Team members to have pleasant expression on their faces. As your Team approaches each door, make sure one person has been _designated to Knock_, _share greetings_, and _identify_ our church and Team members (by first names). Designate another person to _Record Responses_ to the survey on the form.

1. The _Spokesperson_ on the Team should be prepared to—
• *state the purpose of this brief survey: to help our church be more responsive to needs in our community;*
• *ask permission for them to give their opinion on several brief questions; and*
• (if permission is given), *continue by asking the questions.*

2. _Team members_ should be prepared to—
• *listen for clues regarding spiritual needs or interests;*
• *talk about interests and church involvement;*
• *follow up responses to the Key Question in the same ways that was learned in earlier FAITH training* (If a *faith response*, say something like, "That's wonderful; we're so glad you have trusted Jesus as your Savior. Are you participating in a local church?" If not, offer to enroll him/her in Sunday School and give directions to and information about the church. If the person responds with a *works answer*, ask permission to share how the Bible answers the question and move into the gospel presentation.);
• *record as much information as possible about the person/family, including name, address, approximate age, and follow-up opportunities.*
• (If a person makes a decision), *indicate the decision on the appropriate panels of* A Step of Faith. *Provide the information needed for a person to know where to attend Bible study and worship.*

Notes

The Team member responsible for recording information may need to write rapidly. Data may need to be rewritten on another card after the visit to make sure persons at the church can easily read and transfer this information for follow-up.

Realize that many people will not be at home. Some of the ones who are will not permit you to begin a conversation. In most situations, responses will be shared at the door without the Team's entering the house. However, some people will invite the Team inside.

Always be cordial and respectful. If a person chooses not to participate in the Opinion Poll, be gracious. Note all information discovered (even refusals) on the Opinion Poll.

Even if someone provides partial or incomplete information—for example, only answering two questions or not having time to dialogue—he or she may represent a prospect or prospect family for our church. _Success_ in Opinion Poll visits not only occurs when a person accepts Christ during a visit, but also when Teams are sensitive to new prospects and to the potential the church has to build bridges to them in the future.

With this perspective, Celebration Time becomes a wonderful opportunity to celebrate Opinion Poll results and their potential for the future. _Celebrate_ —

- changes in how you and your Team view Opinion Poll visits;
- getting information to help your church be more effective in its ministries;
- new prospects/prospect families discovered; and
- individuals who accepted Christ or for whom a word from the Lord was planted.

Celebrate . . . and begin to follow-up.

Jesus Went to People

Jesus frequently engaged people in a discussion of spiritual matters. He often made Himself available and experienced what we might call divine appointments. A classic example is that of the woman at the well (John 4).

Jesus had to go through Samaria (v. 4), to a place where He knew He might not be welcome. He established common ground with the woman. He made the transition to spiritual matters. He let the woman know how her most pressing need could be met.

When you think about it, this is the only way that most people will have a chance to hear the gospel. Since they are not coming to us, we must go to them. Remember, this is how Jesus communicated.

Visitation Time
DO IT

As you go . . .

A Team member once commented there were not enough prospects to visit. A wise Team Leader assigned this person to his Team one evening. When other Teams got into their cars and headed out for visits, this Team began to walk toward the end of the block. When the man asked why, the Team Leader said he wanted the Team to see that prospects were everywhere.

Before they reached the corner they met a couple walking toward them. The Team Leader greeted them and began a conversation that resulted in the couple's praying to receive Christ. The Team member got the message.

Have *you* gotten the message? People are lost without Christ and our command is to *go* to people, just like Jesus did.

Prayerfully participate in intentional visits to share the gospel and to find out more about who people in our community are and what they need. Especially observe and pray for the outcome of Opinion Poll visits in this session.

Celebration Time
SHARE IT

As you return to share . . .

- Especially highlight "successful" Opinion Poll visits. Does our church have some new opportunities to build bridges?
- Other reports and testimonies
- Session 5 Evaluation Card
- Participation Card
- Visitation forms updated with results of visits

Notes

Home Study Assignments

Home Study Assignments reinforce this session and prepare you for the next session. "Journaling" experiences in Your Journey Continues are an important part of your development as a Great Commission Christian through FAITH training. Other assignments may include additional reading that enhances your experience.

Selected features in this section highlight opportunities the Team Leader has to build bridges to his or her Team, class/department (especially through weekly Sunday School leadership team meetings) church, and community. They can assist you in accomplishing your important responsibilities.

Your Journey Continues

Think about some of the individuals and families you have met during Opinion Poll visits. Did some people seem to be closed to any word from or about the Lord? Pray for these people now. Thank God for using your Team to plant a seed with these people; He has, you know!

_____

_____

_____

_____

_____

Read Isaiah 61:1-3. This is the passage Jesus read when He was in the synagogue and introduced His ministry (Luke 4:18-19).

Listed are four target groups of people identified in the Scripture as being persons Christ reached and we are to reach. Beside each word indicate a possible need (for example, *poor*—spiritual poverty, financial need). List a strategy this Scripture says for us to take to reach and care for persons with that need. Indicate a way your Sunday School class might reach and minister to persons with that need.

Poor

_____

_____

_____

Brokenhearted

_____

_____

_____

Captives

_____

_____

_____

Those who mourn

_____

_____

_____

Notes

Prayer Concerns

_____

_____

_____

_____

_____

_____

_____

_____

Answers to Prayer

_____

_____

_____

_____

_____

_____

_____

_____

Notes

An Important Bridge:
Your Weekly Sunday School Leadership Team Meeting

Use this space to record ways your FAITH Team impacts the work of your Sunday School department or class. Use the information to report during weekly Sunday School leadership team meetings. Identify actions that need to be taken through Sunday School as a result of prayer concerns, needs identified, visits made by the Team, and decisions made by the persons being visited.

Highlight needs/reports affecting your class/department or age group.

_____
_____
_____

Pray now for teachers and department directors.

How does preparation for Sunday need to consider needs of individuals or families visited through FAITH? _____

_____

How will the class begin to follow up on persons discovered through the Opinion Poll? _____

_____

Indicate ways Sunday School leaders can help you and Team members in FAITH. _____

_____

What areas in our Sunday School do we need to start or strengthen based on input from Opinion Poll visits? _____

_____
_____
_____

For the Team Leader

This weekly feature suggests actions the Team Leader can take to support Team members, prepare for Team Time, and consider ways to improve visits. This work becomes part of the Team Leader's Home Study Assignments. Add any actions suggested by your church's FAITH strategy.

Support Team Members
❑ Pray for and personally follow up on any Learner who may need personal encouragement.

❑ Contact Team members during the week to remind them you are praying for them and to discuss their participation in FAITH. Seek to encourage Learners.

Remember, Learners have overviewed the entire gospel presentation in Session 5 and may have questions about their role in making a visit. Record specific needs and concerns in your Journal margin.

❑ Think of appropriate ways to involve an Assistant Team Leader, if assigned to your Team.

Prepare to Lead Team Time for Session 6
❑ Overview "Leading Team Time" for Session 6.

❑ In a review of Session 5, be prepared to overview the entire gospel presentation.

Prepare to Lead Visits
❑ Review the FAITH Visit Outline.

❑ *Think about:* Do you need to begin gently "pushing" some Learners out of their comfort zones during evangelistic visits? Some may be hesitant to participate fully without some encouragement.

❑ Be prepared to model a visit in which a Team member is asked to lead in a visit up to asking the Key Question. Think about who might be ready for this opportunity or to share an evangelistic or Sunday School testimony.

❑ Pray for sensitivity as you involve different members in visits and pick up your part of the presentation appropriately and naturally.

❑ Prepare to lead your Team during Celebration Time.

Build Bridges to Sunday School
❑ Participate in your weekly Sunday School leadership team meeting. Share pertinent information in this meeting using the feature on page 78 and FAITH visit results.

FAITH at Work

❝We hosted a FAITH Awareness Meeting in Spokane, Washington in summer 1998. We sent 3 people to Las Vegas for training.

During our second session of FAITH—our first night of visits—we sent out 3 Teams, had 9 people praying specifically for the Teams and the people being visited, made 5 visits, enrolled 4 people in Sunday School, and saw one profession of faith. We later sent out a senior adult Team.

Until now, I have never as a pastor had 20 people involved in outreach visitation in one week. I have never heard any of my members say, "You mean we have to wait a whole week to go out and do this again?" The prayer team is jealous and impatient because they want to be trained and to go out also. I have never had that 'problem' before.

I thought you might enjoy a FAITH testimony from a once small, flatlined church in the Northwest. We don't feel like we fit that description anymore. ❞

—M.R. Kidwell, Pastor,

Dishman First Baptist Church, Spokane, Washington

SESSION 6

Building Bridges with the

FAITH Visit Outline:

Forgiveness and Available

In this session you will

CHECK IT: engage in Team Time activities;

KNOW IT: review principles and concepts from Session 5;

HEAR IT: learn supplemental verses, illustrations, and meanings for the first two letters of the FAITH Visit Outline;

SEE IT: see video on FORGIVENESS and AVAILABLE;

SAY IT: with a partner, practice FORGIVENESS and AVAILABLE.

STUDY IT: overview Home Study Assignments for Session 6;

DO IT: participate in visits in which Team members share through the Key Question but the Team Leader takes the lead in the visit;

SHARE IT: celebrate.

Notes

Leading Team Time

All Team members participate in Team Time. They are primarily responsible for reciting the assigned portion of the FAITH Visit Outline and for discussing other Home Study Assignments.

As you direct this important time of CHECK IT activities with your Team, keep in mind how Learners also look to you as role model; motivator; mentor; and friend. Team Time activities can continue in the car, as the Team travels to and from visits.

✓ FAITH Visit Outline

❑ Listen while each Learner recites all of *Preparation, Presentation* through the FORGIVENESS statement and verse (Eph.1:7a), as well as other key words in *Presentation* and in *Invitation.*

✓ Other Home Study Assignments

❑ Check to see whether Learners shared their evangelistic testimony with two different believers. Briefly discuss how these two believers responded to the testimony.

❑ Discuss benefits Learners are discovering from assigned reading material in *Evangelism Through the Sunday School* and in the FAITH Tip, "Nurturing a New Christian."

❑ Make sure Learners are writing in "Your Journey in Faith" (their journaling section).

✓ Session 5 (Overviewing the Gospel Presentation) debriefing

❑ Learners have heard the entire gospel presentation by viewing the videotape, hearing the presentation during visits, and overviewing it in Session 5. Ask Learners to share how comfortable they are becoming with understanding the significance of sharing the complete gospel presentation.

❑ Remind Learners that although the gospel presentation is built on the letters in *FAITH, A Step of Faith* is used to help lead a person to make a commitment to Christ and enroll in Sunday School.

Indicate that each of the following six sessions will focus on letters of the gospel presentation and on how to use the leaflet in leading a person to make a decision to follow Christ.

✓ Help for strengthening a visit

❑ Encourage Learners to be constantly in prayer for each other and for the persons being visited. Emphasize the importance of looking for opportunities to build bridges that allow us to share the gospel while, at the same time, being sensitive to the needs of the person being visited. Call attention to the fact that many times a Team might inadvertently close a door to receptivity to the gospel because they come across as "pushy."

❑ Remind Team members of the importance of being available to the Holy Spirit and of relying on Him to prepare someone for the gospel. We are to be prepared to share and to know how to compassionately lead someone to make the commitments that will forever change his or her life.

Notes

_____

_____

_____

_____

_____

Actions I Need to Take with Learners During the Week

_____

_____

_____

_____

_____

Notes

A Quick Review

___ **1. Which of the following statements is** *false* **about use of the Opinion Poll?**

a. Use the Opinion Poll when your FAITH ministry needs more prospects to visit.

b. Ask Opinion Poll questions if you discover a person is already a Christian or a church member.

c. A Team can ask Opinion Poll questions while standing at the door, rather than entering the house to take the brief survey.

d. Even if a person chooses not to answer the questions, try to get basic information to help (begin) building bridges between him and the FAITH Team/your Sunday School class/department.

2. In the space provided, describe the purpose you share for the Opinion Poll with the person you are visiting.

_____

_____

_____

_____

3. Place a checkmark (✔) beside the correct response(s) to the following question: *What should you do if a person answers the last question on the Opinion Poll with a faith answer?*

___ a. Celebrate his/her response, ask that he/she briefly share what Jesus means to them, and ask for prayer for your church's ministry.

___ b. Try to enroll him/her in the appropriate Sunday School class/department if not participating in any ongoing Bible study group.

___ c. Respond with a loud Amen and jump up and down in celebration.

4. Place a checkmark (✔) beside the correct response(s) to the following question: *What should you do if a person answers the last question on the Opinion Poll with a works answer?*

___ a. Record the response, thank him, and move on to the next house.

___ b. Tell him he is going to hell without Jesus, invite him to Sunday School, and leave.

___ c. Ask for permission to share what the Bible says about answering that question. With permission, share the FAITH gospel presentation and use *A Step of Faith* to ask whether the person is willing to accept God's forgiveness.

The Person God Uses
The person God uses is growing in the joy of his salvation.

Psalm 51 is one of the most piercing passages in Scripture. We understand that King David wrote these verses as expressions of his deep remorse for his sin against God and against Bathsheba and Uriah (2 Sam. 11-12:14). Every person who realizes the reality and severity of his or her sins identifies wholeheartedly with this Psalm.

The person God uses realizes that, without the sacrificial death of God's only and perfect Son, he would be judged as unable to be in the presence of Almighty God. The person God uses has accepted God's forgiveness and has been transformed by Christ's love into one who loves and forgives as does Christ Himself. Psalm 51:12 becomes the prayer and focus for the believer: "Restore to me the joy of your salvation and grant me a willing spirit, to sustain me" (NIV).

Have you accepted the joy that comes from being forgiven by God? Do you seek to help others know of the joy that changes your life on a daily basis?

Don't forget that after verse 12 comes verse 13, which says: "Then I will teach transgressors your ways, and sinners will turn back to you." The reality is that unless you remember you have much in common with the unsaved (you once rebelled against God just as they have), you cannot realize that the unsaved person wants the joy that passes all understanding.

Pray that your life will demonstrate the joy of salvation and that sinners will be converted because they see God's joy in you.

God's Forgiveness: Vital to the Gospel

It is important that you have a growing grasp of the biblical concept of God's forgiveness being available to all but not automatic. You may encounter someone who does not understand the need for God's forgiveness. You might dialogue with someone who does not realize that God loves and is willing to forgive him or her. During this session we will identify information designed to help supplement your understanding of forgiveness and to be prepared to further explain it if needed.

First, let's focus on God's forgiveness. Ephesians 1:7a is the verse we quote to highlight FORGIVENESS: "In Him (meaning Jesus) we have redemption through His blood, the forgiveness of sins" (NKJV).

Notes

Several significant words in this verse need to be highlighted to build on our understanding of God's forgiveness. While most presentations of the gospel will go smoothly and without interruption, in a few cases these words might trigger a question. For example, what would you do if someone were to ask for clarification of the word *redemption?*

- Redemption —"To redeem is to buy back something. God paid the ransom to Himself in order to satisfy the demands of His holy, righteous nature. This He did through Jesus' death and resurrection. 'God was in Christ, reconciling the world unto himself' (2 Cor. 5:19)."[1]

First Corinthians 6:20a says, "You were bought at a price" (NIV). This profound statement introduces us to the concept of being redeemed.

One picture that illustrates redemption is a slave market where persons were sold and bought. Redemption describes the action God took in purchasing you from the "slave market of sin." He paid for your release from sin by sacrificing His own Son on the cross.

- Blood —Jesus purchased, or redeemed, us and He did so with His own blood (1 Pet. 1:18-19). Hebrews 9:22 declares, "Without the shedding of blood there is no forgiveness" (NIV). Likewise from 1 John 1:7*b* we read, "the blood of Jesus, his Son, purifies us from all sin" (NIV).

God requires payment for sin, and that payment is death (Rom. 6:23). The cross of Jesus Christ is central in understanding God's forgiveness and salvation. Jesus was put to death for our sins (Rom. 4:25). He came specifically to die for our sins. His blood was shed "for the forgiveness of sins" (Matt. 26:28b, NIV).

"The cross of Christ will never be understood unless it is seen that thereon the Saviour was dealing with the sins of all mankind."[2] The reality is that Jesus was crucified. Spikes were driven through His flesh to suspend Him on the cross. He bled and died and was buried. All four Gospels (Matt. 27:33-61; Mark 15:22-47; Luke 23:23-56; John 19:16-42) describe the brutal execution Jesus endured. Hebrews 9:11-14 is one of many passages that remind us of the significance of Jesus' shedding blood for salvation.

- Forgiveness —Peter climaxed one of his sermons with this declaration: "All the prophets testify about him (Jesus) that everyone who believes in him receives forgiveness of sins through his name" (Acts 10:43, NIV). Forgiveness is defined as "an Act of God's grace to forget forever and not hold people of faith accountable for sins they confess; to a lesser degree the gracious human act of not holding wrong acts against a person."[3]

In the Old Testament, God required the sacrificial system of the covenant relationships to show the seriousness of and payment for sin. "The forgiveness of God, channeled through the sacrificial offering, was an _act_ _of mercy_ freely bestowed by God, not purchased by the one bringing the offering. . . . Jesus is the perfect and final Sacrifice through which God's forgiveness is mediated to every person."[4]

Jesus taught His disciples to pray by emphasizing God's forgiveness as well as our forgiving others (Matt. 6:14). Likewise, Jesus demonstrated a portrait of God's forgiveness when He said, while nailed to the cross, "Father, forgive them, for they do not know what they are doing" (Luke 23:34, NIV).

• _Sin_ —In the Bible *sin* always refers to the actions and attitudes of rebellion against God. The results of sin "are guilt, separation from God, loss of fellowship [with God], and a life of hardship, anxiety and death lived under the wrath of God."[5]

Many people have a difficult time seeing themselves as sinners. The _downplay_ of the concept of sin by certain groups today—who refer to such factors as sickness, heredity, or other forces beyond our control rather than to rebellion against God—has all but stripped the word of its real meaning. The reality is that _everyone has chosen to sin against God_, and the punishment for sin is separation from God.

If, during a presentation of the gospel, someone protests that he is not a sinner, ask whether you can talk more later. You will be talking much more about humanity's sinful nature when you come to letter *I* (IMPOSSIBLE).

If an explanation is requested at the time, suggest this way of thinking: Most people can identify themselves as sinners when they hear three categories of sins: sins of commission (those actions you commit against another, including against God); sins of omission (those good things you fail to do); and secret sins (those attitudes which are against another person or against God).

It is almost impossible to separate the truths of God's forgiveness and love from reference to our sins. We realize how great is His love for us when we learn what He did to redeem us from the consequences of our sins.

Psalm 103:10-12 reminds us: "He does not treat us as our sins deserve or repay us according to our iniquities. For as high as the heavens are above the earth so great is his love for those who fear him; as far as the east is from the west, so far has he removed our transgressions from us" (NIV).

Notes

Notes

God's Forgiveness: Based in His Great Love and Mercy

God's forgiveness is available to all! John 3:16 announces, "For God so loved the world that He gave His only begotten Son, that whoever believes in Him shall not perish but have everlasting life" (NKJV).

The Bible speaks of God's forgiveness as being an expression of His love. Innumerable passages refer to God's loving us so much that He was willing to provide the sacrifice to save us from the serious consequences of our sin. Here are but a few verses that remind us of God's love for the redeemed:

John 15:13, NIV—"Greater love has no one than this, that he lay down his life for his friends."

Romans 5:8, NIV—"But God demonstrated his own love for us in this: While we were still sinners, Christ died for us."

Ephesians 2:4-5, NIV—"But because of his great love for us, God, who is rich in mercy, made us alive in Christ even when we were dead in transgressions—it is by grace you have been saved."

First John 3:1, NIV—"How great is the love the Father has lavished on us, that we should be called children of God!"

First John 4:10, NIV—"This is love: not that we loved God, but that he loved us and sent his Son as an atoning sacrifice for our sins."

Read John 3:16 once more. "For God so loved the world that He gave His only begotten Son, that whoever believes in Him shall not perish but have everlasting life" (NKJV). As simple and straightforward as this verse is, it seems there could be no misunderstanding that God's forgiveness is available to all but is not automatic.

Why AVAILABLE BUT NOT AUTOMATIC Is Essential to the Gospel

Many people are blinded by the word *all* ("whoever") and so do not see "whoever believes in Him (meaning Jesus)" as being the absolute requirement for salvation. This error is called _Universalism_. This belief system teaches that ultimately all people will be allowed to enter into heaven. "All religions lead to God" is the supposed motto of this belief

system. It is "inclusive" in that it _accepts all beliefs_ as long as a person is sincere.

Many churched people may be practicing _"closet" universalism_, likely to their distress if the matter were brought to their attention. Such people share no concern about evangelism and about seeing people come to Christ. There is a major _danger in distorting scripture_ in this way.

"Of course, every Christian believes in religious freedom when it comes to individuals, but there is a tragic danger in thoughtless tolerance. There are beliefs across the land today that quickly are turning our society and civilization into an ungodly wilderness wasteland.

"Yes, Christianity is inclusive in that God meant everyone when He said 'whosoever' in John 3:16. Even so, Christianity is exclusive as Jesus Christ is the only way to the Father and heaven . . . (John 14:6). Any other worldview of Christianity is unbiblical and killing to the church of Jesus Christ and world evangelism."[6]

Many religious groups worship God or include Him as a major part of their belief systems. What they fail to recognize—and which is the distinctive of Christianity—is that _Jesus is the only way_ to God and the only means of receiving God's forgiveness and salvation.

Another way many people overlook the BUT NOT AUTOMATIC part of God's forgiveness is summed up with _works answers_ to the Key Question. The problem here is not believing too much as the universalists do, but in _not believing enough_. These individuals cannot accept the fact that salvation is not attained by their own effort, by being good to others, and by refraining from doing (extreme) bad things.

According to some recent polls, most people see themselves as acceptable to God because they are not bad people. There is no evidence in Scripture to support this erroneous view.

In reality, this view is exactly opposite to what is declared throughout the Scripture. Jesus said: "Enter through the narrow gate. For wide is the gate and broad is the road that leads to destruction, and many enter through it. But small is the gate and narrow the road that leads to life, and only a few find it" (Matt. 7:13-14, NIV). This verse identifies for us the main reason we must give emphasis to the BUT NOT AUTOMATIC point in the FAITH gospel presentation.

This may be the most misunderstood point in the gospel. Many people seem to believe that entering heaven when we die is more or less automatic.

Second Corinthians 4:4 is very instructive at this point: "The god of this age has blinded the minds of unbelievers, so that they cannot see the light of the gospel of the glory of Christ, who is the image of God" (NIV).

Notes

The _blindness_ mentioned in this verse refers to those who do not believe the glorious gospel of Christ.

The longer you are involved in the FAITH evangelism strategy, the more you will realize the truth of this verse. It seems that the reason most people think they are OK is that they judge themselves (horizontally) in comparison to their neighbors and so feel they are as good as other people. The reality and problem is that we are judged (vertically) by the absolute requirements of Holy God.

The *all* of the gospel is like a two-edged sword; it _cuts both ways_ . All have sinned (Rom. 3:23), but all may be saved (John 3:16). The qualifier is belief in the saving work of Jesus. _Without belief in Him there can be no salvation_ . God's forgiveness is available to all, but it is not automatic.

The following is a familiar illustration of this concept, but it is still a good one:

A trapeze performer displayed his skills before a large audience. Several times he walked a tightrope from one point to another high above the floor. He then asked the audience if they believed he could roll a wheelbarrow across the high wire. Everyone raised their hands, but when he asked for a volunteer to sit in the wheelbarrow as he rolled it across the high wire, he had no one to volunteer. This means, of course, that no one truly believed he could do it.

All who truly believe in Christ will enter heaven.

Visitation Time
DO IT

As you go . . .

Be aware that many people expend a lot of effort to look good, act good, appear good or better than their neighbors. The Scriptures tell us no one is good, not even one. People are lost without Christ, just as you were until you decided to accept God's forgiveness in Christ.

Just as this is a significant point in the gospel presentation, so are you at a significant time in your FAITH training and in your growth as a Great Commission Christian.

Celebration Time
SHARE IT

As you return to share . . .

As reports can help Learners clarify ways to respond to how a person answers the Key Question, provide this help. Also handle—

- Reports and testimonies
- Session 6 Evaluation Card
- Participation Card
- Visitation forms updated with results of visits.

Notes

Home Study Assignments

Home Study Assignments reinforce this session and prepare you for the next session. "Journaling" experiences in Your Journey Continues are an important part of your development as a Great Commission Christian through FAITH training. Other assignments may include additional reading that enhances your experience.

Selected features in this section highlight opportunities the Team Leader has to build bridges to his or her Team, class/department (especially through weekly Sunday School leadership team meetings), church, and community. They can assist you in accomplishing your important responsibilities.

Your Journey Continues

Describe at least one visit you have made in which it became obvious a person was challenged or convicted by the fact that God's forgiveness is available to all but not automatic.

_____

_____

_____

_____

What have you learned about God's forgiveness by participating in FAITH training?

_____

_____

_____

_____

_____

_____

Read the following verses and describe their emphasis on God's forgiveness.

Galatians 3:13-14

_____

_____

_____

_____

Colossians 1:13-14

_____

_____

_____

_____

Hebrews 9:11-14

_____

_____

_____

_____

Prayer Concerns

Answers to Prayer

Notes

An Important Bridge:
Your Weekly Sunday School Leadership Team Meeting

Use this space to record ways your FAITH Team impacts the work of your Sunday School department or class. Use the information to report during weekly Sunday School leadership team meetings. Identify actions that need to be taken through Sunday School as a result of prayer concerns, needs identified, visits made by the Team, and decisions made by the persons being visited.

Highlight needs/reports affecting your class/department or age group.

_____

_____

_____

Pray now for this important meeting.

What are ways the department/class can seek to impact the lives of people who do not realize both the availability and the requirements of God's forgiveness?

_____

_____

How does preparation for Sunday need to take into account persons who might consider themselves going to heaven because they are good people (because of a works answer)?

_____

_____

For Further Reading

Read pages 140-45 of *Evangelism Through the Sunday School: A Journey of FAITH* by Bobby Welch.

If you had had the experience with the cab driver (described on p. 141), what would you have said? _____

_____

_____

Read the FAITH Tip, "The Forgiveness of God."

FAITH *Tip*

The Forgiveness of God
"In Him we have . . . the forgiveness of sins . . ." (Ephesians 1:7).

"Beware of the pleasant view of the fatherhood of God: God is so kind and loving that of course He will forgive us. That thought, based solely on emotion, cannot be found anywhere in the New Testament. The only basis on which God can forgive us is the tremendous tragedy of the Cross of Christ. To base our forgiveness on any other ground is unconscious blasphemy. The only ground on which God can forgive our sin and reinstate us to His favor is through the Cross of Christ. There is no other way! Forgiveness, which is so easy for us to accept, cost the agony at Calvary. We should never take the forgiveness of sin, the gift of the Holy Spirit, and our sanctification in simple faith, and then forget the enormous cost to God that made all of this ours.

Forgiveness is the divine miracle of grace. The cost to God was the Cross of Christ. To forgive sin, while remaining a holy God, this price had to be paid. Never accept a view of the fatherhood of God if it blots out the atonement. The revealed truth of God is that without the atonement He cannot forgive—He would contradict His nature if He did. The only way we can be forgiven is to be brought back to God through the atonement of the Cross. God's forgiveness is only possible in the supernatural realm.

Compared with the miracle of the forgiveness of sin, the experience of sanctification is small. Sanctification is simply the wonderful expression or evidence of the forgiveness of sins in a human heart. But the thing that awakens the deepest fountain of gratitude in a human being is that God has forgiven his sin. Paul never got away from this. Once you realize all that it cost God to forgive you, you will be held in a vise, constrained by the love of God."[7]

Notes

[1]Herschel H. Hobbs, *The Baptist Faith and Message* (Nashville: Convention Press, rev. 1996), 49.

[2]*The Illustrated Bible Dictionary* (Wheaton, IL: Tyndale House Pub, 1980), 148.

[3]Earl C. Davis, "Forgiveness," in *Holman Bible Dictionary*, gen. ed. Trent Butler (Nashville: Holman Bible Publishers, 1991), 509.

[4]Ibid., 510.

[5]Ibid., 510.

[6]Bobby H. Welch, *Evangelism Through the Sunday School: A Journey of FAITH* (Nashville: LifeWay Press, 1997), 142.

[7]This material (November 20 devotional) is taken from *My Utmost for His Highest* by Oswald Chambers. Copyright © 1935 by Dodd Mead & Co., renewed © by the Oswald Cambers Publications Assn. Ltd., and is used by permission of Discovery House Publishers, Box 3566, Grand Rapids, MI 49501. All rights reserved. Used by permission.

For the Team Leader

This weekly feature suggests actions the Team Leader can take to support Team members, prepare for Team Time, and consider ways to improve visits. This work becomes part of the Team Leader's Home Study Assignments. Add any actions suggested by your church's FAITH strategy.

Support Team Members

❏ Contact Team members during the week. Remind them you are praying for them. Discuss prayer concerns and answers to prayer.

❏ Record specific needs and concerns of Team members in the space provided.

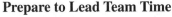

_____

_____

Prepare to Lead Team Time

❏ Review Home Study Assignments of Team members.

❏ Review "Leading Team Time" for Session 7.

Prepare to Lead Visits

❏ Review the FAITH Visit Outline.

❏ Be prepared to explain the significance of God's forgiveness.

Build Bridges to Sunday School

❏ Use information in "An Important Bridge" to share about FAITH during this week's meeting.

SESSION 7

Building Bridges with the
FAITH Visit Outline:
Impossible and Turn

In this session you will

CHECK IT: engage in Team Time activities;

KNOW IT: review principles and concepts from Session 6;

HEAR IT: learn supplemental verses, illustrations, and meanings for IMPOSSIBLE and TURN in the FAITH Visit Outline;

SEE IT: see video on IMPOSSIBLE and TURN;

SAY IT: with a partner, practice IMPOSSIBLE and TURN;

STUDY IT: overview Home Study Assignments for Session 7;

DO IT: participate in visits in which a Team member shares the part of the gospel presentation already learned but the Team Leader leads in the visit (Team Leader asks Learner in advance);

SHARE IT: celebrate.

Leading Team Time

All Team members participate in Team Time. They are primarily responsible for reciting the assigned portion of the FAITH Visit Outline and for discussing other Home Study Assignments.

As you direct this important time of CHECK IT activities with your Team, keep in mind how Learners also look to you as role model; motivator; mentor; and friend. Team Time activities can continue in the car, as the Team travels to and from visits.

Lead CHECK IT Activities

✓ FAITH Visit Outline

❑ Listen while each Learner recites all of *Preparation;* all of *F* and *A* FORGIVENESS and AVAILABLE; the key words for *I, T,* and *H* in *Presentation;* and the key outline words in *Invitation.*

Indicate your approval and any suggestions for improvement.

✓ Practice

❑ Give Learners an opportunity to practice reciting the portion of the FAITH Visit Outline they have learned up to this point.

✓ Other Home Study Assignments

❑ Check to see whether Learners listed two or three persons who might have a particular interest in knowing that God's forgiveness is available for them. Discuss how your FAITH Team can impact their lives with the gospel and with ministry. Also discuss the reading material which was assigned. Encourage Learners to continue writing in "Your Journey in Faith" (their journaling section).

✓ Session 6 (F is for Forgiveness) debriefing

❑ Learners are beginning to learn the gospel presentation. God's forgiveness becomes the foundation upon which the rest of the gospel is shared. It is vital to understand that God's forgiveness is based on the free gift of grace that God gives because of the sacrificial death of Jesus. As part of the gospel presentation, each letter is accompanied by at least one verse.

✓ Help for strengthening a visit

❑ Many people will not be aware of the free gift of forgiveness that God offers. Some are living with guilt and remorse because of sin in their lives. Others are insensitive to the fact that they are sinners who reject God's love and rebel against Him. The message of forgiveness may be an unfamiliar one to them.

Emphasize the importance of showing compassion and understanding with each person being visited. It helps to remember that your Team is not going to be judgmental but to share that there is real hope because God provides forgiveness through faith in Jesus.

❑ Have Learners had opportunities to practice parts of the gospel presentation in home visits? In visiting a Sunday School class member or fellow Christian, sometimes practice becomes an option.

❑ Have Learners seen someone come to know Christ in a home visit?

Notes

_____

_____

_____

_____

_____

_____

Actions I Need to Take with Learners During the Week

_____

_____

_____

_____

_____

_____

Notes

Notes

A Quick Review

The longer you are involved in the FAITH evangelism strategy, the more you will realize the truth of this verse: "The god of this age has blinded the minds of unbelievers, so that they cannot see the light of the gospel of the glory of Christ, who is the image of God" (2 Cor. 4:4, NIV).

Many people you will visit think they are OK. They do not recognize themselves as sinners because they are trying to live right and feel they have not done extremely wrong or harmful acts. They judge themselves in comparison to their neighbors and so feel they are as good as others. The reality and problem is that we are judged by the absolute requirements of Holy God.

The *all* of the gospel is like a two-edged sword; it cuts both ways. *All* have sinned (Rom. 3:23), but *all* may be saved (John 3:16). The qualifier is belief in the saving work of Jesus. Without belief in Him, there can be no salvation.

God's forgiveness is available to all, but it is not automatic.

The Person God Uses
The person God uses is humble before God and with other people.

The person God uses will have a reputation as a Christian who is humble and who lives by the Word of God. Humility is understanding who God is and who we are and then going about living our daily lives showing that we understand those facts!

Humility does not mean spiritlessness, weakness, cowardice, or a sense of inferiority. It does mean a life of high spiritual courage and strength. Humility is meekness.

For the person God uses, there is one scriptural action required: we are "to humble ourselves" (2 Chron. 7:14; 33:12; Matt. 18:4; 23:12; Luke 14:11;18:14; 1 Pet. 5:5-6).

If we refuse to humble ourselves, there are several predictable consequences:
- God Himself can humble us (Matt. 3:12).
- God can allow others to humble us (2 Chron. 33:11-13).
- God can allow us to destroy ourselves because of a lack or loss of humility. Samson (Judg. 13:1—16:31) is a clear example of how pride can take the place of humility and lead to destruction.
- God can allow us to remain unused. This result may be the saddest of all. The person God uses will humble himself or herself.[1]

What are ways you are learning humility as you seek to represent the King of Kings and share His message of hope and good news?

Father, make me humble before Your throne. Help me also to be humble in spirit as I seek to represent You with boldness.

It Is Impossible for God to Allow Sin into Heaven

This is a startling statement, particularly when people think that their "presumed innocence" gets them into heaven. Many people automatically think that heaven is the destination of everyone who has not committed the most horrible of crimes.

Think about how our culture refers to each deceased person automatically as "up there," "at rest," or even "with God." Some people casually refer to heaven as the next automatic destination. *Certainly, God would not keep any good person out of heaven*, they seemingly think.

Look at the statement for the letter *I* (IMPOSSIBLE) once more: "It is impossible for God to allow sin into heaven." We already have learned in FAITH Basic that it is impossible because of who God is and because of who we are. Let's investigate these realities in more detail.

It is impossible because of who God is.—
<u>God is love</u>. We easily acknowledge this fact by reciting the wonderful truths of John 3:16. The Bible expresses over and over the fact that God not only loves us but that He *is* love (1 John 4:16).

God's love is <u>unconditional</u>. He loves us no matter what actions we take. Imagine a loving, caring parent who has a rebellious child. With few exceptions, such a parent will love and cherish the child no matter how old he or she is and no matter what actions the child might take. It is hard for us to realize unconditional love since we often are influenced by people who love "with strings attached."

Notes

God's love _protects_ _and_ _provides_ _for us._
God's love also provides us with a choice of whether to obey or reject Him.

Love is the attribute of God which almost everyone likes and with which almost everyone agrees. It also is this attribute that causes some people to question, "If God is a God of love, how can He not want everyone to go to heaven and be with Him eternally?"

There is more to God's nature than just love. Just as a beautifully cut diamond has more than one facet, so does God have more than one dimension. Each attribute is complete and helps us understand the entire picture of God.

Yes, God is love, but God also is _Holy_ _and_ _just_. Many cults can be traced to a distorted emphasis on one of the attributes of God to the exclusion of others that are vital. God cannot allow sin into heaven because _sin is completely opposite to His perfect holiness and justice_.

God is holy. Nothing in our mind can possibly begin to comprehend the holiness and perfection of God. Words do little to express such grandeur. Pictures help us only a bit.

The Old Testament is full of imagery describing the holiness of God and the consequences of any (unholy) thing or person being in His presence. The entire _Sacrificial system_ was to help people realize the need for their sins to be paid by an unblemished lamb before they could be acceptable to God. The Temple was designed to help show the need for humanity to have a _Mediator_ go into God's presence (then symbolically separated by a curtain).

God is so holy that no one could survive a look at His presence. Isaiah 6:1-5 is a magnificent passage describing Isaiah's dream of being in the holy presence of God. One observation from this passage is that when we come into God's presence our first response is, "I am ruined! For I am a man of unclean lips" (v. 5a, NIV). A further response is, "Here am I. Send me!" (v. 8b, NIV).

God is just. It is important to gain an awareness of God's holiness to understand that God's justice simply *cannot* allow sin into heaven.

God cannot ignore or condone evil. Just as a court judge must pronounce sentence based on the laws of the land, so is God the Almighty Judge who will judge every person according to his or her sin (Rev. 20:4). _His judgment is without mercy_; it does not compromise based on the truth. Every sin is intolerable by God, and He demands that all sin be punished.

God showed His mercy by becoming the Sacrifice to pay for sin for all time. The Bible is clear that whoever believes in Him as that Sacrifice on his or her behalf (John 3:16) will be judged as

righteous because of the righteousness of Christ.

God's great love for us does not stop even when we rebel and sin against Him, but the fact remains that His judgment regarding sin is without mercy. Unless a person has accepted Jesus' blood sacrifice and acknowledged Him as his or her Savior, there is really no mercy in judgment. The stark reality is that when a person dies in unbelief, God's judgment will be without mercy (see John 3:36; Heb. 9:27).

God cannot allow sin into heaven because of who we are.—

Is there any person in this FAITH training who is without sin? The message of Romans 3:23 is to us as well as to folks we are assigned to visit. It is obvious that we are all sinners by nature and that we are visiting people who are sinners by nature. The difference for us (and for the Christians your Team visits) is that we have realized that we are sinners and cannot do anything to be saved apart from acknowledging that Jesus paid the penalty of our sins.

Many Christians have learned that sin is "*Missing the mark*." Although we have only one word for sin, the Bible uses many different words to describe the *different aspects of sin*. Consider some of the following meanings and examples from Scripture.

Old Testament concepts include:
- *a perverted mind (Prov. 12:8);*
- *a perversion of what is right (Job 33:27);*
- *moral and spiritual badness (Prov. 21:10);*
- *ethical wrong (Zeph. 3:4);*
- *moral or spiritual failure (Ex. 10:16);*
- *refusal to obey a command (Ex. 7:14);*
- *rebellion or transgression against God (Hos. 14:9);*
- *wicked behavior, or that which indicates that the nature of the individual is corrupt (1 Kings 8:47);*
- *unfaithful or treacherous acts against God (Num. 31:16) or in the husband-wife relationship (Num. 5:27).*

New Testament concepts include:
- *some wrong done to someone else (Heb. 8:12);*
- *a departure from that which is right (1 John 5:17);*
- *a lack of belief (Matt. 13:58);*
- *unfaithfulness or the betrayal of a trust (Rom. 3:3);*
- *a description of those whose purpose in life is to satisfy desire (Eph. 4:18);*
- *covetousness (Mark 4:19);*
- *a desire for something forbidden as in lust (2 Pet. 2:10);*
- *a hatred or enmity against God (Rom. 8:7).*[2]

Notes

Notes

Be very careful when you are visiting that you *do not come across as judgmental* of others. Remember, you can identify very much with the most hardened of sinners. Until you chose God's way over your own, you were just as guilty.

It is virtually impossible for an unsaved person to be open to the gospel until he understands he is a sinner and in need of redemption. Romans 3:10 states that "*There is no one Righteous, not even one*" (NIV). When we identify ourselves with the truth of the verse, it makes it easier for the person we are visiting to see himself in that same condition.

But how can a sinful person enter heaven, where God allows no sin?

To Turn Means to Repent

The Bible teaches the necessity of changing our attitudes and actions from rebellion against God to submission and obedience to God. The word used most frequently to describe this change is "*Repent*" or "*Repentance*." The reason you share the illustration about the car in the FAITH Visit Outline is because "repent" basically means to turn.

Repentance is an *attitude*. A definition of repentance is "a feeling of regret, a changing of the mind, or a turning from sin to God."[3] There must be a *Remorse for sin and a true decision to change*, an intentional desire to turn from sin to follow Christ.

Repentance is also an *action*. Unless a person changes the actions of sin and turns to living in obedience to the instructions of God, there has been no real repentance. In contrast, *those who Receive Him* are truly repentant.

Jesus preached repentance and associated it with one's acceptance of Him; those who were unrepentant were those who rejected Him. Jesus gave a wonderful description of repentance when He shared the parable of the prodigal son who returned to the father (Luke 15:11-32).[4] Paul's preaching virtually identified repentance with belief in Christ.

The letters *I* (IMPOSSIBLE) and *T* (TURN) are the crux of the gospel message. You are briefly sharing the bad news/good news, both of which must be understood. We move from a hopeless state (as a result of our sins) to a hopeful result (because of Christ, we can turn *from* sin and turn *to* Christ.)

T also stands for *Trust Christ only*. Jesus said that unless we become as little children, we will not be able to see the kingdom of heaven. Just as "repent" is both an attitude and an action, so does trust

describe both attitude and actions.
A person who trusts Christ *believes Jesus is who He says He is*. FAITH Teams may encounter any number of misconceptions about who Jesus is, including that He was merely—

• a miracle worker;
• a great person;
• an esteemed teacher;
• the one who established Christianity;
• leader of the Jews; and/or
• a prophet.

While all of these characteristics are true, they do not fully describe who Jesus is—the only Son of God, fully human and fully divine. Scriptures affirm Jesus to be virgin-born (Matt. 1:18); tempted as we are, yet sinless (Heb. 4:15); the Sacrifice who makes possible our salvation (1 Cor. 15:3b); and our risen Lord (1 Cor. 15:4a). He intercedes for us even now (Rom. 8:34) and promises to come again for us (Acts 1:11).

While Teams will not be able to get into all of the significant biblical doctrines, someone who trusts Jesus is expressing belief that Jesus is Who He says He is—the Son of God and the only One able to save. A person who trusts Christ *believes Jesus means what He says* about His dying on our behalf, being raised by God from the dead, and returning in glory to claim us as His own for eternity.

A person who trusts Christ *does what Jesus teaches*, even though he does not understand all the implications. Many people use the words *trust* and *faith* as synonyms. Reflect on the following story to illustrate trust:

Identical twins grew up in a loving family. Most people could not tell them apart. As they grew older it became obvious that though they looked alike, their actions were quite different. One (John) was good and always showed a concern for others, while the other (Ron) was disobedient and seemed to care for the needs of no one but himself.

When they were grown they went their separate ways. John became good and compassionate and a helper to others. Ron, on the other hand, lived a lawless lifestyle that always kept him in trouble. One night Ron was involved in a failed bank robbery in which he killed someone. He was caught, tried, and sentenced to death.

When John learned of his brother's plight, he knew he must try to save Ron. When John learned that Ron would be in a local

Notes

hospital for tests, he developed a plan. He entered the hospital, changed into prison clothes, and at the right moment allowed his brother to escape while taking his place as the prisoner.

The day for the execution came, and John was put to death instead of Ron. Later, the weight of guilt became unbearable for Ron. He regretted the actions he had taken and his good brother's death in his stead. Ron confessed what had happened. He was told he was free because the sentence for his crime had been carried out.

In a sense, this is what happened for the person who accepts the salvation which Jesus provides. We can be set free only if we will believe that "Christ died for our sins according to the Scriptures, and that He was buried, and that He rose again the third day according to the Scriptures" (1 Cor. 15 3b-4, NKJV). Likewise, "If you confess with your mouth the Lord Jesus and believe in your heart that God has raised Him from the dead, you will be saved" (Rom. 10:9, NKJV).

Visitation Time
DO IT

As you go . . .

We've talked about universalism and beliefs you may encounter when you visit someone with this philosophy. "Do you know anyone in your *church* (italics added) who claims to be a universalist, that is, a person who truly believes that everyone's going to heaven? We live in a society of universalists. *U.S. News and World Report* ran a cover story on hell. A survey was included revealing that 60 percent of Americans believe in a literal hell while only 4 percent think they'll go there.

"Unfortunately, Christians act like universalists if they never share their faith. If we fail to witness, we demonstrate the attitude that all will go to heaven, and this simply is not the case."[5]

As you participate in FAITH visits and FAITH training, you help many people we visit change their thinking and realize that separation from God and hell are realities unless they make a distinct choice. In addition, by your example and your experiences you challenge *church members* who, for whatever reason, fail to share their faith.

Pray not only for prospects we will encounter, but also for church members who may need a greater sense of urgency to share their faith. Pray that the Lord of the harvest will motivate and use them.

Celebration Time
SHARE IT

As you return to share . . .

- Other reports and testimonies
- Session 7 Evaluation Card
- Participation Card
- Visitation forms updated with results of visits

Home Study Assignments

Home Study Assignments reinforce this session and prepare you for the next session. "Journaling" experiences in Your Journey Continues are an important part of your development as a Great Commission Christian through FAITH training. Other assignments may include additional reading that enhances your experience.

Selected features in this section highlight opportunities the Team Leader has to build bridges to his or her Team, class/department (especially through weekly Sunday School leadership team meetings) and church, and community. They can assist you in accomplishing your important responsibilities.

Your Journey Continues

What have been some of the reactions people have had to the concept "It is impossible for God to allow sin into heaven?"

_____

_____

_____

_____

What have you learned about these truths by participating in FAITH training?

God is love

_____

_____

God is just

_____

_____

Man is sinful

_____

_____

There are several wonderful verses throughout Scripture that express God's desire for us to turn from sin and turn to Him. Read these passages and, in your own words, write specific examples that depict turning from and turning to.

Isaiah 55:7, NIV:

"Let the wicked forsake his way and the evil man his thoughts. Let him turn to the Lord, and he will have mercy on him, and to our God, for he will freely pardon."

Turn from: _____

Turn to: _____

Write the verse in your own words:

_____

_____

_____

_____

Second Chronicles 7:14, NIV:

"If my people, who are called by my name, will humble themselves, and pray and seek my face, and turn from their wicked ways, then will I hear from heaven, and will forgive their sin and will heal their land."

Turn from: _____

Turn to: _____

Write the verse in your own words:

_____

_____

_____

_____

Acts 3:19, NIV:

"Repent, then, and turn to God so that your sins may be wiped out, so that times of refreshing may come from the Lord."

Turn from: _____

Turn to: _____

Write the verse in your own words:

_____

_____

_____

_____

Notes

Notes	Prayer Concerns	Answers to Prayer
	_____	_____
	_____	_____
	_____	_____
	_____	_____
	_____	_____
	_____	_____
	_____	_____
	_____	_____
	_____	_____
	_____	_____
	_____	_____
	_____	_____

An Important Bridge:
Your Weekly Sunday School Leadership Team Meeting

Use this space to record ways your FAITH Team impacts the work of your Sunday School department or class. Use the information to report during weekly Sunday School leadership team meetings. Identify actions that need to be taken through Sunday School as a result of prayer concerns, needs identified, visits made by the Team, and decisions made by the persons being visited.

Highlight needs/reports affecting your class/department or age group.

_____

_____

_____

Pray now for teachers and department directors.

What are ways the department/class can seek to impact persons with the truth that we must turn from sin and turn to Christ?

_____

_____

_____

How does preparation for Sunday need to help persons consider the truths of the gospel?

_____

_____

_____

For Further Reading

Read pages 53-56 of *Evangelism Through the Sunday School: A Journey of FAITH* by Bobby Welch. How do the testimonies encourage you at this important time in FAITH training?

Notes

For the Team Leader

This weekly feature suggests actions the Team Leader can take to support Team members, prepare for Team Time, and consider ways to improve visits. This work becomes part of the Team Leader's Home Study Assignments. Add any actions suggested by your church's FAITH strategy.

Support Team Members

❑ Contact Team members during the week. Remind them you are praying for them. Discuss prayer concerns and answers to prayer.

❑ Record specific needs and concerns of Team members in the space provided.

_____

_____

_____

Prepare to Lead Team Time

❑ Review Home Study Assignments of Team members.

❑ Review your "Leading Team Time" responsibilities for Session 8.

Prepare to Lead Visits

❑ Review the FAITH Visit Outline.

❑ Be prepared to explain the significance of God's forgiveness being available to all but not automatic.

Build Bridges to Sunday School

❑ Use information in "An Important Bridge" (p. 111) to share about FAITH during this week's meeting.

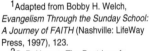

[1] Adapted from Bobby H. Welch, *Evangelism Through the Sunday School: A Journey of FAITH* (Nashville: LifeWay Press, 1997), 123.

[2] C. B. Hogue, *The Doctrine of Salvation* (Nashville: Convention Press, 1978), 22-43.

[3] Naymond Keathley, "Repentance," in *Holman Bible Dictionary,* gen. ed. Trent Butler (Nashville: Holman Bible Publishers, 1991), 1175.

[4] Ibid., 1174.

[5] David Self, *Good News for Adults: The Power to Change Lives* (Nashville: Convention Press, 1998), 14.

SESSION 8

Building Bridges with the
FAITH Visit Outline:
Heaven and the Invitation

In this session you will

CHECK IT: engage in Team Time activities;

KNOW IT: review principles and concepts from Session 7;

HEAR IT: learn supplemental verses, illustrations, and meanings for HEAVEN and the *Invitation* in the FAITH Visit Outline;

SEE IT: see video on the letter *H* (Heaven) and the *Invitation;*

SAY IT: with a partner, practice the letter *H* (Heaven) and the *Invitation;*

STUDY IT: overview Home Study Assignments for Session 8;

DO IT: participate in visits in which Team members share through the Key Question but the Team Leader leads in the visit;

SHARE IT: celebrate.

Notes

Leading Team Time

All Team members participate in Team Time. They are primarily responsible for reciting the assigned portion of the FAITH Visit Outline and for discussing other Home Study Assignments.

As you direct this important time of CHECK IT activities with your Team, keep in mind how Learners also look to you as role model; motivator; mentor; and friend. Team Time activities can continue in the car, as the Team travels to and from visits.

Lead CHECK IT Activities

✓ FAITH Visit Outline

❑ Listen while each Learner recites all of *Preparation*; all of the outline points for the letters *F* (FORGIVENESS), *A* (AVAILABLE), and *I* (IMPOSSIBLE); key words for the letters *T* (TURN) and *H* (HEAVEN); and key words for the *Invitation*.

✓ Practice

❑ Give opportunity for Learners to practice reciting the portion of the FAITH Visit Outline they have learned up to this point.

✓ Session 6 (A is for Available) debriefing/ Other Home Study Assignments

❑ God's forgiveness is available to everyone. Even the most hardened of criminals or the most unloving person is the target of God's love and forgiveness. John 3:16 reminds us of the scope of God's love and forgiveness ("God so loved the world . . . that whoever"). This same verse introduces us to the fact that God's forgiveness is not automatic ("whoever believes in Him").

This passage also focuses on the consequences of not accepting God's forgiveness ("perish"). It is important to remember that many people you visit will not understand that God's forgiveness is available to them but it is not automatic.

✓ Help for strengthening a visit

❏ Many people you seek to visit will indicate they do not have much time for a lengthy visit. Some persons may not allow your Team to enter the house because of time or personal constraints.

Your primary job is to seek to build relationships with people and to introduce them to the idea of enrolling in your Sunday School (class or department). Indeed you look for opportunities to ask the Key Question, hear responses, and share the FAITH gospel presentation. But also look for opportunities to build bridges with the person through Sunday School enrollment.

God may be using you to plant a seed. He also may be using you and your Team members to nurture relationships on His behalf. He also may be using you to prepare the harvest. Be sensitive to opportunities God is providing for you in the midst of visits.

Notes

_____

_____

_____

_____

_____

_____

Actions I Need to Take with Learners During the Week

_____

_____

_____

_____

_____

_____

Notes

Notes

A Quick Review

God cannot allow sin into heaven because of who He is and because of who we are. Were it not for His great love and mercy, we would be forever separated and estranged from God because of our sin. Only Jesus' blood sacrifice made it possible for us, and others we will visit who have not yet accepted His forgiveness, to enter His presence as if we had no sin.

Our responses are many—praise, gratitude, worship. The response God requires and most desires is repentance, a change of heart, and a life redirected in obedience to Him. To choose to trust Christ and Him only reflects this dramatic, life-changing moment—the beginning of one's journey in faith.

The Person God Uses
The person God uses is forgiven and is learning to forgive and be forgiven by others, as Christ commanded.

We understand the need to ask God for His forgiveness. We learn many lessons about our need to forgive others when they fault or grieve us.

The psalmist felt the weight of his sin always before him (Ps. 51:1-10) and separating him from a holy God. Jesus told us to be different—to forgive others (Matt. 6:12,14) and to forgive in unlimited measure, from the heart (Matt. 18:21-35).

It is much easier for us to realize our need to ask God for forgiveness and to forget the persons we have faulted. The person God uses asks God for forgiveness; the person God uses asks forgiveness from others.

Have you experienced the healing that comes when you go to someone whom you have faulted and ask for forgiveness? The words of Christ echo in Matthew 5:23-24, reminding us that the most worthy worship and service is broken by an unforgiving heart.

There is a blockage in the arteries of our life when we are not reconciled with one another. We have a growing cancer in our lives when we do not have an openness with others. If there is anyone whom you have faulted (intentionally or unintentionally) and from whom you have not asked for forgiveness and reconciliation in the name of Jesus, then you are not in a position to be freely used of God to your potential.

Read Ephesians 4:32. Then read the context of the passage by reading Ephesians 4:25-32. Can you recall from recent months, or even years, some individuals who might have a fault against you? What actions might you have intentionally or incidentally done for which you need reconciliation?

What actions will you take to ask forgiveness from and to reconcile with this person(s)?

_____

_____

Dear Father: Give me the strength and courage to follow up on my desire to ask forgiveness from those I have wronged. Help me also to forgive others as You have forgiven me.

A Little Bit of Heaven on Earth

There are two dimensions of heaven on which we focus in this part of the gospel presentation. Heaven is HERE. Heaven also is HEREAFTER.

The phrase "heaven is HERE" describes the *Quality of life available for every believer.* Words such as "eternal," "full," and "abundant" are used to describe this quality of life. Although Jesus promised and provides the quality of life that gives us a hint of the complete joys and satisfaction of heaven, there is a general lack of understanding or awareness of the present dimension of spiritual life now for the believer.

Facts such as the following help remind of us of the *Realty of the abundant life* available to those who believe:

• *We have been set free and are no longer condemned because of Christ's redeeming actions (Rom. 8:1-2).*

• *We are made heirs of God and thus are able to share in His glory (Rom. 8:17).*

• *The Holy Spirit bears fruit in the life of the believer (Gal. 5:22-25).*

• *The Holy Spirit is the pledge of the believer's participation in heaven (2 Cor. 5:5).*

• *We are made as new creation and are reconciled to God (2 Cor. 5:17-18).*

• *We are made alive in Him and brought close to Him (Eph. 2:4-13).*

• *We are able to grow in relationship to Him, and know His power and fellowship (Phil. 2:10).*

• *We are given hope (Heb. 6:17-20).*

In the FAITH video, Andrew tells Tony that his relationship with Christ is "like a little bit of heaven here on earth." Andrew's excitement about his salvation and the abundant life that becomes available immediately to a new

Notes

2 COR 2-7

Notes

believer is a good model. *You,* too, can share briefly personal experiences describing assurance of your salvation and ways your life has changed.

Eternity in God's Presence

The phrase "Heaven is HEREAFTER" refers as much to the *place where God lives* and *where the believer will live* as to the *Kingdom God will Rule* when there is no interference with His glory or temptation which could lure us away from His presence. For the believer, there is great joy and anticipation when we consider heaven in the hereafter.

We are visiting many people who have been influenced by misconceptions about heaven. As we focus on the letter *H* in the FAITH gospel presentation, we need to identify some of the *misconceptions many people hold* about heaven:

Some common misconceptions of heaven include the following:
- *Heaven is not a real or literal place.*
- *When a person dies and goes to heaven, he becomes an angel with wings.*
- *All people will go to heaven when they die.*
- *Heaven is a paradise existence here on earth achieved by only a few persons.*
- *Before a person can get into heaven, he must wait in a place (purgatory) to be purged of his or her sins.*
- *Heaven is a place of (sensuous) pleasure.*

Certainly this is not an exhaustive list, but it does alert us to the fact that not everyone we visit will have the same concept of heaven as we do. As a matter of fact, many young people likely will not have thought of heaven much since, in their perspective, heaven is far off. On the other hand, recent opinion polls have indicated that most people believe in heaven and expect to go there when they die.

While Jesus was painfully enduring the cross, He made the following declaration to one of the crucified thieves who repented and believed: "I tell you the truth, today you will be with me in paradise" (Luke 23:43, NIV). *The Bible gives us many understandings* of the magnificence and significance of heaven, including the following:
- *Heaven is a literal place (John 14:2-3).*
- *Heaven is the dwelling place of God (Matt. 6:9).*

• *Heaven is where Jesus is in bodily form (Acts 7:55-56).*
• *Heaven is eternal (2 Cor. 5:1).*
• *Jesus spoke of heavenly life as eternal time of joy, celebration, and fellowship with God (Matt. 26:29).*
• *Heaven is the place of God's throne and eternal presence (Rev. 22:3).*
• *Heaven is the future home of believers (2 Cor. 5:1-2).*
• *Presently all who have died in the Lord are there (2 Cor. 5:8).*
• *Heaven (the kingdom of God) is without the presence of sin (Gal. 5:19-21).*
• *Multitudes of angels are in heaven praising God and attending to Him (Rev. 5:11).*
• *There is no darkness in heaven (Rev. 22:5).*
• *Pain, suffering, and sorrow are not known in heaven (Rev. 21:4).*
• *Heaven is the place where the believer's inheritance is kept with care until the revelation of the Messiah (1 Pet. 1:4).*

For several reasons it is important to emphasize HEAVEN in the gospel presentation. Particularly important is the fact that *Believers will spend eternity in the presence of God*. Remember, those who reject God's gift of salvation and die in their sins choose eternity away from His presence, fellowship, and care.

Explain HOW Clearly

The letter *H* also means HOW. Review *A Journey in Faith: Journal* to recall details for using *A Step of Faith*: (1) The cover picture dramatically helps someone realize his personal sin, how Jesus died for him and how he, too, can have salvation/forgiveness; (2) sharing another meaning of *FAITH* (**F**orsaking **A**ll **I** **T**rust **H**im) presents yet another visual image of turning and trusting, as well as helps you make transition to the Inquiry question in the *Invitation;* (3) Romans 10:9 focuses the conversation on what the person must do to be saved.

A Step of Faith always can help you assess someone's understanding of the gospel, explain how to be saved, and guide a new believer to make significant commitments. It is especially meaningful for the person being visited.

However, as you are learning, not all visits go by the script. Don't lose an opportunity to ask someone to accept Christ as Savior and Lord by thinking you must have *A Step of Faith* to do so.

Notes

Notes

What Would You Do?

In a daily-life encounter, you find an opportunity to share FAITH. The person gives a works response to the Key Question and permission for you to share how the Bible answers this question. You've moved through the gospel presentation, and the person seems under conviction by the Holy Spirit. You don't have a copy of *A Step of Faith*. What should you do?

You can review the same HOW subpoints in the letter *H* (HEAVEN) by saying something like the following:

_____ *(person's name)*, you may be asking yourself: *How can a person have God's forgiveness, heaven and eternal life, and Jesus as personal Savior and Lord?* We've talked about how *H* stands for HEAVEN; it also can stand for HOW. *(Extend your hand.)*

_____ *(person's name)*, look at your own hand. Remember how we just spelled out meanings of the word *FAITH* on our hands? Another meaning of FAITH can be **F**orsaking **A**ll **I** **T**rust **H**im. And *Him* is Jesus.

_____ *(person's name)*, if you would turn from your own way of trying to make life work and, in a way, reach out with your own hand of faith to Jesus you could find this same forgiveness, heaven and eternal life, and Jesus as personal Savior.

You can know for certain that you are on the right road, and you can receive God's forgiveness, eternal life, and heaven. Remember what we said earlier: "If you confess with your mouth the Lord Jesus and believe in your heart that God has raised Him from the dead, you *will* be saved" (italics added).

_____ *(person's name)*, understanding what we've shared, would you like to receive this forgiveness by trusting in Christ as your personal Savior and Lord?

If the person says yes, lead him to pray a simple prayer for salvation. One of the most important concepts of how a person receives salvation is to turn from sin to trust Christ only. Help the person understand the necessity of realizing he is a sinner, asking God for forgiveness, repenting from his sins, and acknowledging Jesus' death and resurrection as the only way to be saved. The brief prayer should reflect these understandings.

You can begin to help the person understand significant commitments for growth, though follow-up will be important. Since you do not have *A Step of Faith* you do not have a place to record information; it is especially important to recall and record details so meaningful follow-up can be done.

May God be glorified as He uses you and others to share the good news people are dying to hear.

Visitation Time
DO IT

As you go . . .

Are Team members becoming increasingly comfortable with making adjustments as the visit merits? While your Team should plan in advance what is to happen and what responsibilities the various Team members will assume, the best visit is one in which visitors adjust to the needs of the situation.

Team Leader, as you make changes in the FAITH Visit Outline, be sure to explain why. Affirm your Team Learners as they show increasing confidence and ease in sharing their testimonies and in using the FAITH Visit Outline.

Pray for sensitivity to the situations Teams will be encountering in these visits. Always be open to enrolling someone in Sunday School.

Celebration Time
SHARE IT

As you return to share . . .

Ask a Team Learner to take the lead in sharing your Team's reports.

- Reports and testimonies
- Session 8 Evaluation Card
- Participation Card
- Visitation forms updated with results of visits

Notes

Home Study Assignments

Home Study Assignments reinforce this session and prepare you for the next session. "Journaling" experiences in Your Journey Continues are an important part of your development as a Great Commission Christian through FAITH training. Other assignments may include additional reading that enhances your experience.

Selected features in this section highlight opportunities the Team Leader has to build bridges to his or her Team, class/department (especially through weekly Sunday School leadership team meetings) and church, and community. They can assist you in accomplishing your important responsibilities.

Your Journey Continues

Read Ephesians 2:1-10. If all that you knew about God's grace was based on this passage, what would grace mean to you? What would you tell others about God's grace?

_____

_____

_____

_____

Describe some FAITH visitation experiences you have had in which you have seen people respond to God's grace in a new or fresh way.

_____

_____

_____

_____

What have you learned about heaven through your participation in FAITH training?

_____

_____

_____

_____

Prayer Concerns

_____

_____

_____

_____

_____

_____

_____

_____

_____

_____

Answers to Prayer

_____

_____

_____

_____

_____

_____

_____

_____

_____

_____

Notes

Notes

An Important Bridge:
Your Weekly Sunday School Leadership Team Meeting

Use this space to record ways your FAITH Team impacts the work of your Sunday School department or class. Use the information to report during weekly Sunday School leadership team meetings. Identify actions that need to be taken through Sunday School as a result of prayer concerns, needs identified, visits made by the Team, and decisions made by the persons being visited.

Highlight needs/reports affecting your class/department or age group.

_____

_____

Pray now for teachers and department directors.

Highlight needs/reports affecting your class/department or age group.

_____

_____

Pray now for this important meeting.

What are ways the department/class can seek to impact persons with the truth that, for believers, heaven is HERE?

_____

_____

That heaven is HEREAFTER?

_____

_____

How does preparation for Sunday need to help persons consider an explanation of the gospel and invitation to receive Christ?

_____

_____

For Further Reading

Review pages 152-56 and 164-69 of *A Journey in FAITH: Journal* to study the process for using *My Step of Faith* during the **Invitation** segment of the FAITH visit. Read the FAITH Tip, "Salvation and God's Grace."

FAITH *Tip*

Salvation and God's Grace

Foundational to this truth is an understanding of the impact of God's grace on salvation. Herschel Hobbs explained this truth in the following way.

". . . Salvation is by grace through faith in Jesus Christ. When man would not, could not be saved by the law, God provided salvation by grace through faith. By his sordid, sinful record, man proved that he would not obey God's law.

If God knew from the beginning that this would be true, why did He wait so long to provide salvation through His Son? God knew it. But man had to learn by bitter experience that he was too weak and willful to be saved by law. . . . When man would not, could not save himself, he was ready for someone else to do it for him. So in Christ, God did for man what neither he, no one else, nor anything else could do for him. That is the very essence of grace. C. Roy Angell once said that grace means that God gives us what we need, not what we deserve.

Originally the Greek word rendered 'grace' meant to make a gift, then to forgive a debt, then to forgive a wrong, and finally to forgive sin. So basically grace is a gift, as expressed in Romans 3:24. Literally, 'Being declared righteous as a gift by his grace through the full redemption, the one in Christ Jesus.'

This truth is plainly stated in Ephesians 2:8-10. 'For by grace are ye saved through faith; and that not of [out of] yourselves: it is the gift of God: not of [out of] works, lest any man should boast. For we are his workmanship, created in Christ Jesus unto good works, which God hath before ordained that we should walk in them.'

Note that salvation is not 'out of yourselves' or 'out of works' as the source. It is 'of God the gift.' It is by grace made possible in the individual through his faith. Good works are the fruit, not the root, of salvation."[1]

Notes

For the Team Leader

This weekly feature suggests actions the Team Leader can take to support Team members, prepare for Team Time, and consider ways to improve visits. This work becomes part of the Team Leader's Home Study Assignments. Add any actions suggested by your church's FAITH strategy.

Support Team Members

❏ Contact Team members during the week. Remind them you are praying for them. Discuss prayer concerns and answers to prayer.

❏ Record specific needs and concerns of Team members in the space provided.

_____

_____

_____

Prepare to Lead Team Time

❏ Review Home Study Assignments of Team members.

❏ Review "Leading Team Time" for Session 9.

Prepare to Lead Visits

❏ Review the FAITH Visit Outline.

❏ Be prepared to explain the significance of God's forgiveness being available for all but not automatic.

Build Bridges to Sunday School

❏ Use information in "An Important Bridge" (p. 124) to share about FAITH during this week's meeting.

❏ Encourage Sunday School teachers to periodically call on Team members to share reports from their FAITH experiences. Encourage your Team members to give periodic updates in your class.

[1]Herschel H. Hobbs, *The Baptist Faith and Message* (Nashville: Convention Press, rev. 1996), 50-51.

SESSION 9

Building Bridges to People Through Sunday School

In this session you will:

CHECK IT: engage in Team Time activities;

KNOW IT: review principles taught in Session 8;

HEAR IT: highlight purposes, principles, and outcomes of making a Sunday School ministry visit; discuss how to prepare for any situation in which a ministry visit might occur;

SEE IT: see a ministry visit modeled in which the Team visits a chronic absentee and discovers a ministry need in the process;

STUDY IT: overview Home Study Assignments for Session 9;

DO IT: lead the Team to make evangelistic and Sunday School ministry visits (Involve Team members to the extent they have learned the outline and are comfortable sharing; but the Team Leader takes the lead.);

SHARE IT: celebrate.

Notes

Leading Team Time

All Team members participate in Team Time. They are primarily responsible for reciting the assigned portion of the FAITH Visit Outline and for discussing other Home Study Assignments.

As you direct this important time of CHECK IT activities with your Team, keep in mind how Learners also look to you as role model; motivator; mentor; and friend. Team Time activities can continue in the car, as the Team travels to and from visits.

Lead CHECK IT Activities

✓ FAITH Visit Outline

❑ Listen while each Learner recites the FAITH Visit Outline: all of *Preparation;* all of *Presentation*, adding T is for TURN to the gospel presentation, plus the key words for *Invitation*. Be aware of time limits if two Learners are sharing; someone may need to recite in the car going to and from visits.

Sign off each Learner's work in his or her Journal.

Practice other parts of the outline as time allows.

✓ Other Home Study Assignments

❑ Emphasize the importance of involving the Sunday School class in FAITH, whether by prayer support, in training, or in follow-up. Discuss how, in this session, Sunday School will be the focus of building bridges to people.

Ask: Do class/department members who are not participating in FAITH still see themselves as a part of this ministry? In what ways? Are you sharing prayer needs and results of visits with fellow class members? Are they praying for you and for people you and your Team will visit? Is your class, department, and church growing spiritually and numerically?

❑ Home Study Assignments and memorization are reaching their maximum. Make a special effort during the week to personally encourage Learners, especially those who may have fallen behind in memory work or home study.

✓ Session 8 (I is for Impossible) debriefing

❑ Some important theological truths are communicated in this part of the gospel presentation. Are Learners at ease and confident in sharing both about God's love and His justice? About their own sinfulness?

Ask them to recall, from their personal experience—
• their need to be saved,
• their inability to save themselves, and
• God's saving initiative in their lives (their life-changing experience).
Doing so will help them continue to identify with the people they visit. All of us are sinners in need of God's grace. Some of us have been fortunate enough to receive and accept it, while others still need to know of God's forgiveness. Letting them know is a big part of what FAITH is all about.

If needed by your group, overview ways to respond to a works answer to the Key Question.

✓ Help for strengthening a visit

❑ Have most Team members seen someone accept Christ during a home visit by this time? If so, remind Team members of how such a visit should motivate them to continue in their efforts. If not, remind Team members that God is still working, even if they have not seen specific desired results.

Call on the Assistant Team Leader (if on your Team) to encourage other Team members; he or she may have had experiences in earlier FAITH training that can motivate others.

❑ As important as practice is, it is not the same as sharing the gospel in a home visit. Acknowledge that even as you encourage your Team to practice with one another and with other believers, as the opportunity allows.

Notes

_____
_____
_____
_____
_____

Actions I Need to Take with Learners During the Week

_____
_____
_____
_____
_____

Notes

A Quick Review

There are two dimensions of heaven on which we focus as part of the FAITH gospel presentation. Heaven is HERE, and heaven is HEREAFTER.

Heaven HERE describes the quality of life—*abundant* life, as John 10:10 reminds us—which is available to every Christian. There also is great joy and anticipation when we consider heaven in the hereafter—as both the place where God lives and the place where we will live, as well as the kingdom God will rule when there is nothing to lure us away from His presence.

We are visiting many people who may have been influenced by misconceptions about heaven. Our focus on the letter *H* in the gospel presentation helps Teams identify and address some misconceptions.

One of the most important concepts of HOW a person receives salvation is to Turn from Sin and to Trust Christ Only. You will need to help someone understand the necessity of realizing he is a sinner, requesting forgiveness from God, repenting from his sins, and remembering God has saved him. *A Step of Faith,* as you recall, can help you in this process.

You have one of the greatest opportunities anyone can have when you carefully and prayerfully invite someone to accept Jesus as Savior. By making yourself available for God to use you in this most important of encounters, you also experience the joy of seeing Him work to change someone's life.

The Person God Uses
The person God uses is a servant.

What is your attitude about being a servant? Are you willing and available to do whatever the Master says? The Scriptures teach many significant principles about servanthood. The primary concept we are to follow is to obey God and to love Him with all of our heart. We also learn that we are to be a servant in the same way as Jesus modeled servanthood.

Philippians 2:5-11 describes the attitude and actions of Jesus as a servant. Jesus becomes our Example as well as our Mentor:

"Your attitude should be the same as that of Christ Jesus: Who, being in very nature God . . . made himself nothing, taking the very nature of a servant, . . . he humbled himself and became obedient to death—even death on a cross!" (Phil. 2:5-8, NIV).

Read the following words written by Richard Gillard. These words have been placed to music and have become a beautiful hymn. Think about

ways Jesus showed us how to be a servant. Consider ways you can be a servant to God and to those we are to serve.

> *"We are trav-'lers on a journey, Fellow pilgrims on the road;*
> *We are here to help each other Walk the mile and bear the load.*
> *I will hold the Christ-light for you In the nighttime of your fear;*
> *I will hold my hand out to you, Speak the peace you long to hear.*
> *Let me be your servant, Let me be as Christ to you;*
> *Pray that I may have the grace to Let you be my servant, too.*
> *I will weep when you are weeping, When you laugh,*
> *I'll laugh with you;*
> *I will share your joy and sorrow, Till we've see this journey thro'.*
> *When we sing to God in heaven, We shall find such harmony,*
> *Born of all we've known together Of Christ's love and agony."* [1]

Keep in mind, ". . . servanthood is a holy place. It is the place where God and Christ desire each of us to live out our earthly existence. It is the place of great usefulness and great blessings for here and for eternity."[2]

Dear God: Use me as a servant who is obedient to You and who blesses others by following Your example.

The Role of Sunday School in Building Bridges

The Sunday School is designed to build bridges to people. Through ministry, assimilation, and discipleship, it is effective in connecting to and involving both new people and current members.

We focus on evangelism, discipleship (Bible teaching), fellowship, ministry (caring), and worship (prayer) to better focus on people—both current members and those we have yet to reach and assimilate into the class. You already have discovered that FAITH Sunday School Evangelism Strategy helps our church *focus on people*—both members and prospects.

You already know that FAITH is designed to help our Sunday School ministry identify opportunities to share the gospel, particularly to people who are prospective members of the class. FAITH also is designed to identify opportunities to help nonattending members and those with special needs find their way back to a group of caring and supportive individuals who are a part of the class or department. The FAITH Team can help *initiate bridge-building opportunities* and activate class members to build bridges.

Notes

Your Team already has had opportunities to make ministry visits. You will continue to make such visits. Generally, your Team knows to make such a visit by information provided on your *FAITH Visit Assignment Card*. Occasionally, a FAITH Team will learn of a member's need at the last minute and determine to visit without having a specific assignment to do so.

Frequently and ideally, however, the need or situation surfaces each week in Sunday School leadership team meetings. *This meeting is the bridge* that unites FAITH training to effective Sunday School work.

One of the main features of the weekly meeting agenda is to identify situations reflecting personal need and to request a specific age-group FAITH Team to make a visit. You already know that no other group is more likely to know of such a need than the class or department. In some cases, a class member or FAITH Team member will know of a special need in the life of a class member before the leadership does. If this occurs, then an assigned ministry visit can be replaced by an assignment to visit this class member, especially if the need is of a more serious nature.

Then, the next week at the leadership team meeting, a report can be shared to indicate the results of the FAITH Team's visit. Additional follow-up or ministry can be planned and implemented.

On most occasions you will want to be aware, before leaving the church, of the recent *attendance* (*or absence*) *pattern* of the member. Several consecutive weeks of absence could indicate a physical need. Or absences could indicate another kind of need, including a spiritual one. In some instances, you may discover a need that calls for immediate attention. Visiting a member after two to three unexplained absences (such as being on vacation) can keep that member from becoming a chronic nonattender.

Attitude Is Everything

The *attitude* of FAITH Team members is extremely important in making ministry visits. *Sensitivity* and an ability to *listen* are vital.

You are going in the leadership of the Holy Spirit. You are going as a minister in the name of Christ. You will be going to some people who are hurting, some who are lonely, others who may be angry, still others whose busy lifestyles have caused them to brush aside an earlier commitment to discipleship.

Some are under the direct attack of Satan, perhaps even moving into a sinful lifestyle. Others have lost sensitivity to the leadership of God in their lives. No matter what the situation, you will find that a ministry visit has the opportunity to accomplish several significant outcomes:

Notes

• *To let persons know your Sunday School class (and church) cares for them—or otherwise demonstrate personal interest;*
• *To develop or strengthen friendships with class members;*
• *To gain firsthand knowledge, and thus identify additional ministry needs class members might address;*
• *To provide assistance or comfort during a time of crisis;*
• *To discover possible reasons for nonattendance and identify ways to build bridges between the person and the class/church;*
• *To provide resources or some other gift to the person on behalf of the class or church; and*
• *To discuss ways to grow as a Christian and make a commitment to initiate or strengthen discipleship opportunities.*

How to Make a Sunday School Ministry Visit

In general, as you learned from A Journey in FAITH training, Sunday School ministry visits are to three main types of member situations: to _absentees_ (members who have been absent two weeks or more without a known reason such as vacation); to _nonattenders_, or chronic absentees (people who are on roll but do not attend); and to _members_ _with_ _special_ _needs_ (individuals who have experienced or are undergoing some life need).

Again as a review, individuals being visited are members of a specific School class/department. Your weekly FAITH assignment indicates the nature of such a visit, and that determination most often grows out of _weekly_ _Sunday_ _School_ _leadership_ _team_ _meetings_ in which many FAITH Team members participate.

Ministry visits require a strong sensitivity to the leadership of the Holy Spirit and a growing awareness of personal needs. Every situation has the potential of being different since every ministry need is unique. FAITH Team members who are good listeners, who encourage the member, who ask for opportunities to pray for the class member, and who assure him that

Notes

the class/Team will not forget about him are likely to see other good results from Sunday School ministry visits.

Although there is no script or visitation outline to follow, the _FAITH Visit Outline_ used throughout training can help you accomplish your goals. In every Sunday School ministry visit seek to take the following actions:

• _Introduction_

Introduce your Team or become reacquainted.—In visiting an absentee or a member with a special need, everyone should know each other.

Frequently, in visiting a nonattender, it is possible that the Team and the class member do not know each other. The individual may no longer live at the address indicated on the card. Or you may find that the family is attending or considering joining another church. In such a case, record accurate information on the visitation assignment card. One of the benefits of FAITH ministry visits is to keep class rolls up-to-date.

• _Interests_

Discuss common or evident interests, such as family, hobbies, and so forth.—Doing so puts the Team and the member at ease.

• _Involvement_

Focus on types of church involvement and participation.—This is where the Team Leader shares the purpose of the visit. Discuss the fact that class members have missed seeing the person in Bible study/worship. If applicable, acknowledge the ministry need that has come to the FAITH Team's attention.

Listen for clues about the person's spiritual condition.—This step is particularly important in visiting a nonattender, as a spiritual need may be at the heart of nonattendance. Be sensitive in listening for reasons the person no longer is attending. Share appropriate comments (but not confidential or personal information) during Celebration Time to help other Teams who encounter similar situations.

Share a Sunday School testimony.—Once the reason for not attending Sunday School has been identified, _tactfully seek to address it_. One way is by calling for a Sunday School testimony from a Team member. (Make sure the Team member knows in advance.) Whoever shares should describe general benefits of Sunday School and a current personal experience, all of which might encourage a member to return to the class/department. Leaving a copy of current Bible study material also can help the person consider resuming attendance.

Discuss ways the FAITH Team/Sunday School class might build bridges to the member and his family.

Invite the person to be part of specific class/church opportunities.—Take along any printed church information that describes such activities. Offer to meet the person at a specific time/place prior to the event, or otherwise help the individual be more comfortable in returning.

- *Inquiry*

In all ministry visits, especially those with nonattenders, be sensitive to the possibility that the person is unsaved.—Be sensitive to the leadership of the Holy Spirit; you may have been given a divine appointment. If the person is not a Christian and the opportunity presents itself, dialogue with the person about benefits of conversion. Follow the same order of the evangelistic testimony and subsequent points in the FAITH Visit Outline.

If the person being visited is a Christian, ask permission for a Team member to practice.

Invite family members not enrolled in Sunday School to enroll.

Make sure the Team knows of prayer concerns of the member.—Conclude the visit with prayer.

After the visit, *update information* on the FAITH Visit Assignment Card. Share appropriate information as part of Celebration Time.

The goal of a ministry visit is not to "get a person back into Sunday School" although it certainly is a desired outcome because of the personal growth that occurs through the class. It is important that the person being visited does not think this is your main goal.

Instead, your purpose as a Team is to be there for people, to represent your class as a group of caring believers, to show support for members, and to emphasize how welcome they will be if they choose to return.

Preparing for a Ministry Visit

Since every visit is unique, it is difficult to identify every scenario that can be anticipated. On the other hand, you can do some things to be better prepared for the variety of ministry visit opportunities.

1. Work on *personal qualities* **needed by a Christian minister.**

Compassion—This characteristic means sharing the pain, the hurt, the plight of another person and wanting to do something to change the outcome, lessen the pain, or meet the need.

Notes

A desire to help and a willingness to be involved—Identifying another person's point of hurt or area of need is one thing; taking the risk of becoming involved to alleviate the pain or meet the need is entirely different.

Listening skills—Listening includes hearing what the person is saying, as well as understanding what he or she is not saying.

Sensitivity—By listening and observing, a person can become sensitive to another person's needs, moods, likes, and dislikes.

Accepting others even when disapproving their actions—To be effective, try to relate to people as they are. That does not mean approving what they do; it simply means acknowledging the reality of their lifestyle. Your goal is to lead person(s) to become what Christ would have them become.

Confidentiality—During a visit, personal information may be revealed. A person may say more than he intended. You also may learn some things intuitively. Whatever the case, the person being visited needs assurance that information will be kept in confidence. If there is any question about reporting certain information, be certain to ask for his/her permission. Then be careful how and with whom the need is shared.

Emotional stability—Help Team members be in control of their emotions and avoid extremes in Christian zeal. Inappropriate displays of emotion might upset the person being visited or make him or her uncomfortable. On the other hand, learn to laugh and to cry with the person.

Spiritual maturity—Study the Word; pray regularly; apply God's Word by working in the church; and manifest concern for people. In other words, the spiritually mature are in a constant spiritual growth pattern. Second Peter 3:18 reminds us, "But grow in grace and in knowledge of our Lord and Savior Jesus Christ" (NIV).[3]

2. *Learn Skills* of an effective cultivator.

Build trust.—You must be genuinely sincere. The skeptical mind will quickly detect pretense. You must be open, credible, responsible.

Demonstrate a servant spirit.—You are a servant of Christ, and you are learning to serve others in the name of the Savior.

Be a Christian conversationalist.—Grow in your ability to ask questions that probe the person's interest without being too personal. Conversation related to the person's family, vocation, hobbies, and other interests is most productive.

Be available.—On many occasions, a FAITH visit will merely open the door for future bridge-building opportunities. Make yourself available for the person to contact you at home, at work, and in other settings.

Follow up with meaningful expressions of care.—Unless you lead your Team and Sunday School class members to take the steps to actually

respond to the needs, your commitments will be meaningless. Be sure to demonstrate Christian integrity so that the words you say and the actions you take are consistent.[4]

3. _Look for Reasons_ a person is not attending. Identify ways class members can respond to these concerns and build bridges to him or her.

Following are some general concerns that may contribute to a person's becoming inactive in Sunday School or other church ministries:
- *Occupational or financial transitions*
- *Need for transportation*
- *Extended illness*
- *Family problems*
- *Lack of interest*
- *Lack of concern or friendship shown by class members/leaders*
- *Lack of class ministry during time of need*
- *Poor teaching/dislike of the teacher/personality clash with member*
- *Dislike of music (or other aspect of the worship)*
- *Conflict with church leader(s) or member(s)*
- *Lack of youth or children's activities*
- *Disagreement over church practices and procedures*
- *Doctrinal questions*
- *No one to care for a sick family member*
- *Development of sinful attitudes/lifestyle*
- *Individual is lost.*

Many of the same issues appearing in an absentee visit also surface in a nonattender visit, but are more pronounced. If you are a Team Leader, help your Team anticipate the reasons and the increased complexity of a visit to a nonattender.

4. _Be sensitive to special needs_.
Often needs that have not been anticipated will surface in a home visit; they require sensitivity and prayerful handling. These examples represent needs many people have that keep them from participating fully in Sunday School:
- *Member or family member in the hospital*
- *Recovery from illness*
- *Death in the family*
- *Diagnosis of a serious illness*
- *Concern about a potential move*
- *Loss of job*

Notes

• *New birth in the family*
• *Emotional trauma (divorce, separation, and so forth).*

Many people drop out of attending Sunday School and church because they do not feel they have a support group during life transitions and challenges. Although Sunday School is designed to minister to members and prospects, many classes/departments merely focus on meeting the needs of persons who are regular attenders.

Your FAITH Team can help build bridges to absentees, nonattenders, and members who are experiencing unique needs or crises. Your ministry as a FAITH Team will be rewarded as you help persons focus on ways they can grow as Christians.

Visitation Time
DO IT

As you go . . .

Go out in the attitude and spirit of Christ Jesus, humbling yourself and allowing someone else to see Christ in you.

How are you able to serve others through the visits and contacts you make this week? Are there ways you can meet someone's need? Lift someone's load? Hold out the "Christ light" to someone else? How are you allowing others to serve you during any times of need? Remember, your Sunday School class is there for you, too!

As the Team returns to the church from its visits, the Team Leader should guide in an evaluation of what happened and what follow-through should be made by the Team and/or class/department. Discuss how the report should be presented during Celebration Time; be careful not to tell things of a personal or sensitive nature that surfaced during the visit(s).

Celebration Time
SHARE IT

As you return to share . . .

Highlight the results of ministry visits as you debrief with your Team. Indicate the different types of ministry visits and why certain topics were discussed. What would Team members suggest as actions for follow-up?

- Other reports and testimonies
- Session 9 Evaluation Card
- Participation Card
- Visitation forms updated with results of visits

Home Study Assignments

Home Study Assignments reinforce this session and prepare you for the next session. "Journaling" experiences in Your Journey Continues are an important part of your development as a Great Commission Christian through FAITH training. Other assignments may include additional reading that enhances your experience.

Selected features in this section highlight opportunities the Team Leader has to build bridges to his or her Team, class/department (especially through weekly Sunday School leadership team meetings) and church, and community. They can assist you in accomplishing your important responsibilities.

Your Journey Continues

John 11 begins with the sickness and death of Lazarus and Jesus' ministry to his sisters. This situation is full of ways we can identify with the need for ministry. It also can help us identify benefits of ministry, both from the perspective of the one receiving and the one giving a ministry.

Read particularly John 11:17-36. Look for ways Jesus—

• helped them deal with the seriousness of their need

_____

_____

_____

• demonstrated compassion

_____

_____

_____

• taught truths of the kingdom during the visit

_____

_____

_____

• listened

_____
_____
_____

What lessons have you learned through FAITH about ministering to members of your own Sunday School class?

_____
_____
_____

Recall your most challenging experience in FAITH. What did you learn?

_____
_____
_____

Who are some class members for whom you pray because of your contact(s) through FAITH ministry visits?

_____
_____
_____

Prayer Concerns

_____
_____
_____
_____
_____
_____
_____
_____
_____

Answers to Prayer

_____
_____
_____
_____
_____
_____
_____
_____
_____

Notes

Notes

An Important Bridge:
Your Weekly Sunday School Leadership Team Meeting

Use this space to record ways your FAITH Team impacts the work of your Sunday School department or class. Use the information to report during weekly Sunday School leadership team meetings. Identify actions that need to be taken through Sunday School as a result of prayer concerns, needs identified, visits made by the Team, and decisions made by the persons being visited.

Highlight needs/reports affecting your class/department or age group.

_____

_____

_____

Pray now for teachers and department directors.

How does preparation for Sunday need to consider needs of individuals or families visited through FAITH?

_____

_____

_____

How will the class begin to follow up on persons who received a ministry visit?

_____

_____

_____

What areas in our Sunday School do we need to start or strengthen based on input from ministry visits?

_____

_____

_____

For Further Reading

Read pages 66-72 in *Evangelism Through the Sunday School: A Journey of FAITH* by Bobby Welch.

For the Team Leader

This weekly feature suggests actions the Team Leader can take to support Team members, prepare for Team Time, and consider ways to improve visits. This work becomes part of the Team Leader's Home Study Assignments. Add any actions suggested by your church's FAITH strategy.

Support Team Members
❏ Pray for and personally follow up on any Learner who may need personal encouragement.

❏ Contact Team members during the week to remind them you are praying for them and to discuss their participation in FAITH.

❏ Learners are memorizing the gospel presentation, T is for TURN. As you discuss this content with Team members, remind them that this is the heart of the gospel.

Prepare to Lead Team Time
❏ Overview "Leading Team Time" for Session 10.
❏ Review the FAITH Visit Outline.

Prepare to Lead Visits
❏ Be prepared to explain the benefits and procedures of making Sunday School ministry visits.

❏ Be prepared to model a visit in which Team member(s) are asked to lead in a visit up to the point of T is for TURN.

❏ Be prepared to lead your Team to participate during Celebration Time.

Build Bridges to Sunday School
❏ Participate in weekly Sunday School leadership team meetings.

❏ Share pertinent information in this meeting using information on page 142 and other FAITH visit results.

[1]1997 Scripture In Song (a div. of Integrity Music, Inc) All rights reserved. International copyright secured. Used by permission. c/o Integrity Music, Inc., 1000 Cody Road, Mobile, AL 36695.
[2]Bobby H. Welch, *Evangelism Through the Sunday School: A Journey of FAITH* (Nashville: LifeWay Press, 1997), 125.
[3]Neil E. Jackson, Jr., "Qualities Needed for Personal Visitation," in *Going . . . One On One: A Comprehensive Guide for Making Personal Visits* (Nashville: Convention Press, 1994), 34-36.
[4]C. Ferris Jordan, "Making a Visit to Cultivate a Prospect," in *Going . . . One On One: A Comprehensive Guide for Making Personal Visits* (Nashville: Convention Press, 1994), 53-54.

FAITH at Work

❝The first semester our church went from having 3-4 people coming to outreach, to 18 people. Last night two Teams had professions of faith. One man (visited) is 78 and has cancer; the Team went to see his wife, who had visited our church.

At Christmas, our church adopted children through a prison ministry project. Last night, in a visit to one of those families, a teenager and two older children accepted Christ. They want to come to Sunday School if we can get transportation arranged.

Two weeks ago a Team couldn't find anyone at home for whom they had assigned names. Their Team Leader told them they were going to do Opinion Poll visits. At the first door they got to share the gospel, and the woman accepted Christ. She told them she had been praying for someone to come see her that day. That was a divine appointment.

A couple of weeks ago my Team visited a family from Nigeria who are members of our church. The wife had been absent for several weeks because she works on Sundays. We were strengthened by the testimony from committed believers who have had to flee their country because of political problems. Last week a lady joined our church whose Chinese father had been saved through the effort of Baptist missionaries.

The pastor and I believe that FAITH may be the tool that helps move our church from being inwardly focused to reaching out to our community in a focused way. We cannot put limits on what might happen in our church and our denomination if we get focused on what we need to be about.❞

—Jerry Frazier,
Groveton Baptist Church, Alexandria, Virginia

SESSION 10

Building Bridges to the Entire Family

In this session you will

CHECK IT: engage in Team Time activities;

KNOW IT: review selected principles from Session 9;

HEAR IT: consider the implications of other family members' being in a home during a visit and learn ways to build bridges to them;

SAY IT: with a partner, practice as much of the FAITH Visit Outline as time allows;

STUDY IT: overview Home Study Assignments for Session 10;

DO IT: make visits in which a Team member takes the lead, with the Team Leader's support;

SHARE IT: celebrate.

Notes

Leading Team Time

All Team members participate in Team Time. They are primarily responsible for reciting the assigned portion of the FAITH Visit Outline and for discussing other Home Study Assignments.

As you direct this important time of CHECK IT activities with your Team, keep in mind how Learners also look to you as role model; motivator; mentor, and friend. Team Time activities can continue in the car, as the Team travels to and from visits.

Lead CHECK IT Activities

✓ FAITH Visit Outline
❑ Listen while each Learner recites all of the *Preparation* and *Presentation* content and key words for *Invitation*.

✓ Practice
❑ Give opportunity for Learners to practice reciting the portion of the FAITH Visit Outline they have learned up to this point.

✓ Other Home Study Assignments
❑ This may be a good time to discuss the benefits of writing a weekly journal as part of the FAITH training. Discuss some of the truths or understandings gained through the weekly Bible studies. Dialogue about how the reflective questions have impacted Learners' training experience.

✓ Session 9 (T is for Turn) debriefing
❑ T is for TURN. This is the point in the gospel in which a person makes a significant choice—whether or not to receive salvation. To be forgiven, a person must turn from his sin and turn to Christ. He must trust Christ and Christ only.

The imagery of turning is reinforced with the simple question, "If you were driving down the road and someone asked you to turn, what would he or she be asking you to do?" *(change direction)*. Most people can easily understand the idea of changing from one direction to another.

The Bible uses the word *repent* to depict the same thing. The Bible is clear about the need for a person to repent of sin and to live for Christ (change direction) by committing to and trusting Him. Team members will need to remember the significance of the concepts behind the letter *T* to help explain and emphasize the how of the gospel.

✓ Help for strengthening a visit

The illustration of changing directions in a car is the only dialogue that is planned as part of the actual gospel presentation. It is important to ask the person to share his or her answer to the question. The response is predictable, but by asking the question you call the person's attention to the gospel and increase his or her participation in the discussion.

You might be talking with a child, a younger youth, or someone who obviously does not drive. If so, adapt the question to something like, "If you were riding down the road and you asked the driver to turn, what would you be wanting the driver to do?"

It usually will be significant to use the word *repent* only after the question has helped you explain what the word means. Use of the turning analogy to emphasize faith in Christ also helps clarify the meaning of *repent.* For many unsaved or unchurched people, *repent* is associated with religious or churchy terms; without a relevant, contemporary explanation, this word might lose much of its significance.

❏ Remind Team members to listen during each visit for ministry opportunities, as well as for things a person might say to help you identify with his or her spiritual journey.

❏ Discuss how, as Team Leader, you communicate follow-up information to the appropriate age group/class/department when you encounter family members of different ages in a home visit.

Notes

_____
_____
_____
_____
_____
_____

Actions I Need to Take with Learners During the Week

_____
_____
_____
_____
_____
_____

Notes

Notes

A Quick Review

As you recall, your FAITH visits include several main types:
- *prospect or evangelistic visits,* in which the Team may have the potential to share the gospel;
- *follow-up visits,* in which the Team visits someone who has made a significant commitment, most often a decision to accept Christ as Savior, during the previous visit;
- *Opinion Poll visits;* and
- *Sunday School ministry visits.*

The last type of visit has the potential to—
- help our Sunday School keep in touch with members;
- meet specific and unique needs in their lives; and
- reactivate absentees before they become chronic nonattenders.

Information to be addressed through ministry visits often surfaces during weekly Sunday School leadership team meetings. Other details are recorded on weekly FAITH Visit Assignment Cards, enabling Teams to make contacts using the most up-to-date information possible. Class members are praying and are sensitive to needs they can address.

While the different situations may vary significantly, the FAITH Visit Outline, especially the INTRODUCTION section, is a good framework for involving the Team and the Sunday School member in a meaningful visit. A capacity to listen with sensitivity, among other skills and personal characteristics, can make the difference in a good visit.

A "good visit" can reclaim someone for our church and for a Sunday School class. A number of FAITH churches have experienced significant results and meaningful personal impact when visiting chronic absentees or inactive members. It some cases, a ministry visit may surface for the first time a Sunday School member's need for God's forgiveness and salvation.

Ministry visits are a significant part of the FAITH strategy.

The Person God Uses
The person God uses gives the glory to Him.

Acts 2:43 declares that a simply remarkable thing took place in the early church: "Everyone was filled with awe, and many wonders and miraculous signs were done by the apostles" (NIV). The amazing thing is not that God was at work among His people, but that the believers were available to God so He could do marvelous things through them. They opened their spiritual eyes and saw God at work in their midst. They gave the glory to God for what only He could do (Acts 2:47).

A danger for churches is the tendency toward spiritual pride. We are honored to see God at work saving people and drawing them to Him. Yet it becomes easy for us to take credit even for some of the work with which He allows us to be associated. Many believers pray diligently for God to do something wonderful and unique. Yet when God acts, it is so easy to forget Who did the work and to seek to take some of the credit.

Be careful to give glory to God for the work He has done and continues to do in people's lives—action that results in salvation. Remember to humbly walk in footsteps that follow the Master. Remember Who does the work of salvation. Remember that God alone deserves the glory!

Lord, forgive us for failing to recognize You at work in our midst. Forgive us for our spiritual pride. Let us be faithful in giving You the glory that is due You and You alone!

You committed to be part of the FAITH Sunday School Evangelism Strategy training in order to focus on persons in your Sunday School class or department. You have spent nearly two semesters in FAITH focusing on ways to minister to and share the gospel with individuals in your class. In doing this, you have discovered many opportunities for visits with persons who have been in an age division other than the one you are assigned. Although the principles and approaches have focused on making a visit to an adult, you have experienced and heard of visits with persons of all ages. As you train others in FAITH, it becomes important to be sensitive to and address the distinctive needs and issues of all age groups.

This session will help you overview some important considerations when visiting in a home in which at least one person is in a different division than is assigned to your Sunday School department.

As we briefly focus on preschoolers, children, youth, and adults, look for ways you can help your Team adjust a visit when someone from that age division is present in the home. As you do, you may be building bridges in different ways to help reach the entire family for Bible study or Christ.

Notes

What If . . . a Preschooler Is in the Room?

As a general rule, Preschool Sunday School workers visit homes to contact parents and to make ministry visits with preschool members or prospects. However, you are a Sunday School worker with children, youth, or adults and find your Team visiting a home in which a preschooler is present and active. What should you do?

Begin by being prepared for the __dynamics__ of such a visit. Observe these and other guidelines as developed with your church's preschool ministry:

• *Be sensitive to the* __potential presence and needs__ *of preschoolers.*—Preschoolers demand a schedule in which at least one parent must respond immediately to physical, social, and emotional needs. Often loud, unfamiliar voices cause strain and disruption for young preschoolers. Parents will appreciate Team members who are conscious of the timing and effects of visits during such important times as sleeping, eating, and bathing.

There may be times when it is appropriate to consider scheduling the visit at another time, especially if doing so might allow adults in the home to give better attention to your message. Especially when young preschoolers are in the home, be sensitive to this potential need.

• *Sit near the preschooler.* —If the family gives permission for a visit now, __acknowledge__ *the child with* __your presence__. Some preschoolers may be shy or hesitant around strangers, while others will want to be the center of your attention.

At least one Team member might offer to sit with and give attention to the preschooler as needed during a visit targeting older family members. Such involvement and help by a Team member is especially important if the adults you are visiting are open to hearing the gospel presentation.

• *At the same time, never allow a Team member to be alone with a preschooler for any period of time.*

• *Be sensitive to* __ministry needs and opportunities__.—On occasion, a ministry visit will reveal situations in which preschoolers and their families are hurting or have special needs. Parents will appreciate someone who listens and provides care, comfort, and help in meeting needs. You may be able to build bridges to Sunday School for parents and the preschooler.

• *Build bridges for the preschooler's* __involvement in Sunday School__ *by taking along a sample of appropriate materials.*—Leaflets such as *Early Bible Steps* or *Preschool Bible Fun* are

good to give to preschoolers because they are suitable for the age of the child. Also, offer to parents Bible study material and information that identifies _Church policies_ on security, safety, and teaching of preschoolers while they are at church.

Preschoolers and their families quickly can sense the comfort and security provided by caring adults. Parents will welcome knowing that their child will be part of a church/Sunday School that cares about their child.

• *In building bridges of relationship, be open to opportunities to* _Introduce simple Bible truths_ *to preschoolers.*—Every moment with a preschooler is a teachable moment. In talking about God, Jesus, the church, and the Bible with preschoolers, use simple Bible verses, phrases, or thoughts. Such Bible phrases and verses as "God loves you" or "Jesus loves you" help a preschooler feel secure and can build trust in other adults at church. Simple Bible stories—such as Jesus and the children or the birth of Jesus—will help preschoolers begin to build foundations of faith.

As you build relationships with and introduce important Bible thoughts to preschoolers, you lay foundations for a future decision for Christ—one that the individual will understand and which will guide and direct his life.

• _Talk appropriately_ *with the preschooler.*—Remember, preschoolers are literal-minded. Avoid abstract or symbolic concepts—for example, "let Jesus live in your heart." Instead, use language that is clear and simple.

• *If an opportunity has not come up earlier,* _ask permission To enroll the entire family_ *in Sunday School.*

What If . . . a Child (Grades 1-6) Is in the Home?

How should a FAITH Team best handle the presence of elementary-age children in the home when visiting their parents? A person who makes a visit into a home where a child is present needs to keep several important principles in mind.

• *Just as there are major differences between younger and older preschoolers, so are there* _major differences between children_ .—In particular, children are active in their physical, mental, and social development. They are beginning to move from almost exclusive concrete thinking to more abstract thinking.

Notes

• *Recognize that children are at a significant time in their* _spiritual development_.—Many children are privileged to be raised in loving, caring homes that build strong foundations for their understanding of God's love. Other children are in homes that lack such support.

• _Talk with children_.—Children are not adults; but they can think, talk, and ask and answer questions. Children appreciate someone who talks with them and not merely at them. It helps if a Team member can talk with children on their level—for example, to ask questions about school activities, interests, and hobbies.

• *Children like to be with other children in fun, meaningful experiences.*—Tell the child about the type of activities he or she would engage in in _Sunday School_. Provide a sample of material used on Sundays.

• *Help the child feel comfortable with you and with the idea of participating in Sunday School and church experiences.*—One way, if known, is to indicate some of the children who are in the department to which the child would be assigned. Seek to _enroll the entire family_ in Sunday School.

• *Team members should* _become sensitive to difficult issues_ *many children are facing.*—Such issues include, but are not limited to, having parents who are divorced and/or who have remarried; being in a single-parent home; facing challenges with schoolwork; exhibiting a low self-image; and being limited by physical disabilities.

• *It may be helpful for one Team member to focus attention on the child while other Team members relate to other family members.*—It also is important to relate necessary information to Children's Sunday School leaders by writing appropriate details on the FAITH Visit Assignment Card.

• *Never leave a Team member alone with a child for any period of time.*

• *Even though the concepts shared in the FAITH gospel presentation are simple, many facts of the gospel are particularly abstract for a child.*—Remember that many children will be hearing these concepts for the first time and will not understand the personal significance of such truths as the availability of God's forgiveness, the need to turn from their sin to Christ, and the implications of heaven.

The Holy Spirit works in the tender lives of children, and children certainly can make the decision to accept Jesus as their Savior. However, be sensitive to the need many children have to _think about and ask personal questions_ over a period of time about their relationship to and understandings of the gospel.

What if . . . a Youth Is in the Home?

Many times youth whose parents or younger siblings are being visited tend to make themselves inaccessible. In such a FAITH visit, let it be known that you are interested in the opinions of and opportunities to visit with teenagers. Keep these characteristics in mind when visiting a youth.

• *Youth are in a significant* ___life   transition___ .— They are growing physically at alarming rates. They also are developing a search for personal spiritual significance that sometimes leads through various tests of or rebellion against traditional religious expressions.

• *Youth are* ___testing   the   parameters___ *of their decision-making skills.*—They want to make good decisions that affect them no matter what other family members have done. They want to know the facts. They certainly do not want anyone to look down on nor to talk down to them.

• *Youth tend to relate well and personally to each concept in the gospel presentation with the exception of HEAVEN in the hereafter.*—Although this is a significant truth most youth can begin to grasp, eternity is a long way off in the minds of most youth. ___Do   not   compromise___ the truth about heaven, but realize that youth need to consider how a relationship with Christ will impact their lives now and in the immediate future.

"We must be sure that we are sharing the good news of a relationship, not just a religion. The commitment God seeks from us is not primarily a commitment to be good people, to attend church, to pray, or even to read the Bible (even though all of these activities should characterize a growing Christian.) He expects a commitment of trust in His Son, Jesus Christ. . . .

"We must present clearly to teenagers what it means to become a Christian. We must encourage them to count the cost of deciding to follow Jesus in a lifelong relationship of surrender and obedience."[1]

When Other Adults Are in the Home

In some homes, adults not only care for young children but also for one or more aging parents. The "sandwich" generation faces a combination of pressures in that situation. A spouse may not have been present for an

Notes

earlier visit. For whatever reason and circumstance, other adults may be in the home in addition to the person you were assigned to visit. Be aware of the many differences and needs adults represent.

• *Adults are distinctive from one another.*—Each person has a wonderfully unique personality and background. Many adults have learned to respond negatively to other people because of abuse or other hurtful factors. Other adults are going through extreme transitions of life. Most lead very busy and complicated lives. In general, adults are searching for meaning and purpose in life, no matter their marital, financial, or physical status. It is important that you treat each person as a *God-Created and lovable individual*, no matter how he or she responds to your Team's overtures.

• *Many adults are very protective of their time, family matters, and home space.*—They are resistant to allowing a stranger to intrude on their time or space. Many persons feel strangers at the door are only there to sell some unwanted item or to get something from them. Sometimes our timing is not the best for them.

• *A related principle is to quickly and carefully gain the trust of adults.*—We must demonstrate respect. Building bridges starts with building trust.

• *All adults have a story to share.*—Their lives are invested with both positive and negative experiences. They want to be understood and loved no matter what their stories. Bridge-building involves *listening*, *caring*, and *understanding*.

• *Many adults desperately desire meaningful relationships.*—But some tend to reject persons who seek to reach out to them. Others have been hurt in the past and fear that any new relationship will result in added pain. We must be willing for some people to reject us while patiently looking for ways to initiate and demonstrate a safe, caring relationship.

• *Not every adult you encounter will be ready to hear the message of the gospel.*—Many will need to watch you, as well as the integrity of your message, before they will begin investigating the potential impact of the gospel for their lives.

We have been told that it takes a business an average of 13 contacts before a customer begins considering the potential of purchasing its product or service. In the same way, many adults need to *think long and hard about the implications* of such a powerful message before they commit their lives to Christ.

• *The Holy Spirit works in the lives of adults no matter their background, status, experience, successes, or failures.*—In many situations, when you read the adult, you have an inroad to reaching the entire family.

Visitation Time
DO IT

As you go . . .

Think about the long-reaching bridges of relationship and time that your FAITH Team is building, as preschoolers and children feel love expressed to them in a home; as relationships of love and good experiences extend to the church; as the church extends its support to families. Remember the children who some day will meet Christ and begin to grow in Him.

Remember the youth in that home you visited and the untapped potential that teenager seemed to have. Does he or she need the support and love of peers, the encouragement to take risks and to grow, and the insights from God's Word? Does he or she need God's initial touch on his life?

Remember senior adults (and other adults) who are still growing and seeking to find meaningful ways to leave their imprint on the world. What a joy when an adult has the life-changing experience only Christ can provide!

Remember and reflect, . . . could one of those persons have been you?

Celebration Time
SHARE IT

As you return to share . . .

Ask a Team member to take the lead in sharing reports.
- Reports and testimonies
- Session 10 Evaluation Card
- Participation Card
- Visitation forms updated with results of visits

Notes

Home Study Assignments

Home Study Assignments reinforce this session and prepare you for the next session. "Journaling" experiences in Your Journey Continues are an important part of your development as a Great Commission Christian through FAITH training. Other assignments may include additional reading that enhances your experience.

Selected features in this section highlight opportunities the Team Leader has to build bridges to his or her Team, class/department (especially through weekly Sunday School leadership team meetings) and church, and community. They can assist you in accomplishing your important responsibilities.

Your Journey Continues

Describe the most meaningful visit you have made where more than one age group was represented in the home.

_____
_____
_____
_____
_____
_____

Read Acts 16:22-24. What are some ways persons have built barriers or have demonstrated resistance to your Team's coming and sharing but still allowed you to share?

_____
_____
_____
_____
_____
_____

Read Acts 16:25-34. Describe some of the lessons you are learning about impacting an entire family with the ministry of the gospel.

_____

_____

_____

_____

_____

_____

Notes

Prayer Concerns   Answers to Prayer

_____   _____

_____   _____

_____   _____

_____   _____

_____   _____

_____   _____

_____   _____

_____   _____

_____   _____

_____   _____

Notes

An Important Bridge:
Your Weekly Sunday School Leadership Team Meeting

Use this space to record ways your FAITH Team impacts the work of your Sunday School department or class. Use the information to report during weekly Sunday School leadership team meetings. Identify actions that need to be taken through Sunday School as a result of prayer concerns, needs identified, visits made by the Team, and decisions made by the persons being visited.

Highlight needs/reports affecting your class/department or age group.

_____
_____
_____

Pray now for teachers and department directors.

How does our preparation for Sunday need to consider the varying needs of families represented by selected FAITH visits?

_____
_____
_____

How does our teaching appropriately focus on life needs of various ages? How could it be more effective? What training needs might we identify and follow up on?

_____
_____
_____

For Further Reading

Read the FAITH Tips: "Talking with Children About Salvation"and "What You Need to Know About Today's Youth."

FAITH *Tip*

Talking with Children About Salvation

From their birth, God is at work in the lives of girls and boys. He desires for parents and other adults to nurture and to instruct children in such a way as to provide a foundation leading them toward faith in Jesus Christ. At some point, often during the first- through sixth-grade years, most children become aware of their sin.

When the opportunity presents itself to talk with children about salvation, these guidelines can help in sensitively assessing a child's readiness to accept Christ.

1. *Counsel children individually.* When possible, invite parents to be present.

2. *Be conversational.* Often when adults talk with children, the conversation sounds like a monologue. Talk with, not to, the child.

3. *Ask open-ended questions.* For example, ask, "Juan, why do you want to become a Christian?" or "Judy, why do you think a person needs to become a Christian?" Open-ended questions require the child to think and give you an answer other than yes or no. Often when adults ask a yes or no question, they unconsciously answer the question for children with their body language, such as a nod of the head to indicate yes. Toward the end of the conversation at the time of commitment, you will use some yes and no questions; but at that point the questions are simply to confirm what the child has already told you.

4. *Give the child time to think.* Adults are not comfortable with silence. When children are asked questions they often need time to think. Wait for the answers.

5. *Listen carefully to the child's questions and answers.* The insight you gain from the responses will guide you as you continue the conversation and help you know if the child understands the information. To become a Christian, a child must be able to comprehend that his personal sin separates him from a relationship with God, express sorrow over his sin, and willingly repent of his sin.

6. *Use the Bible.* The Bible gives authority to what you say. As you use your Bible, you model how to use it. Use five or six key verses, if possible, from the child's Bible.

7. *Show sincere concern, but avoid becoming emotional.* Children are easily influenced emotionally. They are eager to please adults. If you become teary-eyed, you will confuse them. Most children still associate tears with negative emotions.

8. *Speak in your normal tone of voice.* Adults have a special high-pitched voice they often use with children. Older children may be distracted or annoyed by the condescending tone.

9. *Avoid talking about sin in such a way that you penetrate the child's privacy or elicit an unhealthy sense of guilt.* Adults can easily make a child feel guilty. Just because a child agrees she has lied does not mean she can relate her sin to rebellion against God. God holds a person morally responsible or accountable when she is able to relate her actions to Him.

10. *Be sincere.* In 17 years of full-time children's ministry, I have found that when a child is truly ready to hear the plan of salvation, the Holy Spirit places in him a willingness to listen to the presentation.[2]

FAITH *Tip*

What You Need to Know About Today's Youth

David Scott describes the following six characteristics of youth, based on George Barna's profile of today's teenagers in *Generation Next: What You Need to Know About Today's Youth.*

"They are SERIOUS about life. Though they love humor and can at times be sarcastic, today's teenagers realize that their decisions today will shape aspects of their lives tomorrow.

They are STRESSED out. Teenage stress and anxiety comes from a variety of sources—school, family, peer pressure, sexuality, technology, financial woes, crime, and political correctness.

They are SELF-RELIANT. . . . Some are self-reliant out of necessity. Many have parents who are unable to provide assistance with schoolwork because of technological advances, while others have parents who do not take the time. . . Still others demonstrate an arrogance and rebelliousness that is often typical of the teenage years.

They are SKEPTICAL. Many teenagers have little faith in the reliability of people. . . . Their skeptical attitude has become a security system to shield them from disappointment.

They are SURVIVORS. . . . Today's teenagers have an entirely different criteria for success and excellence (than their parents). . . . Says Barna, 'The truth is that teenagers are realistic, not idealistic. As such, they can handle a difficult circumstance far better than many of their predecessors might have.'

They are highly SPIRITUAL. . . . Barna says, 'Many teenagers believe that a major component of America's illness is that we have lost our sense of the divine and the mystical.'

Millions of teenagers are seeking to incorporate their spiritual understanding into their daily existence, making faith more than a Sunday experience but rather a 'life filter.' . . ."Some teens are attaching themselves to established religious groups, while others are customizing a religious belief system that is personally appealing. We must, however, realize that for many teenagers spiritual is no longer synonymous with Christian.

Today's teens are a relational generation and they love to do things in a group setting. . . . Regardless of their understanding of the spiritual purposes of the church, these youth love the 'togetherness' of the church-based activities.

So, Barna says, there is some good news about the Church and teenagers. Many teenagers are interested in spiritual matters and will give the local church a shot at proving its worth. This means that many (if not most) teens are somehow connected to a Christian body of believers today."[3]

For the Team Leader

This weekly feature suggests actions the Team Leader can take to support Team members, prepare for Team Time, and consider ways to improve visits. This work becomes part of the Team Leader's Home Study Assignments. Add any actions suggested by your church's FAITH strategy.

Support Team Members

❑ Contact Team members during the week. Remind them you are praying for them. Discuss prayer concerns and answers to prayer.

❑ This week Learners are memorizing the FAITH presentation through the *Invitation.* As you discuss this content with Team members, remind them that this is when someone has the opportunity to make a life-changing decision.

❑ Learners have a significant amount of reading during home study this week. The information is important to read and understand since it interprets *A Step of Faith.* Encourage Learners to read the FAITH Tips and to be prepared to discuss the significance of this leaflet in preparation for Session 11.

❑ Record specific needs and concerns of Team members in the space provided.

_____

_____

_____

Prepare to Lead Team Time

❑ Review Home Study Assignments of Team members.
❑ Overview "Leading Team Time" for Session 11.

Prepare to Lead Visits

❑ Review the FAITH Visit Outline.

Build Bridges to Sunday School

❑ Use information in "An Important Bridge" (p. 158) to share about FAITH during this week's meeting.

[1]David Scott, *Good News for Youth: The Power to Change Lives* (Nashville: Convention Press, 1998), 9.
[2]Adapted from Cindy Pitts, in *Good News for Kids: The Power to Change Lives* (Nashville: Convention Press, 1998), 28-30.
[3]David Scott, *Good News for Youth: The Power to Change Lives* (Nashville: Convention Press, 1998), 15-17.

FAITH *Tip*

"I would just like to let you know of the awesome opportunity that I had on Thursday evening. I was in the SGA Lounge talking with a friend and there were some other people there. Our conversation turned towards faith and things of God.

One of the girls that was there became very interested. She began to ask a lot of questions, and I felt that it was a time that I needed to share the gospel. Well, I did and she was still a little confused. She could not understand the whole idea of God sending Jesus to forgive us of all our sins. She began to talk about evolution and stuff, and I was never able to reiterate the whole idea of Jesus and forgiveness.

It was a little challenging, but she asked if she would see me again and said that we may be able to continue the conversation then. I would just like you to pray for this young lady. She was interested, but not ready.

I would like to thank God for giving me the opportunity to even discuss the things of the Lord with people. This made me realize ever more that people are searching and we as Christians have those answers and we mustn't keep them to ourselves.

A Christian is called to keep the faith, but not to himself. **"**

—Stewart Parker, Student FAITH participant,

First Baptist Church, Daytona Beach, Florida

SESSION 11

Building Bridges for Divine Appointments

In this session you will

CHECK IT: engage in Team Time activities;

KNOW IT: review principles and concepts from Session 10;

HEAR IT: overview ways to be more open to God's intervention and appropriate principles for handling potential divine appointments;

SAY IT: with a partner, practice the FAITH Visit Outline beginning with the Key Question;

STUDY IT: overview Home Study Assignments for Session 11;

DO IT: participate in visits in which Team members share through the letter *I* (IMPOSSIBLE) but the Team Leader leads in the visit;

SHARE IT: celebrate (share any divine appointments experienced).

Notes

Leading Team Time

All Team members participate in Team Time. They are primarily responsible for reciting the assigned portion of the FAITH Visit Outline and for discussing other Home Study Assignments.

As you direct this important time of CHECK IT activities with your Team, keep in mind how Learners also look to you as role model; motivator; mentor; and friend. Team Time activities can continue in the car, as the Team travels to and from visits.

Lead CHECK IT Activities

✓ FAITH Visit Outline

❏ Listen while each Learner recites the FAITH Visit Outline beginning with HOW and including all of the *Invitation*. Indicate any notes for improvement.

✓ Practice the *Invitation* using *A Step of Faith*

❏ Make sure Team members know the correct sequence in using *A Step of Faith* in making transition from the gospel presentation to leading someone to declare commitments to Christ as Savior and Lord, to enroll in Sunday School, and to publicly acknowledge new faith in Jesus.

Since several Home Study Assignments dealt with use of *A Step of Faith,* you may not need additional review of Session 10 assignments.

❏ Make certain Team members are able to lead a person to pray to receive Christ and to pray for Christian growth. Also, be certain Team members are comfortable in leading a person to record commitment(s) they have made and to provide the information the church needs.

✓ Session 10 (H is for Heaven) debriefing

❏ HEAVEN HERE and HEAVEN HEREAFTER are fundamental beliefs of the Christian. Do Learners demonstrate a sense of comfort in sharing their joy in Christ and their assurance of eternal life in God's presence?

❏ H also stands for HOW. This becomes the hinge on which a Learner is able to clarify for another person how a person can have God's forgiveness, heaven and eternal life, and Jesus as personal Savior and Lord.

Make sure the person is becoming increasingly comfortable in using the picture on the front of *A Step of Faith* to identify with the need for God's forgiveness. You received earlier training to help your Team know what to do if *A Step of Faith* is not available.

✓ Help for strengthening a visit

❏ Remind Team members that they are seeing the Holy Spirit at work as they make themselves available for visitation. Recall examples of ways you have seen the Holy Spirit at work when a person has heard the FAITH gospel presentation.

❏ One of the great privileges and responsibilities in FAITH training is to encounter family members of someone you are assigned to visit. Although your Team is focusing on people from your Sunday School department or class, you quickly learn that there are many opportunities to minister to and share the gospel with persons of other age divisions.

Dialogue about ways to meaningful include in a visit preschoolers, children, youth, and adults who would not be assigned to your department or class.

❏ Indicate that next week's practice session is a good way to improve skills and increase confidence. Share schedule adjustments.

Notes

_____
_____
_____
_____
_____
_____

Actions I Need to Take with Learners During the Week

_____
_____
_____
_____
_____
_____

Notes

Notes

A Quick Review

Take the following brief quiz. It (and similar questions from previous sessions) will help prepare you for the written review in Session 16.

___ **1.** *True or False:* **Your Team is responsible only for persons who are or would be assigned to your Sunday School department or class.**

___ **2. Actions you can take with family members in the home include** *(Place a check mark beside all that apply in a FAITH visit)*—

___ a. Ask to enroll the person(s) if not participating in Sunday School.

___ b. Engage the person in conversation and include the person(s) in the ministry or evangelistic visit as appropriate to their age or situation.

___ c. Have a Team member work with the person one-on-one, particularly if with a young family member, while the other Team members focus on older member(s) of the family.

___ d. Gather information on the person(s) and be prepared to share it using the FAITH Visit Assignment Card for the appropriate Sunday School class/department.

The Person God Uses
The person God uses is fit to stand against the devil's schemes.

When you agreed to participate in FAITH training, you realized you would be going completely against the plans and plots of Satan. You have come to realize that this is not a game and that we are in a spiritual warfare against the Evil One. Read carefully the familiar passage from Ephesians (6:10-18) and identify ways you need to strengthen your stance in the warfare against the devil.

"[10] Finally, be strong in the Lord and in his mighty power.

[11] Put on the full armor of God so that you can take your stand against the devil's schemes.

[12] For our struggle is not against flesh and blood, but against the rulers, against the authorities, against the powers of this dark world and against the spiritual forces of evil in the heavenly realms.

[13] Therefore put on the full armor of God, so that when the day

of evil comes, you may be able to stand your ground, and after you have done everything, to stand.

[14] Stand firm then, with the belt of truth buckled around your waist, with the breastplate of righteousness in place,

[15] and with your feet fitted with the readiness that comes from the gospel of peace.

[16] In addition to all this, take up the shield of faith, with which you can extinguish all the flaming arrows of the evil one.

[17] Take the helmet of salvation and the sword of the Spirit, which is the word of God.

[18] And pray in the Spirit on all occasions with all kinds of prayers and requests. With this in mind, be alert and always keep on praying for all the saints" (NIV).

What are ways you need to strengthen your stance in the warfare against the devil?

_____

_____

Father, use me to be strong in warring against Satan and in bringing glory to Your name. Help me to effectively use the armor You have provided for the battle.

Be Ready for Divine Appointments

You are leading other Team members to be prepared to minister to and share the gospel with Sunday School members and prospects. Your assigned visits usually will be in the homes of members or prospects. In addition, you are leading Team members to conduct Opinion Poll visits. At this point you realize that most of the visits you make, though bathed in prayer by many people, are those for which you are prepared. They are to places and to people you know about in advance.

After you have made several visits with your Team, you begin to realize that some encounters are more spontaneous than others. Although you cannot explain it, you may "chance upon" some people who seem more responsive than usual to the ministry or evangelistic overture of Team members. You may discover that some individuals are not necessarily those who have been assigned to the Team. This session will focus on the challenges and opportunities for divine appointments you may experience as a Team.

Notes

Divine appointments can be defined as those encounters where it can only be explained that God has been at work directing the specific Team to intersect and engage a specific person at a given time. It becomes apparent that God has been at work so that the person is particularly inclined to hear and respond to the gospel or to the Team's ministry. This kind of encounter reminds us yet again that it is God who makes just the right time, just the right person, and just the right thing(s) to say and do.

Every ministry and gospel presentation contact, in reality, is a divine appointment when God is in charge. When you begin to grasp this reality, you realize that even when one person is not at home or someone rejects the gospel, you are intentionally _placing   the person in God's hands_. God may have sent you to a house or to a neighborhood to encounter someone He has prepared and placed at that site to intersect with Team members who are prepared to be used by Him.

Principles for heightened preparation for divine appointments include the following:

1. _Prayer_ is an integral part of divine appointments. We pray for God to use us. Moreover, we join other believers in praying for—

• a Team to be in the right place at the right time;

• nonbelievers to be prepared and receptive;

• God to be active in and to "soften" the hearts of individuals who need to be touched by the message and ministry of the gospel.

When it becomes apparent that God has led your Team to a given person who is convicted or convinced by the Holy Spirit, it is vital that Team members pray for each other and for the specific leadership of the Spirit in all that is said. It is a holy moment when God is working; it also is an intensified battle in which Satan combats God's plans and His people.

2. The _Holy Spirit_ is ultimately in control of every situation of the believer's life and places people in situations in which He can most appropriately use them for His glory. God uses all of your experiences for His good. He may assign you to encounter someone who can relate to the gospel message only because you can relate to the particular situation. Many times a believer discovers that his previous experiences (trials, valleys, learning experiences) are used by God to help someone who needs the gospel to better relate to the good news.

3. _Believers who are available to God_ become more sensitive and usable for spontaneous situations. God may close some doors of planned visitation in order to place you at open doors of opportunity, in which you minister and/or share the gospel. God will let you know what to say and do at the appointed time. Remember Jesus' words: ". . . do not worry about what to say or how to say it. At that time you will be given what to say, for it will not be you speaking, but the Spirit of your Father speaking through you" (Matt. 10:19-20, NIV).

4. Often it takes an _Awareness of God's direct intervention_ to intersect our lives with the people who need God's message. God uses people at every stage (FAITH Group Leaders, Sunday School leaders during weekly leadership team meetings, outreach secretaries, and others who coordinate making visitation assignments) to link a specific Team with someone who needs to hear the gospel. God can and does use a believer even when that person is not aware of the situations leading up to an encounter. Recognize that every visit will be a good one because God is at work both in the lives of the Team members as well as of those who are being visited.

5. _God's timing_ is not the same as ours. On many occasions, you may be assigned to visit where no one is at home or where all the "doors" are closed for any effective visit. It is then that you encounter a person who is in need of and receptive to the ministry of the gospel. The world may call such occasions "chance encounters" or "coincidences"; Christians know them as divine appointments.

Ways to Prepare the Team

1. _Emphasize dependence on the Holy Spirit_ in all aspects of training and personal encounters.

2. Emphasize and _model the need for prayer_ for Team members, for the persons assigned to be visited, for situations that block some encounters and open up others.

3. _Keep your spiritual eyes open_. Look for open and closed doors to the gospel. Try to view individuals as Jesus sees them.

4. _Keep your spiritual ears open_. Listen for questions and comments that might indicate the movement of God's Spirit in the person's life. Listen for the still, small voice of God as He teaches and uses you.

5. _Find where God is at work_ and go be part of it.[1]

6. _Keep your heart pure_ and in touch with God's leadership. Although God can use anyone, He seeks persons who are obedient and submissive to Him. "A tender and sensitive heart will be ready to respond to God at the slightest prompting."[2]

7. Realize that divine appointments may be to _plant a seed_ so that someone will begin considering the gospel for his or her life, to _perform a ministry action_ that opens the gospel for someone, and to _share the gospel_ with a person at just the right time.

Notes

8. Understand that <u>Satan places every possible obstacle</u> in your way to obscure your sensitivity to and availability for divine appointments. However, never forget that "the one who is in you is greater than the one who is in the world" (1 John 4:4, NIV).

Divine appointments can take place as a result of or during a planned visit. They can take place in lieu of a planned visit (for example, you try to make a visit and find no one at home; upon leaving, you encounter someone with whom you begin talking, only to discover he or she has been looking for someone to explain how to have assurance of God's forgiveness).

Such encounters can take place en route to or from a planned visit. Often these are spontaneous encounters. These encounters likely are away from the home setting. Although such a visit could be in a home as part of the planned visit where the entire visitation outline is initiated, you could find yourself in a store or restaurant, on the side of a street, in a parking lot, in a yard, or by a car. Be particularly sensitive to the leadership of the Holy Spirit in anticipation of and in response to divine appointment encounters.

What Would You Do?

Tom and his Team members, Carlos and Cindi, attempted three visits. No one was at home, and time was becoming a factor. Carlos had yet to share the entire gospel presentation during a visit, and Tom was certainly hoping for Carlos to have the experience. Thus far, Tom had gone "by the book" and wanted his Team to return in plenty of time for Celebration Time.

He decided to return to the church. Down the street from the church, the Team decided to pull into a fast-food restaurant to sit and drink a cup of soda together. *Besides,* Tom thought, *they could at least practice on each other and give Carlos the opportunity to share the gospel with them.* After placing their orders and finding a table in the near-vacant restaurant, a young couple came in and sat near them.

Carlos observed that the man looked familiar. He struck up a conversation with him and soon realized that the man had come into his store recently. Carlos told the couple that the Team was visiting for their church as Cindi and Tom moved closer and entered into the conversations. The man responded that he and his girlfriend wanted to get married but did not have any connection with a church. He shared that she was pregnant and had been ostracized from her family who lived in another state.

Tom looked at his watch and realized it was time to return to the church. Without realizing what was happening, Cindi shared her Sunday School testimony. A few customers came into the restaurant, and Tom thought the conversations would die down. Yet he began to pray for God's leadership. Cindi also was praying. No one seemed to know what to do.

Maximize the Potential

Consider these guidelines to help your Team members anticipate and respond to significant opportunities.

1. _Approach_ the person(s) and _begin a conversation_ with him. Keep in mind the kinds of things you ordinarily would talk about during the INTRODUCTION of a FAITH visit.

2. _Introduce Team members_ and briefly explain what you are doing (visiting Sunday School members and prospects on behalf of your church).

3. Learn to _become comfortable asking questions_ to discover a person's spiritual journey in a spontaneous situation.

4. _Listen for needs_ and ways to identify/associate with the person.

5. _Look for and respond to opportunities_ to share your evangelistic testimony, to ask the Key Question, and to share the FAITH gospel presentation. You will be surprised at how many people will be open, interested, and responsive!

6. Humbly _Anticipate that God may do a great work_ and that you may have the privilege of being His instrument in leading a person to faith in Christ.

7. Look for ways to _Follow up_ on needs, concerns, and decisions.

The Story Continues

Although there was more noise in the restaurant than when the conversations began, Carlos asked the Key Question and for permission to share what the Bible has to say. The man's response was, "I never thought I'd say this, but now more than ever, I really want to know. Please tell us." Carlos took the few minutes to share. Tom and Cindi realized that the Holy Spirit was the One in charge as both the man and his girlfriend listened carefully and committed their lives to Christ. All this happened while trying not to be too early for Celebration Time. Tom realized that one of their challenges would be to identify ways to begin follow-up.

What would be appropriate ways to ensure follow-up in this situation?

Notes

Visitation Time
DO IT

As you go . . .

The weather is messy. The family needs you. Recent visitation assignments have not been very promising. Last week's maps/directions were confusing, and the Team got lost rather than having quality visits. You're tired and have an important meeting tomorrow. It would be a lot easier not to go on FAITH visits this week.

By going out to visit even when it would be easier not to, you show your obedience to God and your desire to serve. You also position yourself more firmly against the devil as you "put on the full armor of God."

Recognize that, in God, every visit is a good visit. During times like these, you may find yourself refreshed and revived by a divinely orchestrated appointment. Don't allow yourself to miss out!

Celebration Time
SHARE IT

As you return to share . . .

- Reports and testimonies
- Session 11 Evaluation Card
- Participation Card
- Visitation forms updated with results of visits

Home Study Assignments

Notes

Home Study Assignments reinforce this session and prepare you for the next session. "Journaling" experiences in Your Journey Continues are an important part of your development as a Great Commission Christian through FAITH training. Other assignments may include additional reading that enhances your experience.

Selected features in this section highlight opportunities the Team Leader has to build bridges to his or her Team, class/department (especially through weekly Sunday School leadership team meetings) and church, and community. They can assist you in accomplishing your important responsibilities.

Your Journey Continues

Read Acts 16:14-21. This passage could represent a situation in which Paul and his FAITH Team were assigned to visit the slave girl (v. 16). What were some results of this assigned visit?

_____

_____

_____

In what situations in which your Team has shared the gospel and a person has received Jesus has it seemed as though God were placing you in an uncomfortable situation? How did He prove to be at work in that situation?

_____

_____

_____

Read Acts 16:22-33. This passage begins with Paul and his "Team" being placed in prison because they were faithful to Christ in proclaiming the gospel. What about this passage could be described as a divine appointment?

_____

_____

_____

Notes

Describe some of the divine appointments you and your Team have experienced during FAITH training.

_____
_____
_____
_____
_____
_____

Prayer Concerns

_____
_____
_____
_____
_____
_____
_____
_____
_____
_____
_____
_____

Answers to Prayer

_____
_____
_____
_____
_____
_____
_____
_____
_____
_____
_____
_____

An Important Bridge:
Your Weekly Sunday School Leadership Team Meeting

Use this space to record ways your FAITH Team impacts the work of your Sunday School department or class. Use the information to report during weekly Sunday School leadership team meetings. Identify actions that need to be taken through Sunday School as a result of prayer concerns, needs identified, visits made by the Team, and decisions made by the persons being visited.

Highlight needs/reports affecting your class/department or age group.

_____

_____

_____

Pray now for teachers and department directors.

How does preparation for Sunday need to anticipate divine appointments that may be encountered during Sunday School? By class members during the week? By FAITH Team members as they make visits?

_____

_____

_____

How will the class begin to follow up on persons FAITH Team members discover as a result of divine appointments?

_____

_____

_____

What are ways to involve members in praying for and celebrating God's leadership during divine appointments?

_____

_____

_____

For Further Reading

Read *Evangelism Through the Sunday School: A Journey of FAITH* by Bobby Welch, pages 48-51.

Read the FAITH Tip, "My Most Discouraging Night."

FAITH *Tip*

My Most Discouraging Night

It was a dark and stormy Monday night in Fort Lauderdale when I was sent out with a pastor and his wife to demonstrate the use of a gospel questionnaire. Since I was teaching the clinic on evangelism, they naturally sent me to the hardest location during this spring break, the infamous Fort Lauderdale strip.

That night, a U.S. Navy carrier was in port, so the beachfront was filled not only with drunken college students but also with drunken sailors. Surrounded by thousands of crazy, jostling people, I scarcely could find anyone interested in taking the questionnaire, much less in hearing the gospel. Just when I was feeling as low as I thought I could feel, it began to rain!

The rain actually encouraged me. Now I had an excuse to head back to the car, drive slowly back to the church, and not be ashamed about being the first team to report back. As I trudged through the rain, seemingly surrounded by people who didn't care about the gospel, the pastor's wife spoke up for the first time all evening. "Are we going back already?" Guilt stabbed me in the heart; I became defensive. "Sure," I replied. "We're not doing any good here. If we have some extra time, I'll help you review your homework." She persisted. "Would you mind checking to see how many of those questionnaires we completed?"

A fresh wave of depression swept over me. Just that afternoon in class, I had made the rather authoritative statement that on the average, for every ten people who were asked, at least one would want to hear the gospel. Furthermore, I had cheerfully said that God was in charge of reaping a harvest; our only charge was to not give up. Now my credibility was on the line. Was I really giving up? I tried to push my way through.

"One in 10 is an average. I've talked to as many as 25 people in an evening with no response. Other times, the first person I talk to wants to hear the gospel. It's not a mechanical process of percentages. But, for the record, we have nine completed questionnaires."

"Just for me," she said, "could you ask one more person?"

She would not let it go! Determined to prove my point, I looked around for the most carnal person (other than myself, at that moment) that I could find. There: A guy was hulking in an alley near the exit to a night club. I vividly remember his long, shaggy hair, multiple tattoos, earrings, and his biker T-shirt and dirty jeans. *I'd show her that the expert on evangelism knew when to quit!* I thought.

Within five minutes the guy was in tears! He literally begged me to share the good news of Jesus Christ. Out of all the people I've encountered in a street-witnessing situation, he was the most obviously prepared to hear the gospel.

"I can't believe you people had the guts to walk up to me," he said. "Nobody does that. A buddy of mine conned me into going to a Baptist church yesterday. I sat on the back pew and was overcome with emotion as I heard what Jesus did for me. During the invitation I clung to the pew in front of me until my knuckles turned white. All day long I've been praying to God to give me another chance because I knew I was headed straight to hell."

What a strange-looking group we must have been! The biker was crying, I was dumbfounded, the pastor was in shock, and the pastor's wife was dancing a jig —figuratively speaking, anyway. In all the intervening years, whenever I am tempted to give up, I remember that humbling-yet-happy experience on the Fort Lauderdale strip.[3]

For the Team Leader

This weekly feature suggests actions the Team Leader can take to support Team members, prepare for Team Time, and consider ways to improve visits. This work becomes part of the Team Leader's Home Study Assignments. Add any actions suggested by your church's FAITH strategy.

Support Team Members

❑ Pray for and personally follow up on any Learner who needs personal encouragement.

❑ Contact Team members during the week to remind them you are praying for them and to discuss their participation in FAITH.

Prepare to Lead Team Time

❑ Overview "Leading Team Time" for Session 12 (practice).

Prepare to Lead Visits

❑ Review the FAITH Visit Outline.

❑ Be prepared to explain the benefits and procedures for making ministry visits.

❑ Be prepared to model a visit in which Team member(s) are asked to lead in a visit up to the point of the letter *H* (HEAVEN).

❑ Be prepared to lead your Team to participate during Celebration Time.

Build Bridges to Sunday School

❑ Use information in "An Important Bridge" (p. 175) to share about FAITH during this week's meeting.

[1]Henry T. Blackaby and Claude V. King, *Experiencing God: How to Live the Full Adventure of Knowing and Doing the Will of God* (Broadman & Holman Publishers, 1994).

[2]Ibid., 122.

[3]David Self, *Good News for Adults: The Power to Change Lives* (Nashville: Convention Press, 1998), 37-39.

FAITH *Tip*

❝Charlie, a youth worker in our ministry, was having trouble with the brakes on his truck. So he took it to the garage to get them repaired. As they began working on the truck, he noticed a fast-food restaurant next door and decided to go eat. As he entered the restaurant, he was greeted by Chad, a former student of our ministry.

They chatted a minute or two and Charlie asked if he could join him for lunch. After getting his food, Charlie went over to the table and sat down with the student and his friend, Shannon (another boy).

As the conversation developed, Charlie began asking "probing" questions and assessed that he needed to ask the Key Question. Chad had given his life to Christ, and Shannon gave a "works" answer. Charlie asked for three minutes to share how the Bible answered the question; they consented. When he had finished, Shannon prayed to receive Christ! Praise God! However, it gets better.

Charlie went back over to the garage and was greeted with all smiles. The mechanic said, "You need to come back here a minute. There's nothing wrong with your brakes." Charlie disagreed. In fact, Charlie made the man put the tires on the truck and they rode around for 10 minutes, stopping every way possible— no problems with the brakes!❞

—Dwayne Morris for Charlie Thames
First Baptist Church, North Spartanburg, South Carolina

SESSION 12

Building Bridges Through Practicing FAITH

In this session you will
CHECK IT: use the entire time to engage in extended Team Time/practice activities;
STUDY IT: overview Home Study Assignments for Session 12;
DO IT: make visits in which a Team member may take the lead in a visit;
SHARE IT: celebrate.

Notes

Leading Team Time

All Teams remain together during this session for an extended Team Time. All Team members participate in Team Time. They are primarily responsible for reciting the assigned portion of the FAITH Visit Outline and for discussing other Home Study Assignments.

As you direct this important time of CHECK IT activities with your Team, keep in mind how Learners also look to you as role model; motivator; mentor, and friend. Team Time activities can continue in the car, as the Team travels to and from visits.

Lead CHECK IT Activities

✓ FAITH Visit Outline

Spend the entire time with your Team members, leading them to practice the entire FAITH Visit Outline. Consider rehearsing appropriate approaches to take in strengthening the skills and confidence of Learners in leading the visit. It may be helpful to suggest that the Team role-play several situations which your Team(or others) have encountered during FAITH training.

You have been preparing your Team members to take the lead in a visit. Make sure a Team member is informed that he or she will be taking the lead in the specific visits. As always, be prepared to assist; but do everything you can to encourage the person to lead the entire visit.

FAITH VISIT OUTLINE
Preparation

INTRODUCTION
INTERESTS
INVOLVEMENT
> **Church Experience/Background**
>> **Ask about the person's church background.**
>> **Listen for clues about the person's spiritual involvement.**
> **Sunday School Testimony**
>> **Tell general benefits of Sunday School.**
>> **Tell a current personal experience.**
> **Evangelistic Testimony**
>> **Tell a little of your pre-conversion experience.**
>> **Say: "I had a life-changing experience."**
>> **Tell recent benefits of your conversion.**

INQUIRY

Key Question: In your personal opinion, what do you understand it takes for a person to go to heaven?

   Possible answers: Faith, works, unclear, no opinion

Transition Statement: I'd like to share with you how the Bible answers this question, if it is all right. There is a word that can be used to answer this question: *FAITH (spell out on fingers).*

Presentation

F is for FORGIVENESS.

We cannot have eternal life and heaven without God's forgiveness.

   "In Him [meaning Jesus] we have redemption through His blood, the forgiveness of sins"—Ephesians 1:7a, NKJV.

A is for AVAILABLE.

Forgiveness is available. It is—

AVAILABLE FOR ALL

   "For God so loved the world that He gave His only begotten Son, that whoever believes in Him should not perish but have everlasting life"— John 3:16, NKJV.

BUT NOT AUTOMATIC

   "Not everyone who says to Me, 'Lord, Lord,' shall enter the kingdom of heaven"—Matthew 7:21a, NKJV.

I is for IMPOSSIBLE.

It is impossible for God to allow sin into heaven.

GOD IS—

   • **LOVE**
      John 3:16, NKJV
   • **JUST**
      "For judgment is without mercy"—James 2:13a, NKJV.

MAN IS SINFUL

   "For all have sinned and fall short of the glory of God" —Romans 3:23, NKJV.

Question: But how can a sinful person enter heaven, where God allows no sin?

T is for TURN.

Question: If you were driving down the road and someone asked you to turn, what would he or she be asking you to do? *(change direction) Turn* means repent.

Notes

TURN from something—sin and self

"But unless you repent you will all likewise perish"—Luke 13:13b, NKJV.

TURN to Someone; trust Christ only

(The Bible tells us that) *"Christ died for our sins according to the Scriptures, and that He was buried, and that He rose again the third day according to the Scriptures"—1 Corinthians 15:3b-4, NKJV.*

"If you confess with your mouth the Lord Jesus and believe in your heart that God has raised Him from the dead, you will be saved" —Romans 10:9, NKJV.

H is for HEAVEN.

Heaven is eternal life.

HERE

"I have come that they may have life, and that they may have it more abundantly"—John 10:10b, NKJV.

HEREAFTER

"And if I go and prepare a place for you, I will come again and receive you to Myself; that where I am, there you may be also"— John 14:3, NKJV.

HOW

How can a person have God's forgiveness, heaven and eternal life, and Jesus as personal Savior and Lord?

Explain based on leaflet picture, F.A.I.T.H. (Forsaking All I Trust Him), Romans 10:9.

Invitation

INQUIRE

Understanding what we have shared, would you like to receive this forgiveness by trusting in Christ as your personal Savior and Lord?

INVITE

Pray to accept Christ.

Pray for commitment/recommitment.

Invite to join Sunday School.

INSURE

Use *A Step of Faith* to insure decision.

Personal Acceptance

Sunday School Enrollment

Public Confession

Visitation Time
DO IT

As you go . . .

Throughout FAITH, you have been preparing your Team members to take the lead in a visit. Make sure a Team member is informed that he or she will be taking the lead in specific visits. As always, be prepared to assist; but do everything you can to encourage the person to lead the entire visit.

Celebration Time
SHARE IT

As you return to share . . .

Reports and testimonies
Session 12 Evaluation Card
Participation Card
Visitation forms updated with results of visits

Notes

Home Study Assignments

Home Study Assignments reinforce this session and prepare you for the next session. "Journaling" experiences in Your Journey Continues are an important part of your development as a Great Commission Christian through FAITH training. Other assignments may include additional reading that enhances your experience.

Selected features in this section highlight opportunities the Team Leader has to build bridges to his or her Team, class/department (especially through weekly Sunday School leadership team meetings) and church, and community. They can assist you in accomplishing your important responsibilities.

Read the following passages. In the space provided, list reasons the passage gives to praise the Lord.

Psalm 30:1-5

_____
_____
_____
_____
_____

Psalm 65:1-8

_____
_____
_____
_____
_____

Psalm 66:16-20

_____
_____
_____
_____
_____

Psalm 103:1-18

Describe some of the things you have seen and experienced during FAITH training which elicit praise to the Lord regarding—

• your own growth as a Christian

• the experiences of your Team members

• people your Team has visited

Prayer Concerns

Answers to Prayer

Notes

SUNDAY SCHOOL FAITH ADVANCED™ EVANGELISM STRATEGY

Notes

An Important Bridge:
Your Weekly Sunday School Leadership Team Meeting

Use this space to record ways your FAITH Team impacts the work of your Sunday School department or class. Use the information to report during weekly Sunday School leadership team meetings. Identify actions that need to be taken through Sunday School as a result of prayer concerns, needs identified, visits made by the Team, and decisions made by the persons being visited.

Highlight needs/reports affecting your class/department or age group.

_____

_____

_____

Pray now for teachers and department directors.

Evaluate the degree to which department leaders and members are following up on and assimilating prospects being contacted through FAITH visits.

_____

_____

What actions need to be started or strengthened to help assimilate persons into the Sunday School department or class?

_____

_____

What are ways to involve members in praying for and celebrating God's leadership in raising up new persons to begin FAITH Sunday School Evangelism Strategy training?

_____

_____

For Further Reading

Read pages 138-40, *Evangelism Through the Sunday School: A Journey of FAITH* by Bobby Welch. Begin thinking about people to whom you might "pass it on."

Read the FAITH Tip: "How Can People Be Assimilated into a Class?"

FAITH *Tip*

How Can People Be Assimilated into a Class?

Assimilating new members begins with a plan to welcome, include, and actively involve people in Bible study and in the entire life of the class. Until people feel they have been accepted, not enough has been done to assimilate them.

Jackie Robinson was the first black to play major league baseball. Breaking baseball's color barrier, he faced jeering crowds in every stadium. While playing one day in his home stadium in Brooklyn, he committed an error. The fans began to ridicule him. He stood at second base while the fans jeered. Then shortstop Pee Wee Reese came and stood next to him. He put his arm around Robinson and faced the crowd. The fans grew quiet. Robinson later said that arm around his shoulder saved his career.

Folks who come to your Sunday School are not likely to be turned away by others who are jeering at or criticizing them. But they may be turned away by the feeling that no one is interested in them. The interest of another person, particularly someone who has influence with other people, can make a tremendous difference to a new member.

Assimilation is a process for enabling members to express their interest in a new member and for the new member to experience that interest from others. The goal is to lead the person to that point where he or she begins to assimilate new members into the life of Sunday School and church.

Here are some ways classes can create opportunities for expressing interest and concern for others and build personal relationships with new members:

• *Sunday morning Bible study*—Sunday mornings provide an opportunity for members and guests to enjoy regular Christian fellowship. They may visit informally before and after the session. During the session participation in Bible study becomes a common bond that can draw people together.

• *Get-acquainted activities*—Occasional get-acquainted activities can stimulate relationships. In the case of adults and youth, groups of three or four members (or couples) can be formed for informal get-togethers during a given quarter. These get-togethers can be anytime other than Sunday mornings.

• *Use of name tags*—No one wants to be addressed as "Hey, You!" But failing to call people by name is not much better. Knowing people's names indicates you have enough interest to remember who they are. Name tags can help everyone get to know one another, and help leaders in calling everyone by name in every class session.

• *Words of encouragement and affirmation*—Let newcomers know in class that their contributions are appreciated. Affirmations can be given outside class as well; for example, make a phone call during the week to express appreciation to a newcomer for attending a class.

• *Celebrate special occasions*—Birthdays are something all people have, whether they want them or not! When everyone's birthday is celebrated in simple ways, everyone is affirmed. Monthly birthday activities can build fellowship.

• *Social events*—Activities with a social purpose allow relationships to grow and barriers to disappear. When newcomers are included in fellowship events, everyone's "comfort zone" grows. Make sure that prospects are not ignored during the events. Enlist someone to "adopt" newcomers or prospects.

• *Newsletters and printed information*—Regardless of whether newcomers enroll immediately, including them on class mailing lists will let them know someone already considers them part of the group. Add newcomers and prospects to the list for at least six months. After this time, ask prospects whether they want to continue receiving the newsletter.

• *One-on-one mentoring*—In adult and youth classes, a spiritually mature member might be assigned as a mentor to a new member to encourage spiritual growth and development. The mentor and new member may meet together regularly for prayer and additional study periods.[1]

Other helpful resources include—
Taking the Next Step: A Guide for New Church Members (Nashville: Convention Press)
Taking the Next Step: A Guide for New Church Members Leader Guide (Nashville: Convention Press)
Basic Church Stuff: A Guide for Assimilating New Youth Church Members (Nashville: Convention Press)
Now That I'm a Christian, Revised (older children's workbook and leader's guide)
After They Join: 10 Ways to Assimilate New Members

For the Team Leader

This weekly feature suggests actions the Team Leader can take to support Team members, prepare for Team Time, and consider ways to improve visits. This work becomes part of the Team Leader's Home Study Assignments. Add any actions suggested by your church's FAITH strategy.

Support Team Members

❑ Pray for and personally follow up on any Learner who may need personal encouragement.

❑ Contact Team members during the week to remind them you are praying for them and to discuss their participation in FAITH.

❑ Learners are taking the lead in making the visits from this point on. Look for opportunities to encourage each Team member regarding ways he or she is successfully leading in the visit. Continue to identify ways each Learner can improve.

Prepare to lead Team Time for Session 13.

❑ Overview "Leading Team Time" for Session 13.

Prepare to Participate in Visits

❑ Review the FAITH Visit Outline.

❑ Identify the Team member who will be responsible for leading specific visits.

❑ Be prepared to lead Team to participate during Celebration Time. Look for ways to encourage Team members to take the lead in reporting during Celebration Time.

Build Bridges to Sunday School

❑ Prepare to share with other Sunday School leaders using "An Important Bridge" (p. 186) information.

❑ Ask Sunday School leaders to think about others who may become involved in FAITH training.

[1] Adapted from Bill L. Taylor, *The Power to Change Lives: The Complete Guide for Building a Great Commission Sunday School* (Nashville: Convention Press, 1998), 46-48.

Notes

Notes

_____

_____

_____

_____

_____

_____

Actions I Need to Take with Learners During the Week

_____

_____

_____

_____

_____

_____

SESSION 13

Building Bridges in Daily Life

In this session you will

CHECK IT: engage in Team Time activities;

KNOW IT: review selected principles from Session 11 (Session 12 was practice);

HEAR IT: discover how evangelism is both a lifestyle witness and a verbal witness; by using a witness-awareness exercise, develop greater sensitivity to daily opportunities;

SEE IT: use the video segment to remind participants again that people need the Lord;

SAY IT: practice the FAITH Visit Outline with a partner;

STUDY IT: overview Home Study Assignments for Session 13;

DO IT: make visits in which a Team member takes the lead;

SHARE IT: celebrate.

Notes

Leading Team Time

All Team members participate in Team Time. They are primarily responsible for reciting the assigned portion of the FAITH Visit Outline and for discussing other Home Study Assignments.

As you direct this important time of CHECK IT activities with your Team, keep in mind how Learners also look to you as role model; motivator; mentor; and friend. Team Time activities can continue in the car, as the Team travels to and from visits.

Lead CHECK IT Activities

✓ FAITH Visit Outline
❑ Listen while each Learner recites the FAITH Visit Outline. Since there is no new memory work, it may be best to ask Learners to recite the segment they have the most difficulty sharing during a visit.

✓ Session 11 (Inviting Persons to Saving Faith) debriefing
❑ Since Session 12 was a practice session with no new material, debrief Session 11 (Inviting Persons to Saving Faith) now. Session 11 focused on the important time when a person is given the opportunity to personally accept God's forgiveness and salvation, so it is important that Team members be well trained. It is even more important that they be growing in their sensitivity to the Holy Spirit's prompting in a visitation situation.

❑ Discuss ways Team members are finding *A Step of Faith* helpful in prompting discussion in a visit. If time permits, allow Team members to practice the *Invitation* using *A Step of Faith*.

✓ Help for strengthening a visit
❑ Discuss some of the difficulties the Team has encountered in leading someone to hear and consider the FAITH gospel presentation. Evaluate ways the Team responded to selected experiences, and identify appropriate ways to improve responses. Indicate that, while most visits go smoothly, next week's session will help all Team members better handle challenges in a visit.

Difficulties are those things that happen or are said that could keep you from sharing the gospel and leading someone who is ready to respond to make a commitment to Christ.

Notes

Principles for dealing with difficulties relate primarily to building bridges of relationships with the person, dealing with questions and objections, and working through the obstacles and distractions that take place.

❑ As you talk with Team members during the week, share ways you are seeking to take advantage of the daily-life witnessing opportunities you have. Also talk with them about opportunities they have to share the gospel during the week with persons they encounter.

Notes

_____

_____

_____

_____

_____

_____

Actions I Need to Take with Learners During the Week

_____

_____

_____

_____

_____

_____

Notes

A Quick Review

Tom's FAITH Team (see "What Would You Do?" case study, Session 11) exercised sensitivity and openness to God's leadership during a seemingly nonproductive Visitation Time. A "chance" fast-food encounter opened up opportunities for which the Team was able to respond.

Your Team, like Tom's, can learn how to build bridges in the most unlikely situations. You do so as you become more sensitive to those settings non-Christians might characterize as chance encounters but which Christians know to be God's direct intervention. A growing dependence on the Holy Spirit's leading and a greater availability to Him will be the most important things you can learn.

Being ready for God to do a great work—and joining Him in it—is one of the joys of participating in FAITH. Through such experiences we are reminded again that it is God who brings together the right people, the right timing, and the right words. As we continue to pray and make ourselves available to God, such experiences will become a regular part of our Celebration Time reports.

The Person God Uses
The person God uses is consistent.

One of the biggest challenges faced by Christians is that so many believers say one thing and do something else. Many nonbelievers are resistant to the gospel because of us; they do not see enough examples of Christians who are consistent in doing what they say they believe. We understand that no person is perfect except Christ alone. On the other hand, we are called to live holy lives.

The person God uses is growing in head knowledge of what Christ has done for him or her. The person God uses is growing in a personal relationship with Christ, Who became the Sacrifice on our behalf.

Are you learning to place your trust in Christ through the joys as well as the trials of life? Are you demonstrating a growing understanding that Christ wants to direct all areas of your life and to show you the abundant life that results in knowing and serving Him? Are you learning to talk with other believers about what Christ means to you? Can others tell that you are maturing in your relationship with Him?

Lord, continue to help me depend more and more on You in every aspect of my life.

FAITH Is a Both/And Approach

We tend to go through periods of change in how we emphasize or encourage Christians to do evangelism. Sometimes divergent, conflicting views crop up at the same time.

In the mid-1980s, two books appeared on the scene, and both had a direct impact on personal evangelism. One book's approach pointed away from a method of presenting the gospel as a planned presentation toward an approach that emphasized cultivation before a verbal witness would be attempted. The word *confrontational* was coined to describe any evangelism method or strategy designed to train a person in how to share the message of the gospel with another person.

Another philosophy was the lifestyle approach. This philosophy struck a responsive chord in most churches as an alternative to a perceived negative approach to "pushing" the gospel message on another person.

The problem became an "either/or" approach to evangelism. Personal training and equipping in how to witness were perceived as too confrontational, as compared to the relational approach of living the results of salvation so that an unsaved person (hopefully) would ask the Christian to share the gospel with him or her.

While both approaches have important merits, each is incomplete in and of itself. Lifestyle evangelism becomes a lifestyle without evangelism if a person does not know what to share and how to share it. One-on-one evangelism becomes impersonal unless bridges are built to the individual before, during a presentation, and after the gospel is shared.

A biblical model for evangelism takes an appropriate balance in a both/and approach: _____ _____
_____ and demonstrating a lifestyle that draws people to faith _____ _____ __ _____ _____.
The _____ _____ _____ _____
_____/_____ _____ to evangelism.

It is important to remember that we are training in FAITH on a specific day of the week, but we are to be witnesses each and every day. We are to intentionally share the gospel both as a lifestyle and with words that communicate to others. _____ is the key word, meaning a Christian is predisposed and contemplative of opportunities to witness.

Once a Christian discovers that he or she can share the gospel with another person without fear, he realizes there are _____

Notes

_____ ___ _____. Many people have the kind of personality that enhances spontaneous conversations with individuals they have just met. Others are shy and reserved and feel more comfortable talking with individuals with whom they have developed a relationship.

Nonetheless, the more you participate in FAITH visits, the more comfortable you will feel in sharing with persons in spontaneous situations.

During FAITH Basic, your Team members have been introduced to the fact they can share the gospel with persons they may encounter during situations such as the following:

During travel
In social events with neighbors, work associates, and so forth
Through casual contacts with service personnel (waiters, mechanics, clerks, and so forth)
At family gatherings
During telephone surveys/opinion polls
At parks, beaches, and other recreational facilities
At sporting events
At school events
At civic clubs
In waiting rooms or offices (doctor, hospital, nursing home, hospice, and so forth)
Through written communication (mail to family and friends)
While visiting prisons or correctional institutions
At drug or alcohol rehabilitation centers

As you are aware, there are many other opportunities in which a Christian has the opportunity to share both a verbal and a lifestyle witness.

In training your Team members, you have the opportunity to encourage them to identify and take advantage of sharing the gospel in daily-life experiences. As you talk with Team members during the week, share ways you are seeking to take advantage of opportunities you have; also talk with them about opportunities they have to share the gospel during the week.

Most persons are well aware of IQ, or Intelligence Quotient, as an attempt to measure a person's mental capacities. Consider a "WAQ" as a "Witness Awareness Quotient." Although not intended in any way to be scientific or to draw permanent conclusions, a Witness Awareness Quotient can help you identify areas in which you already are strong and ways you can grow in sharing both a verbal and a lifestyle witness.

Such a tool can help raise the awareness of opportunities and encourage a person in his or her commitment as a Great Commission Christian.

My Witnessing Opportunities

The following list of witness opportunities that you have attempted can help you determine your witnessing opportunities. As you respond, consider the encounters and opportunities you have apart from weekly FAITH visits with your Team. This exercise is designed to help you determine the extent to which the FAITH strategy is influencing your daily life.

How many people do you know or regularly come in contact with during a given week? How many of that number are unsaved?

Your Learners will have as a Home Study Assignment this week a FAITH Tip, "Identifying Your Outreach Networks." Part of that FAITH Tip is the assignment to complete "Your Network Potential." In preparation for completing the Witness Awareness Quotient and as a reminder of what Learners have experienced, write your own responses to this assignment in the space below.

Your Network Potential

Calculating your network potential: Take a typical day of a typical workweek. Estimate the number of people with whom you had some kind of contact that day. Total the numbers.

____ Family members

____ People at work or school

____ People talked to on phone or by computer

____ People met casually during day (gas station, restaurant, and so forth)

____ People met during recreational activities

____ Others

____ **TOTAL**

Multiply your total for one day times five (typical workweek)

____ **My weekly networking potential**

Although there is likely an adjustment in the number in some categories from week to week or month to month, write an estimated number which realistically reflects your situation. In each category write the number of individuals you encounter who are unsaved.

Notes

Immediate family	Number of Unsaved _____
Relatives	Number of Unsaved _____
Friends	Number of Unsaved _____
Work associates	Number of Unsaved _____
Acquaintances	Number of Unsaved _____
Strangers	Number of Unsaved _____
	Total Number of Unsaved: _____

Verbal Witness Opportunities

Place a checkmark in each Yes space beside those opportunities in which you attempted to share a verbal witness during the past week; if more than once, put multiple checkmarks. Check No if you have not attempted to take advantage of such verbal witnessing opportunities.

A verbal witness can be defined as "taking advantage of an opportunity to share the message of the _____ _____ ___ _____."

1. Who?
Immediate family	Yes ____ No _____
Relative	Yes ____ No _____
Friend	Yes ____ No _____
Work associate	Yes ____ No _____
Acquaintance	Yes ____ No _____
Stranger	Yes ____ No _____

2. Where?
In my home	Yes ____ No _____
In a neighbor's home	Yes ____ No _____
In a friend's home	Yes ____ No_____
In a relative's home	Yes ____ No _____
In the workplace	Yes ____ No _____
In a shop	Yes ____ No _____
In a public place (such as a sports complex)	Yes ____ No _____
In a private place (such as a counseling room)	Yes ____ No _____

3. How?
In person	Yes ____ No _____
Over the phone	Yes ____ No _____
By mail	Yes ____ No _____

Add the total of Yes responses. Add the total of No responses. Write your total of Verbal Witness Opportunities here.

Verbal Witness: Yes _____   No _____

Lifestyle Witness Opportunities

Place a checkmark in the Yes space beside each opportunity in which you offered a lifestyle witness during the past week; if more than once, put multiple checkmarks. Check No if you had no lifestyle witness attempts.

A lifestyle witness could be defined as "taking advantage of an opportunity to share the message of the _____ _____ ___ _____."

1. Who?
Immediate family	Yes _____ No _____
Relative	Yes _____ No _____
Friend	Yes _____ No _____
Work associate	Yes _____ No _____
Acquaintance	Yes _____ No _____
Stranger	Yes _____ No _____

2. Where?
In my home	Yes _____ No _____
In a neighbor's home	Yes _____ No _____
In a friend's home	Yes _____ No _____
In a relative's home	Yes _____ No _____
In the workplace	Yes _____ No _____
In a shop	Yes _____ No _____
In a public place (such as a sports complex, airport)	Yes _____ No _____
In a private place (such as a counseling room)	Yes _____ No _____

3. How?
Enroll the person in Sunday School	Yes _____ No _____
Visit in the home or at work	Yes _____ No _____
Write a letter, card, or email message.	Yes _____ No _____
Present gift (flowers, resource, meal)	Yes _____ No _____
Provide service (transportation, repairs, lawn maintenance)	Yes _____ No _____

Add the total of Yes responses. Add the total of No responses. Write your total of Lifestyle Witness Opportunities here.

Lifestyle: Yes _____   No _____

Notes

Notes

Rewrite your totals here:

Number of Unsaved: _____

Verbal: Yes _____   *No* _____

Lifestyle: Yes _____   *No* _____

*Total Yes Responses*_____

Total No Responses _____

This simple Witness Awareness Quotient can build attentiveness to the fact you *can* strengthen your lifestyle and verbal witnessing opportunities.

The higher the Number of Unsaved, the more potential you have for sharing a witness. The more Yes responses you have, the more you are taking advantage of these witnessing opportunities.

If your No responses are greater than your Yes responses, then you can consciously strengthen your awareness of opportunities to sharing the gospel. If your Yes responses are greater than the No responses, then you can model comfortably for others the significance of sharing FAITH during daily-life opportunities.

Do not see your numerical results as being a definitive response. Do not perceive the test as a pass-fail experience or results for an active witness as indicating a "Super Witness." Always look for opportunities where you can share your faith.

Maximize Your Opportunities

Witnessing _____ _____ _____.
You will have more opportunities to share the gospel when you are in one-on-one settings than you ever will when you are with your FAITH Team.

One reason for providing the FAITH Sunday School Evangelism Strategy training is to give you a heightened confidence to share as you build bridges to unsaved people throughout your busy schedule. Many FAITH trainees have declared that, for them, FAITH has taken the fear out of witnessing.

Remember you also are helping Team members identify an awareness of sharing the gospel throughout the week by completing the FAITH Participation Card each week. The _____ _____ _____ on the Participation Card and the FAITH Report Board

calls attention to the need to take advantage of the natural opportunities we are given each day to share the gospel.

We need to _____ _____ _____ _____ to sharing the gospel. "The first-century Christians . . . were so convinced of the difference Jesus made that they came to see their former existence outside of Christ as a sort of living death (Eph. 2:1; 4:17-19; Col. 2:13).

"Sadly, however, this perspective is lacking in today's evangelistic circles. To make matters worse, the generation with which we seek to share the gospel is generally not the least bit interested in seeking us out. The result is sort of a spiritual truce: they don't bother us, and we don't bother them."[1]

We must unapologetically share the good news with those who are in need of hearing and seeing it lived out. We must stop waiting for them to come to us so we can refer them to someone else.

Pray that your sensitivity to daily opportunities to witness will increase. Pray for Team members as they learn to share their faith during FAITH visits as well as during the daily opportunities given them.

Notes

Notes

Visitation Time
DO IT

As you go . . .

Be aware that every witness you share can have a rippling effect: to other family members, friends, acquaintances, even total strangers. That rippling effect may be even greater in daily-life settings in which you share your faith; for example, a non-Christian often has a large number of unsaved friends.

The network of people who might be reached by one contact is known only to God. He has allowed you to join Him in His work.

Celebration Time
SHARE IT

As you return to share . . .

Ask a Team member to share your Team's reports.
• Reports and testimonies
• Session 13 Evaluation Card
• Participation Card
• Visitation forms updated with results of visits

Home Study Assignments

Notes

    Home Study Assignments reinforce this session and prepare you for the next session. "Journaling" experiences in Your Journey Continues are an important part of your development as a Great Commission Christian through FAITH training. Other assignments may include additional reading that enhances your experience.

    Selected features in this section highlight opportunities the Team Leader has to build bridges to his or her Team, class/department (especially through weekly Sunday School leadership team meetings) and church, and community. They can assist you in accomplishing your important responsibilities.

Your Journey Continues

    Describe some experiences you have had in sharing the gospel other than with your FAITH Team.

_____

_____

_____

_____

_____

_____

    Record some of the highlights of testimonies you have heard others share during Celebration Time. Highlight experiences they have had in sharing the gospel other than with their FAITH Team.

_____

_____

_____

_____

_____

_____

Notes

Acts 3 records the account of Peter and John walking to the temple when the Holy Spirit used them to minister to a crippled man who was asking for money. The man was healed and immediately made a scene by jumping up and down, praising God. The people who saw what was going on "were filled with wonder and amazement at what had happened to him" (Acts 3:10, NIV). Peter took advantage of the situation by sharing the gospel. This is recorded in Acts 3:11-26.

Read Acts 3:12-21. Based on these words Peter shared, rewrite the message of the gospel in your own words.

_____

_____

_____

_____

_____

_____

_____

_____

_____

Prayer Concerns

_____

_____

_____

_____

_____

_____

_____

_____

_____

_____

Answers to Prayer

_____

_____

_____

_____

_____

_____

_____

_____

_____

_____

An Important Bridge:
Your Weekly Sunday School Leadership Team Meeting

Use this space to record ways your FAITH Team impacts the work of your Sunday School department or class. Use the information to report during weekly Sunday School leadership team meetings. Identify actions that need to be taken through Sunday School as a result of prayer concerns, needs identified, visits made by the Team, and decisions made by the persons being visited.

Highlight needs/reports affecting your class/department or age group.

_____

_____

_____

Pray now for the important leadership meeting.

What are ways the department/class can follow up on life-witness opportunities shared by class members?

_____

_____

_____

What actions can be taken to encourage members and leaders to share both a lifestyle, as well as a verbal, witness during the week?

_____

_____

_____

How does preparation for Sunday need to consider persons who might attend because they received a witness by members during the week?

_____

_____

_____

For Further Reading

Read the FAITH Tip, "The Ripple Effects of FAITH."
Read pages 97 and 155 of *Evangelism Through the Sunday School: A Journey of FAITH* by Bobby Welch.

FAITH *Tip*

The Ripple Effects of FAITH

During the last months of 1997, Tony Antolino hit bottom. Suicidal, the heroin-addicted gang member made a call to a friend in Daytona Beach, Florida. This call saved not only his life, but also his soul.

The person he turned to was Laura Parks. A new Christian who had made a profession of faith only months earlier, Laura had become involved in a College and Career Sunday School class at First Baptist Church, Daytona Beach, and was eager to share her newfound faith.

"I just wanted the Jesus in me to be the Jesus in other people," she explained, "but I didn't know how. So, I did the FAITH thing." After counseling and encouraging Antolino, Parks led her friend to Christ over the telephone and launched him on a new course for life.

"Back in New York, all my friends thought I'd be the first one to die. Now I'm the first one with eternal life," Antolino testified during a January 20, 1997 FAITH enlistment banquet at The Ocean Center in Daytona Beach, Florida, drawing a standing ovation from the more than 1,000 attendees.

Parks and Antolino are living examples of the "ripple effect" of the FAITH Sunday School Evangelism Strategy. Antolino accepted Christ after Parks shared with him over the phone. She became a Christian partly through the witnessing efforts of her sister, Patricia, and friend Anthony Orzo, both of who were going through FAITH training.

A year earlier, Orzo was an alcoholic who spent his events partying at local nightclubs. After accepting Christ through Parks' witness, he became actively involved at First Baptist, ministering to kids through the church's bus ministry. A short time later, he went on his first mission trip, sharing his faith with youth in Brazil.

Another First Baptist Daytona Beach member shared her testimony during the banquet. Following her conversion, Karen Adams of Port Orange, Florida, said God "lit a fire in me that was almost overwhelming." Raised as a Roman Catholic, she became involved in a Lutheran church before meeting her husband, Mack, a retired Baptist missionary, over the Internet. Largely through his witness, she accepted Christ about a year before sharing the testimony; the couple became members of First Baptist Church, Daytona Beach.

Eager to share her faith with others, Adams enrolled in FAITH training at her church. On the fifth week of training, she and her two-member witnessing Team were going through their visitation assignment cards when she discovered one listing the name and address of her oldest son, 25-year-old Kyle.

"I couldn't believe it. I knew he had visited our church, but he had refused to fill out a visitor card," Adams said in an interview after the banquet. "He didn't want anyone visiting him. We have no idea how that card got there."

Though she hadn't yet shared the plan of salvation using the FAITH gospel presentation, she asked if she could present it to her son. "For the next half hour, I talked to my son on my fingers," Adams said, using them to share the five-point FAITH presentation.

"When I asked him if he wanted to pray to receive Christ as Savior, he said yes. The feelings I had that night I cannot describe. To me, that was the greatest moment a mother could ask for. FAITH has been a gift to me."[2]

For the Team Leader

This weekly feature suggests actions the Team Leader can take to support Team members, prepare for Team Time, and consider ways to improve visits. This work becomes part of the Team Leader's Home Study Assignments. Add any actions suggested by your church's FAITH strategy.

Support Team Members

❑ Contact Team members during the week. Remind them you are praying for them. Discuss prayer concerns and answers to prayer.

❑ As you talk with Learners this week, discuss opportunities they have for witnessing during the week. Encourage them as they seek to be a witness to persons they encounter.

❑ Record specific needs and concerns of Team members in the space provided.

_____

_____

_____

_____

_____

Prepare to Lead Team Time

❑ Review Home Study Assignments of Team members.

❑ Overview "Leading Team Time" for Session 14.

Prepare to Lead Visits

❑ Review the FAITH Visit Outline.

Build Bridges to Sunday School

❑ Use information in "An Important Bridge" (p. 205) to share about FAITH during this week's Sunday School leadership team meeting.

[1] Mark C. McCloskey, *Tell It Often—Tell It Well: Making the Most of Witnessing Opportunities* (HERE'S LIFE PUBLISHERS: San Bernardino, CA: 1986), 133.

[2] *The Sunday School Leader*, September 1998, 17. © LifeWay Christian Resources of the Southern Baptist Convention. Adapted from a Baptist Press release.

FAITH at Work

"We celebrate the FAITH process at Myrtle Grove Baptist Church, Pensacola, Florida. God has truly blessed our efforts through FAITH. Our first semester was conducted with 21 participants and 7 Teams.

Our first semester was tremendous. Every one of our Teams experienced at least one time leading someone to faith in Jesus Christ. We ended up baptizing the majority who were saved and enrolling dozens of new people in Sunday School.

As a result, the excitement penetrated the entire church family. This excitement has resulted in a second semester enrollment of 45 participants, with 15 Teams and 2 floater-trainers who will fill in during absences of other FAITH participants.

We are anticipating great results in the second semester and as a result have hired a consultant to help us expand our Sunday School—all in an effort to better assimilate those who are reached in the FAITH process.

Baptisms are up, Sunday School enrollment is up, and the spirit of our people is at an all-time 'up.'"

—Ron Lentine, pastor

SESSION 14

Building Bridges to People During Difficult Visits

In this session you will

    CHECK IT: engage in Team Time activities;

    KNOW IT: review selected principles from Session 13;

    HEAR IT: learn principles that apply to a variety of difficult situations and consider actions to take that can build bridges of relationship;

    SEE IT: view video footage in which principles for handling difficult or distracting situations are reviewed;

    SAY IT: practice the FAITH Visit Outline with a partner;

    STUDY IT: overview Home Study Assignments for Session 14;

    DO IT: begin to take the lead in visits, according to your Team Leader's cue;

    SHARE IT: celebrate.

Notes

Leading Team Time

All Team members participate in Team Time. They are primarily responsible for reciting the assigned portion of the FAITH Visit Outline and for discussing other Home Study Assignments.

As you direct this important time of CHECK IT activities with your Team, keep in mind how Learners also look to you as role model; motivator; mentor; and friend. Team Time activities can continue in the car, as the Team travels to and from visits.

Lead CHECK IT Activities

✓ FAITH Visit Outline
❑ Listen while each Learner recites as much of the FAITH Visit Outline as time allows. Make sure each person has a turn. It may be best to ask Learners to recite the segment they have the most difficulty sharing during a visit.

✓ Practice
❑ As time permits, allow for additional practice on any part of the visit presentation, sequence, and materials *(My Next Step of Faith—Baptism,* for example).

✓ Session 13 (FAITH in Daily Life) debriefing
❑ Review:
The FAITH Sunday School Evangelism Strategy is designed to help equip the Sunday School member and leader to share the gospel and minister to prospects and members. A strength of this evangelism training is that participants learn a simple, yet direct, approach to talking with people about the message of the gospel when visiting with a Team of three.

Another wonderful benefit is that someone who learns to share the gospel becomes more aware of witnessing opportunities during encounters throughout the week. Remind Team members that, as they continue training, they will become more aware of opportunities to share both a verbal and a lifestyle witness with people whose lives they intersect.

✓ Help for strengthening a visit

❏ Discuss some of the difficulties Teams have encountered in leading someone to hear and consider the FAITH gospel presentation. Call attention to the fact that this session formally introduces Learners to ways to deal with difficulties and distractions. At the same time, Team Leaders and other Building Bridges participants will be learning still other ways to help their Teams respond appropriately.

❏ As time allows, consider sharing a copy of the Witness Awareness Quotient for Team members to use at their convenience. Or discuss some things you learned as a result.

Briefly help Team members see the impact of increasing their awareness of witnessing opportunities. It is one way to focus attention on strengthening both lifestyle and verbal opportunities to witness.

Notes

Actions I Need to Take with Learners During the Week

Notes

Notes

A Quick Review

Many Christians have daily encounters with the unchurched and the unsaved. Until we begin to be more sensitive to everyone we encounter as potentially in need of the gospel, many of these relationships and opportunities may go overlooked.

The FAITH strategy already is helping us respond with a positive verbal witness, and you could recount instances in which someone seemed to be waiting for such a witness. As FAITH becomes increasingly integrated into your life, you will find yourself more aware of daily-life encounters.

What casual comments might indicate a need? What surface conversation might lead to a more serious one? What cultivation of a friendship might result in a verbal witness? What relationships have been established for the first time? You will find yourself becoming more aware than ever before of the meaning of events and words.

Because you are trained and available to God, the potential increases.

The Person God Uses
The person God uses depends on the Holy Spirit.

The Holy Spirit is the Spirit of God sent forth to do His work. The Holy Spirit's role is to—

- reveal God's will;
- guide persons in understanding and doing God's will;
- convict people of sin and enable lost sinners to turn to Christ in faith; and
- take up His abode in the believer's life.

The Holy Spirit is the Comforter, the One who walks alongside the believer through all situations. The Holy Spirit provides and cultivates a spiritual gift for each believer.[1]

Jesus said, " 'If you love me, you will obey what I command. And I will ask the Father, and he will give you another Counselor to be with you forever—the Spirit of truth' " (John 14:15-17a, NIV).

The Holy Spirit indwells every believer. "One may be filled with the Holy Spirit but not filled with His power. To be filled with the Holy Spirit, one must be submissive and available to the indwelling Spirit. It is not how much of the Holy Spirit the Christian has, but how much of the Christian the Holy Spirit has."[2]

How much of your life does the Spirit of God control? In what ways do you depend on the Holy Spirit to guide your thoughts and actions? To work in leading unsaved people to recognize their need for God's grace? To use you in sharing the good news of God's salvation through Jesus' death and resurrection?

Pray that God will help you learn the joys and results of depending totally on His Holy Spirit.

All Visits Don't Go "By the Script"

Throughout our FAITH training, we have viewed—and Learners are seeing for the first time—video segments of Andrew, George, and Myra making a model FAITH visit to Tony. Nearly everything in these visits goes "by the script." Tony hears the gospel presentation, recognizes his need, and prays to receive Christ.

By now you have realized that obstacles often arise during a visit—problems that can keep a person from hearing, considering, or accepting the gospel presentation. Generally, _distractions_ are those kinds of interruptions related to the _context_ of the visit—the dog barking, people in and out during the visit, the TV staying on, and so forth. We use the word _difficulties_ to describe problems that come up related to the _content_ of the visit—"I don't believe the Bible" or "I don't understand what it means to repent."

In most cases, the simplicity of the gospel presentation answers many questions people might have at the beginning. Most visits go smoothly and without major problems. However, for those times when obstacles do arise, this session will help us focus on ways to deal with difficulties and distractions. You will learn to handle problems so that, by building bridges of relationship, you still have an opportunity to present the gospel.

During each FAITH training course, a Team Leader continues to develop skill in dealing with difficulties; no one ever "graduates" from this subject. Many people who attempt to witness are rendered ineffective because they are not equipped to relate to the difficulties they encounter.

Although the problems we encounter will be varied, the principles we use to deal with them are few.

When they do occur, problems can be encountered during all three parts of a FAITH visit: *Preparation, Presentation,* and *Invitation.* Potential problems in a FAITH visit can crop up as—

1. A _Question_ (for example, "Why wouldn't a loving God allow everyone into heaven?")

Notes

2. An ___*Objection*___ (for example, "I don't think I've ever done anything that bad.")

3. A ___*Misunderstanding*___ (for example, "Are you saying, 'For me to turn from my sin I have to . . . ?' ")

4. A ___*Negative Reaction*___ (for example, "I don't think much about organized religion. I've had some bad experiences in the past.")

5. A ___*Distraction*___ that interrupts the flow and the discussion of a visit (for example, the TV stays on during the visit, phone calls interrupt, the dog barks.)

Here's another way to think about potential difficulties: Comments you may encounter generally can be categorized as *philosophical* (growing out of issues related to the gospel message; for example, "I don't see why it is necessary to have a life-changing experience") or *practical* (based in someone's personal experiences or preferences; for example, "I want to receive Christ, but I want to do it later"). In your Team's response it is important to know where people are coming from, to acknowledge that perspective, and to try to address their concern appropriately.

Session 14 of FAITH Basic introduced us to some principles for dealing with difficulties (especially those categorized as distractions). This session will help you focus on actions to take—especially when encountering other, more complex difficulties—in each part of the visit.

Minimize Difficulties: Build Bridges to Get Acquainted

The same guidelines that get any visit off to a good start can help your Team avoid difficulties. The **Preparation** portion of the visit is significant as you build or strengthen bridges. Consider the following guidelines.

1. Clearly and cordially ___*introduce*___ yourself and your Team. Do everything you can to put the person at ease. Remember, you are asking a person to take his or her time to allow your Team to enter the home.

Many people feel awkward permitting strangers into their homes. Your sensitivity to this reality can help you build bridges in many challenging situations. Many people will be glad to discover that you are from the same group they would identify with in the church. They may welcome you as they discover you share common interests and concerns.

2. ___*Spend appropriate time*___ getting to know the person and helping him feel comfortable with you and your Team members. Often, it is good to bring up information you have about the person that would help begin or strengthen the conversation. Some details may have

been provided on the FAITH Visit Assignment Card—for example, the person visited the church or was referred by someone he knows.

Do not rush the time to get acquainted. Realize that it is vital in building bridges of trust and friendship. At the same time, recognize you have a limited amount of time, so do not spend so much time getting acquainted that you never get to the gospel presentation (if appropriate).

3. Be a _good listener_. Many times a person subtly shares information that can help identify a ministry need or a spiritual condition.

If your Team comes across as more interested in sharing a presentation than in building bridges, you open yourselves up to resistance and closed doors. Sometimes you must be willing to listen to someone's story—even when it includes criticism, questions, denial, or resistance—before he or she will feel comfortable trusting you with the truth of the gospel.

4. _Share testimonies_ to build bridges. The Sunday School testimony is one of the most simple, yet significant, features of the FAITH Sunday School Evangelism Strategy. Many people will be surprised to discover that your Sunday School class has something to offer and that you are impacted personally by your class.

The evangelistic testimony is intended to briefly whet the appetite of the person and determine whether there is interest in a similar life-changing experience. As you help Team members with their evangelistic testimonies, you enable them to share naturally and meaningfully from their experience. Your Team is seeking to _build bridges of Relationships_ that ultimately allow you to share the gospel, if appropriate.

Minimize Difficulties: Transition from the Key Question

A person who realizes you really care for him will be more receptive to hearing the good news you have to share.

1. Know how to _make transition_ between the Key Question and the way(s) a person responds to the question. Generally, a response will indicate that the person—

• *Already believes in and has accepted Christ.*—If so, celebrate the person's faith response. Ask for some events that led to this experience.

Also, look for opportunities to ask whether a Team member could practice the gospel presentation. Look for opportunities to enroll the person in Bible study if not already participating.

Notes

• *Has yet to realize he cannot save himself.*—What we call a works response usually will reflect the person's belief that one goes to heaven primarily as a result of "good, clean" living. Some people believe that, ultimately, all will be saved. When such a response occurs, help the person understand that many people respond this way.

Then, rather than telling the person his answer is wrong or dealing with a side issue, ask permission to share how the Bible answers the Key Question. In many situations, the Holy Spirit has used the gospel presentation to convict the person of his wrong thinking and his need for Christ.

• *Is giving mixed responses.*—The prospect sometimes gives a combination of answers—for example, "I believe the Bible and that you have to live a good life to go to heaven." Gently probe to clarify what the person means.

Someone who gives an unclear answer usually will gravitate toward a works answer when asked to clarify his response. If and when a works answer surfaces, restate it to find out whether it reflects the person's belief. If a works answer is established, ask for permission to share how the Bible answers this question.

• *Seems to have no definite opinion.*—When this occurs, consider suggesting an answer (other than a faith response) and see whether the person agrees with it. If he or she does not agree with your suggested answer, rephrase it

If the person fails to agree with any works answer you supply, help him to understand that a no-opinion response concerning heaven really is not an option; at some point everyone must come to a decision regarding whether to accept Jesus. Ask for the privilege to share how the Bible answers the Key Question.

2. Sometimes at this point in a FAITH visit (Key Question/Transition) people will __Resist__ hearing what the Bible has to say. Some will wonder how long it will take you to share the answer. Others have personal needs that make it difficult for them to listen to you.

You can overcome many difficulties by being sensitive to the barriers people will try to place for not hearing the answer. Remember, the answer to the Key Question often comes in the presentation of the gospel. Be sensitive to the leadership of the Holy Spirit.

Minimize Difficulties: During the Presentation

Be aware of ways to minimize the potential of difficulties that could arise in sharing the gospel presentation. If during the FAITH presentation

itself a difficulty arises, attempt to follow these guidelines while recognizing that each situation is unique:

1. If a person asks a question while you are sharing the FAITH gospel presentation, generally it is best to __*delay*__ answering until you are ready for the Inquiry question in the ***Invitation.*** Frequently, if you are allowed to share the gospel presentation in its entirety, the questions a person might have asked at the beginning of the visit are answered. Usually, you will have the opportunity to completely share the brief gospel presentation.

2. __*Answer   now*__ if the question comes at the point at which you are sharing and and if it clarifies your response. You also can supplement the presentation with information about the message of the gospel.

For example, if the question "What does it mean to repent?" comes when you are addressing T is for TURN, it is best to clarify at that time.

3. If a question is asked that you cannot answer, simply __*say so*__ and ask for permission to continue.

4. __*Be sensitive to others needs*__ reflected by a seemingly negative comment. Someone who says, "We can't listen to this right now" may be indicating a serious personal need or situation for which the family needs help. Actually, there may be greater openness to the gospel than ever before.

Minimize Difficulties: At the Point of *Invitation*

Be aware of ways to deal with difficulties that could arise after sharing the gospel presentation and as you are inquiring about further commitment.

1. Some people who answered the Key Question by saying their good works will enable them to enter heaven may give a different answer to the ***Invitation*** Inquiry question. In such a case, tactfully remind them of an earlier works answer, and __*clarify*__ the importance of trusting in Jesus and Jesus only for forgiveness. Also, __*Reemphasize*__ the *T* (TURN) part of the FAITH gospel presentation.

2. If you have asked permission to delay your answer to the person's question, do __*acknowledge*__ the question again when you are ready to answer it. Doing so lets the person know you have not forgotten about it.

3. On occasion, a person may make a comment, interrupt you, or share

Notes

a response because of something he or she misunderstands. This misunderstanding may grow out of some personal background or experience or from something you said.

Be glad for this type of interruption or response. It gives you an opportunity to <u>clear</u> <u>up a misunderstanding</u>.

4. Some people will object to something you said during the **Presentation**. Many times you can <u>diffuse objections</u> by saying something like (if appropriate), "I used to feel the same way; let me share what helped me change my mind." If this response does not match your experience, choose an answer that does and that helps you relate to the other person.

Another response would be to <u>listen</u> to the objection and to <u>restate</u> it in a way you can answer. Continue by clarifying the gospel presentation.

5. Some people will try to get off the subject of spiritual commitment by talking about such things as church participation, family heritage, or even a negative situation (perhaps something that happened to them).

You may merely need to <u>be a good listener</u> during this kind of situation; let the person <u>vent</u> his or her negative emotions. Remember the importance of building bridges to help the person be open to hearing and responding to the gospel. Also remember that you reflect Christ and His church in how you act as well as what you say.

6. Some people will indicate a lack of belief or trust in something that is important to you or something that is the basis of your message, including—

- the Bible,
- heaven/hell/life after death, or
- other aspects related to the gospel presentation.

Even though you may be able to briefly share some historical evidences of the truth or doctrine, remember that you are not to debate or argue.

A strong yet positive way to answer such a response is to share your <u>personal experience</u>. One appropriate response to make is (for example) "<u>What if the Bible</u> (heaven/hell/life after death, and so forth) <u>is indeed true</u>?" and proceed by sharing.

Perhaps the following story recounted by Billy Graham will be helpful.

"In Wellington, on New Zealand's North Island, I spoke at the university. Among many other things, I spoke on the reality of Hell . . . . After the meeting (late) at night, there came one of the students, and he was angry— *very* angry.

" 'What do you mean coming over here from America and talking about Hell? I don't believe in Hell, and you have no right

to come over here and talk about it!'

"'Let me ask you a question,' I responded. 'Suppose you went to Auckland to catch a plane for Sydney. And suppose they told you there was a 10 percent chance the plane would not make it but was going to crash. Would you get on?'

"'No,' he replied, 'I wouldn't.'

" 'Well, what if there were only a 5 percent chance the plane wasn't going to make it? Would you get on then?'

" 'No, of course not.'

" 'Now suppose there's only a 10 percent—or even just a 5 percent chance—that Jesus was right and there *is* a Hell. Do you think there's at least a 5 percent chance that He might have been right?'

" 'Well, yes, I suppose there is.'

" 'Then is it worth taking the risk and ignoring those odds?'

" 'No. No it isn't,' he admitted.' "[3]

Principles for Dealing with Difficulties and Distractions

Based off what already has been presented, a few significant principles emerge for dealing with the varied situations you will encounter. Remember, as you approach a FAITH visit expecting God to work, you will be relying on Him to help your Team resolve difficulties.

Following are what we might call some *ABC's* of handling difficulties. As you think of each key word, perhaps in new situations you encounter, you also may easily recall a possible solution.

Much of what we are discussing becomes easier and more natural with prayer and with practice as you continue to make evangelistic and ministry visits. Review this content as needed throughout FAITH training.

Avoid *being the difficulty.*

Make sure the actions or attitudes of your Team are not the source of someone's problem. A Team member who is more interested in getting to and through the gospel presentation while overlooking the needs of a person may lose the privilege of sharing the gospel with that individual.

Be *a good listener in dealing with negative reactions.*

In a situation in which someone has had a negative experience,

Notes

especially with the church, you likely need to let the person vent his or her emotions. Those emotions may be strong and deep-seated. At the same time you are exercising patience, especially rely on the work of the Holy Spirit to bring grace into the situation.

Clear *up misunderstandings.*

Be grateful for opportunities the person gives you to clear up any misunderstandings. This is especially important as misconceptions relate to the gospel presentation. Perhaps the individual simply has not heard all of what you said. He or she may have misunderstood a point. Unless the point can be handled later, clear up the misunderstanding at the time. If not clarified at the time, the misunderstood concept may influence a person's entire understanding of the gospel.

Diffuse *objections.*

To be able to continue with the presentation after an objection is voiced may require a capacity to listen carefully and to relate personally to the comment or the experience. Avoid becoming defensive. Seek to maintain the relationship and to continue the communication.

For example, after an objection you are better able to continue by saying something like (be truthful!), "I used to feel the same way about _____; here's what help me change my mind." Another way to deal with objections is to restate the person's statement in such a way that you can respond.

Expect *the Holy Spirit to work in difficulties.*

Be aware that Satan will do everything possible to distract and confuse in any situation. At the same time, you can approach every visit with confidence, knowing that the Holy Spirit is at work and that He is using you and your Team as His instruments. He already may be working in the lives of people you are visiting.

Knowing that God is at work, you can be assured that He can make any difficulty a positive experience. Go in an attitude of prayer and dependence.

Function *as a Team to cover distractions.*

To deal effectively with the distractions posed by TV or stereos playing, the telephone ringing, children coming in and out requires teamwork. While one person shares the gospel, the other two Team members can allow the person to hear it by talking to the child, petting the cat, and so forth. Team members should do whatever is necessary to provide opportunity for the person to hear and respond to the gospel presentation.

God *uses you in different ways.*

God uses you and your Team in different ways in visits. In some cases, you may till the soil, while in other visits you may plant a seed. Occasionally you will nurture a young seedling. In some memorable visits, your Team will be there to harvest fruit.

You will not see the results of every visit. Nor will you see professions of faith in every visit. Your part is to go and to share, leaving the results to God and to further opportunities for cultivation.

Handle *responses to the Key Question appropriately.*

Understand the type of answer the prospect gives to the Key Question, and respond appropriately. Your Team frequently will encounter answers that indicate dependence on his own efforts to achieve heaven. Sometimes the answer reflects uncertainty. Be grateful for such a response; it allows you a God-given opportunity to share the gospel.

A person's response may represent a combination of answers. In this case, try to restate the response or probe for more information. In some cases, it will be important to clarify, perhaps by putting an answer in your own words and seeing whether it reflects the person's opinion.

Improve *your debating skills elsewhere.*

Dealing with difficulties is not about improving your debating skills; it is about handling situations in such a way that you still have an opportunity to present the gospel. *Remember, your goal is to gain a hearing for the gospel.* Many questions someone might have had at the beginning of the visit ultimately are answered by the FAITH presentation.

An individual also has allowed you a limited amount of time; make best use of this time by moving to the main point of your visit—discovering whether a person has received God's forgiveness in Christ and, if appropriate, sharing the gospel. Bridges for sharing the gospel are best laid at the beginning of the visit, when needs are assessed and trust is established.

Even if questions or difficulties cannot be resolved in one visit, one very positive result can be to enroll the person/family in Sunday School—or to follow up with that possibility in mind. Over time, with caring Christian friends and exposure to God's Word, difficulties may become opportunities!

In all situations, seek to build bridges so that additional cultivation and relationship-building can take place.

Notes

Notes

Visitation Time
DO IT

As you go . . .

Think about: Are your Learners ready to take the lead in a visit? Have you built a strong yet sturdy bridge to the Learners on your Team? Are they growing in their faith and in their capacity to share their faith? Are they learning to recognize when the FAITH Visit Outline needs to be adjusted in visits? Are they helping establish bridges of relationship between the community and your Sunday School?

How far have Team members come since Session 1? Have you taken the time to affirm them for their progress and to thank the Lord for this mentoring experience?

What changes in your class/department might be attributed to FAITH? How are Sunday School and church members growing in their faith?

Hopefully, you are continuing to grow in your faith, too!

Celebration Time
SHARE IT

As you return to share . . .

- Reports and testimonies
- Session 14 Evaluation Card
- Participation Card
- Visitation forms updated with results of visits

Home Study Assignments

Home Study Assignments reinforce this session and prepare you for the next session. "Journaling" experiences in Your Journey Continues are an important part of your development as a Great Commission Christian through FAITH training. Other assignments may include additional reading that enhances your experience.

Selected features in this section highlight opportunities the Team Leader has to build bridges to his or her Team, class/department (especially through weekly Sunday School leadership team meetings) and church, and community. They can assist you in accomplishing your important responsibilities.

Your Journey Continues

Describe two to three specific difficulties you have encountered during previous FAITH visits.

What were ways a Team member appropriately dealt with each situation? What have been ways you have seen the Holy Spirit at work in the midst of these situations?

_____

_____

_____

_____

_____

_____

Read Acts 9:1-2. Most people would consider Saul one of the greatest threats and challenges to the Christian faith. Imagine what a FAITH visit would be like to someone like Saul. Write those thoughts here.

_____

_____

_____

_____

_____

_____

Notes

Read Acts 9:3-19. What are some things you are learning about how the Holy Spirit works, even in the life of someone like Saul?

Imagine how you would feel knowing God has called you (your FAITH Team) to be in such a position as Ananias was—to visit someone like Saul. Write your thoughts in the space provided.

_____

_____

_____

_____

_____

_____

Prayer Concerns   Answers to Prayer

_____   _____

_____   _____

_____   _____

_____   _____

_____   _____

_____   _____

_____   _____

_____   _____

_____   _____

_____   _____

_____   _____

An Important Bridge:
Your Weekly Sunday School Leadership Team Meeting

Use this space to record ways your FAITH Team impacts the work of your Sunday School department or class. Use the information to report during weekly Sunday School leadership team meetings. Identify actions that need to be taken through Sunday School as a result of prayer concerns, needs identified, visits made by the Team, and decisions made by the persons being visited.

Highlight needs/reports affecting your class/department or age group.

_____

_____

_____

Pray now for teachers and department directors.

What are ways the department/class can learn from difficulties encountered during FAITH visits?

_____

_____

_____

How does preparation for Sunday need to consider persons who raised questions and difficulties during a FAITH visit? How do their questions challenge us to look at our teaching, assimilation, and outreach efforts?

_____

_____

_____

For Further Reading

Read pages 140-43 of *Evangelism Through the Sunday School: A Journey of FAITH* by Bobby Welch. What church-devouring monsters have been represented by some FAITH visits this semester?

Notes

For the Team Leader

This weekly feature suggests actions the Team Leader can take to support Team members, prepare for Team Time, and consider ways to improve visits. This work becomes part of the Team Leader's Home Study Assignments. Add any actions suggested by your church's FAITH strategy.

Support Team Members

❏ Contact Team members during the week. Remind them you are praying for them. Discuss prayer concerns and answers to prayer.

❏ Record specific needs and concerns of Team members in the space provided.

_____

_____

_____

Prepare to Lead Team Time

❏ Review Home Study Assignments of Team members.

❏ Be prepared to remind Team members to draft a "What FAITH Has Meant to Me" testimony, due Session 16.

Prepare to Lead Visits

❏ Review the FAITH Visit Outline.

Build Bridges to Sunday School

❏ Use information in "An Important Bridge" (p. 225) to share about FAITH during this week's Sunday School leadership team meeting. Add other information appropriate to your class/department/FAITH Team's experiences.

[1]Herschel Hobbs, *The Baptist Faith and Message* (Nashville: Convention Press, rev. 1996), 40-41.
[2]Ibid., 41.
[3]Billy Graham, *Just As I Am: The Autobiography of Billy Graham* (Billy Graham Evangelistic Association, 1997) 331-332.

SESSION 15

Building Bridges for a Stronger FAITH Strategy

In this session you will

CHECK IT: engage in Team Time activities;

KNOW IT: review selected principles from Session 14;

HEAR IT: consider reasons and motivations to continue in FAITH training;

SEE IT (optional): view again, if desired, the Session 1 Part 1 segment ("Tony Remembers") as a reminder of reasons to continue in FAITH;

SAY IT: practice the FAITH Visit Outline with a partner;

STUDY IT: overview Home Study Assignments for Session 15;

DO IT: make visits in which a Team member takes the lead;

SHARE IT: celebrate.

Leading Team Time

All Team members participate in Team Time. They are primarily responsible for reciting the assigned portion of the FAITH Visit Outline and for discussing other Home Study Assignments.

As you direct this important time of CHECK IT activities with your Team, keep in mind how Learners also look to you as role model; motivator; mentor; and friend. Team Time activities can continue in the car, as the Team travels to and from visits.

Lead CHECK IT Activities

✓ FAITH Visit Outline
❑ Listen while each Learner recites as much of the FAITH Visit Outline as time allows. It may be best to ask Learners to recite the segment they seem to have the most difficulty sharing during a visit.

✓ Practice
❑ As time permits, allow for any additional practice that is needed on the visit presentation and sequence.

✓ Session 14 (Handling Difficulties in a Visit) debriefing
❑ Briefly talk about distractions Team members have encountered in earlier visits.

❑ While reminding Team members that most visits go very smoothly, help them begin to recognize principles and actions for handling difficulties. As you model ways to handle difficult situations during visits, be sure to explain what you did and why.

It is important to deal appropriately with difficulties that could take place at any time during the visit. Difficulties are those things that happen or are said during the visit that could keep you from sharing the gospel and leading a person who is ready to respond to make a commitment to Christ.

Principles for dealing with difficulties relate primarily to building bridges of relationship with the person, dealing with any questions and objections, and working through the distractions that take place.

✓ Other Home Study Assignments
❑ Remind the group of the assignment, due next week, to write a testimony indicating what FAITH has meant personally.

✓ Help for strengthening a visit

❏ Remind Team members to listen during each visit for ministry opportunities and for ways to follow up appropriately.

❏ If you have shared the Witness Awareness Quotient with Team members, reemphasize as follows:

The greater the Number of Unsaved identified, the greater the potential for sharing a witness. The greater the number of Yes responses, the more someone is taking advantage of witnessing opportunities.

If No responses are higher than Yes responses, then someone can consciously strengthen awareness of opportunities to sharing the gospel. If Yes responses are higher, then a witness can comfortably model for others the significance of sharing FAITH during daily-life opportunities.

Notes

_____

_____

_____

_____

_____

Actions I Need to Take with Learners During the Week

_____

_____

_____

_____

_____

Notes

Notes

A Quick Review

In all evangelistic visits, your goal is to build bridges that ultimately provide an opportunity to share the gospel. Your Team's attitude and approach should be part of what attracts people to Christ; they should never be barriers to the gospel message or to the person of Christ and His church.

When difficulties present themselves, realize that cultivation may be needed or the person may not be ready. Initially you may be planting a seed, ministering to a person's need, or cultivating the work of someone else. Some difficulties may reflect the convicting power of the Holy Spirit already at work in someone's life.

Your purpose is not to establish the rightness of your position, but to lovingly find out whether a person has need of God's forgiveness and salvation. You respond to that need by words, as well as by example and respect.

Rather than being judgmental, always be ready to share the hope that is in you. Difficulties may be opportunities in disguise.

The Person God Uses
The person God uses is a disciple and one who disciples others.

Jesus said, "Follow me, and I will make you fishers of men" (Matt. 4:19, NKJV). The word *disciple* comes from the same root word as "learner." A disciple is someone who follows his Master; a disciple is one who learns from the Master. God uses Christians who give themselves completely to follow and serve the risen Christ.

Jesus requires a high level of commitment from those who follow Him. As Dietrich Bonhoeffer wrote, "When Christ calls a man, he bids him come and die."[1] There were times when many people wanted to follow Jesus because of His popularity and His miracles; then, when Jesus declared the commitment that was required, many abandoned Him.

Jesus demonstrated that He teaches His followers to disciple others. Your job as a Great Commission Christian is to train others to follow Christ. Indeed, we have the teachings of Holy Scripture to study and the perfect model of Christ to imitate. Without question, we are to train others to learn from Christ by what we say as well as by what we do. Great Commission work is about going, teaching them to observe, baptizing—and remembering that He is with us always.

As you seek to be obedient, look for opportunities to continue training people to be disciples of Christ.

Imagine . . .
What Can Happen

The FAITH Sunday School Evangelism Strategy is designed to be an intentional multiplier concept: One person who has been trained to share his or her faith trains two more persons. Those two individuals are equipped and encouraged to train two more people from their Sunday School department or class. The strategy is designed to be continuous. Imagine the benefits for a church of having every Sunday School member equipped and functioning as a Great Commission Christian.

Read through the following scenarios. Imagine . . . every member of your Sunday School class receiving a ministry visit at least once every few months. Imagine . . . every prospect receiving a personal visit by a Team of members (from his or her own age group), each of whom is prepared to share a simple but direct gospel presentation. Imagine . . . members who are excited about witnessing and training others to do so. FAITH is designed to help accomplish all of these outcomes and more.

The FAITH Sunday School Evangelism Strategy depends on constant cultivation of Sunday School leaders and members who have not been trained. More and more benefits are realized as additional people become actively involved in FAITH.

Some individuals have been able to be involved in FAITH as prayer partners, and that is so important. Some have been involved by providing names and information about prospects who need to be visited, and that is essential. Others have assisted by helping prepare visitation packets, update information in Sunday School records about prospects who are visited, and provide meals or child care for those being trained; the process would not have been as effective without these involvements. All of these responsibilities are vital for the success of this strategy.

But imagine what would happen if even one person who has received training chooses not to reenlist and commit to train two additional persons. Think about the _Impact_ in —
- _Your Life_ if you were not to reenlist. Write it here.

_____

- _Your Sunday School class_. Write it here.

_____

- _Lives of your Team members_. Write it here.

_____

_____

Notes

Now do some math and consider the possible outcomes for your FAITH strategy and your church.

Do the Math . . . and Consider

If one Team Leader were to drop out of FAITH training, the following results take place.

1 — One Team Leader drops out of the next semester of FAITH.

Plus 2 — The number of Learners who cannot be trained by this leader during the next semester.

Equals 3 — The FAITH strategy would have 3 fewer people than would have been involved in making ministry and evangelism visits after 16 weeks of FAITH training.

Times 3 — Each of these 3, in turn, would have trained a new Team.

Minus 9 — The FAITH strategy would have 9 fewer people than would have been involved after 32 weeks of FAITH training.

Times 3 — Each of these 9, in turn, would have trained a new Team.

Equals 27 — The strategy would have 27 fewer people than would have been making ministry and evangelistic visits after 1 1/2 years

Times 3 — Each of these 27, in turn, would have trained a new Team.

Equals 81 — In less than 2 years, the strategy would have 81 fewer people than would have been making ministry and evangelistic visits.

Times 3 — Each of these 81, in turn, would have trained a new Team.

Equals 243 — If one Team Leader drops out of FAITH, in less than 2 1/2 years the strategy potentially could have 243 fewer people involved in making ministry and evangelistic visits.

Do you begin to get the picture of the impact if only one Team Leader chooses to drop out of active participation in FAITH training? This could be called " <u>Satan's math</u> ." The evil one can deceive us into thinking we are too busy to do the basics of Great Commission work. He can deceive us in thinking our "1" does not matter. Begin to think about the number of people who would not hear or respond to the ministry of the gospel because of the <u>One person who does not commit</u> to stay in training and train two more members.

Soon the Official Kickoff Begins

During this session Team Learners are being introduced to reenlistment in FAITH. This session officially begins the period of time when your church begins making transition to the next semester of FAITH. Some Learners are beginning to realistically consider how God may be leading them to train two other people from their class or department. Others are considering reenlistment to repeat training as an Assistant Team Leader.

As a Team Leader, you are concerned about enlisting two people for your own future Team. You also are involved in helping your present Team members identify persons who might be on their Team, particularly if they will be Team Leaders.

Consider the following actions you can take as you and other Team members consider reenlistment in the FAITH strategy.

1. _Help Team members consider persons_ who might be interested or would benefit by participating in FAITH training. Some Sunday School class members have shown an interest or expressed excitement by hearing testimonies of FAITH participants. Some members have become convicted by their lack of commitment or participation in Great Commission work. Others have expressed a desire to participate some day in training.

On many occasions, those who have been reached by FAITH visits may be among the first to consider their own participation in learning how to share their faith; they have realized firsthand the benefits of this ministry.

God may have placed on your heart the name of someone who should be contacted as a participant in this significant strategy. _Don't say no_ for anyone in your class or department. You may be reluctant to ask someone to be on your Team because you think he or she is too busy, would not be interested in FAITH, or would have another excuse. If you fail to ask the person after prayerfully considering God's leadership, then, in effect, you have said no for him or her. Too many people make this mistake.

2. Encourage Team members to preenroll in the next semester of training. You will need to be prepared to _Review the ways a person can participate_ in FAITH training. During the next semester, a Team member can serve as—

• *a Team Leader*, by taking additional training and modeling visits for two other persons;

• *an Assistant Team Leader*, by taking additional training and assisting in training someone else.

3. As always, it is best to _Make a personal visit_

Notes

to the individual(s) you are seeking to pre-enlist as Team Learners. It becomes a very important model for you to take your current Team members as you seek to pre-enlist your future Team members. As a current Team, you can work together in assisting the other Team members in pre-enlisting their future Team Learners.

Use enlistment material from FAITH Basic that Learners are overviewing during this session, plus helps in the Administrative Guide.

4. Although pre-enlistment is not the official enrollment for the next 16 weeks of training, you already are getting a good indication of potential participation. _Encourage persons To prayer fully consider_ their participation. One of your most meaningful responsibilities is to help Team members understand their realistic role in the next semester of FAITH. Some are ready to take the responsibility of serving as a Team Leader. They need your encouragement. Some Team members will do better by reenlisting as an assistant on a Team before they take on the commitment as Team Leader.

5. _Be a positive model_ by reenrolling in FAITH training as a Team Leader. You will be needed in the next semester even more than you are in this current semester if your church's FAITH strategy is to grow. Your church needs individuals who are trained to model the training. Your church needs people to model reenlistment.

6. The time to actually enroll in the next semester of FAITH is always important. Although you can pre-enlist a potential Team member at any time, it is best to _officially enroll a person_ on a FAITH Team approximately _three weeks before the first session_ of the next training course. You will be working in conjunction with your church's publicity and prayer efforts.

7. _Plan To participate in publicity and enrollment efforts_ planned by your church. Encourage class members to participate with you in the following actions:

- *Participate in the Kickoff Banquet.*
- *Be ready to share a testimony of what FAITH has meant to you.*
- *Volunteer to serve on a FAITH planning committee to help publicize and begin the next semester of FAITH.*
- *Be positive and encouraging in your remarks about FAITH training.*

With such a simple step as reenlistment, you are turning "Satan's math" into Great Commission math, as the disciple indeed becomes more involved in making disciples of others. It was what Jesus had in mind when He gave us the Great Commission, and FAITH is a strategy to help us help our church do Great Commission work. Imagine what could happen.

Visitation Time
DO IT

As you go . . .

Realize that by going, you are actively involved in obedience to the Great Commission. You are indicating the availability and obedience God desires and needs. Recognize that not everyone you visit will have the same understandings and motivations as you do. But you can approach your visits knowing that as you go, three-by-three, you are helping reach your Judea and Samaria for Christ.

Celebration Time
SHARE IT

As you return to share . . .

Know that you have reason to celebrate and rejoice together in the efforts made. If you do not have this realization, think about reasons to celebrate as you read the testimonies and FAITH Tip this week.

Ask a Team member to share your Team's reports.
- Reports and testimonies
- Session 15 Evaluation Card
- Participation Card
- Visitation forms updated with results of visits

Notes

Home Study Assignments

Home Study Assignments reinforce this session and prepare you for the next session. "Journaling" experiences in Your Journey Continues are an important part of your development as a Great Commission Christian through FAITH training. Other assignments may include additional reading that enhances your experience.

Selected features in this section highlight opportunities the Team Leader has to build bridges to his or her Team, class/department (especially through weekly Sunday School leadership team meetings) and church, and community. They can assist you in accomplishing your important responsibilities.

Your Journey Continues

Read Jeremiah 1:4-9. Imagine God speaking these words to you. What would be your response to God?

_____

_____

_____

_____

_____

_____

What have you learned through the FAITH training that you would want another Christian to experience?

_____

_____

_____

_____

_____

_____

Who are some people you would want to receive FAITH training? Would they be open to hearing about and considering your experiences in FAITH?

_____

_____

_____

_____

_____

_____

On a separate piece of paper, write a "What FAITH Has Meant to Me" testimony to turn in at the beginning of Session 16.

Prayer Concerns   Answers to Prayer

_____   _____

_____   _____

_____   _____

_____   _____

_____   _____

_____   _____

_____   _____

_____   _____

_____   _____

_____   _____

Notes

Notes

An Important Bridge:
Your Weekly Sunday School Leadership Team Meeting

Use this space to record ways your FAITH Team impacts the work of your Sunday School department or class. Use the information to report during weekly Sunday School leadership team meetings. Identify actions that need to be taken through Sunday School as a result of prayer concerns, needs identified, visits made by the Team, and decisions made by the persons being visited.

Highlight needs/reports affecting your class/department or age group.

_____

_____

Pray now for this important meeting.

With what issues does the class need to deal because new and reclaimed members are participating in the class because someone visited them during the past several months?

_____

_____

How does preparation for Sunday need to help persons consider participating in FAITH Sunday School Evangelism Strategy?

_____

_____

What are some changes FAITH leaders might want to make in future training courses? How has participation this semester of FAITH strategy met or exceeded expectations by Sunday School leadership?

_____

_____

For Further Reading

Read "Testimonies of FAITH at Work" and the FAITH Tip, "Why I Am in FAITH Training." Unless otherwise indicated, testimonies are from FAITH participants at Lynwood Baptist Church, Cape Giradeau, Missouri.

Testimonies of FAITH at Work

"FAITH is a method of presenting the gospel that is complete and easy to learn and to present. It is a great feeling to know how to lead someone to Christ and is exciting when God brings you together with someone who is ready to do so. FAITH is not pushy."

—*Mike Jones*

"Words cannot truly express how God has blessed me through FAITH. To see our church sharing God with the unsaved is what we should do, but to see how God has given me the courage and enthusiasm in spite of my many fears is amazing.

"Thank God someone cared for my soul years ago to share God's Word with me, and thank God our church is reaching out and caring for other lost souls.

"It is humbling when our FAITH groups come together at the end of each night's visits to share decisions and prayer requests made that night and to see how God works through us and how great He is."

—*Judy Rayburn*

"I joined FAITH to lead others to the Lord. However, a couple of weeks into the semester I accepted Jesus Christ as my personal Savior for the first time. Shortly thereafter, I had the blessing of leading a couple to salvation. I have experienced the Lord's using FAITH to change my life and the lives of others with whom I have shared it."

—*Mendy Burgess*

"We read in the Bible how Jesus said, 'Come, follow me and I will make you fishers of men' or how He tells us to 'go and make disciples' in the Great Commission. I believe most Christians, as well as myself, say "I want to do that."

"But we don't know what to share or how to go about sharing. And sometimes we are afraid to share. For me, FAITH has taught me what to share and how to share in a sensitive manner, and it has given me the experiences to know firsthand that God will provide the courage to overcome the fears that Satan will throw at us.

"If I had to put into one sentence what FAITH has done for me, it would be this: FAITH has allowed me to be a part of what God is doing where I work and live and worship."

—*Bob Sheets*

"It blesses me to be a part of a church that has a staff fully committed to reaching the lost for the kingdom of God.

"My first semester in FAITH has given me the training and encouragement to share my faith as God opens the doors of opportunity. Being together each week with a staff and group of lay people for prayer, training, visitation, and sharing has strengthened me. I have seen God working through people just like me to win others into His family.

"I have also learned that with very ordinary people committed to His service, He accomplishes very extraordinary and life-changing results."

—*Frank Rayburn*

"As I read Bobby Welch's book *(Evangelism Through the Sunday School: A Journey of FAITH),* I was stopped cold when I read the statement, "Think about the last time you led someone to the Lord." I was embarrassed to admit after all the years I had taught Sunday School (25) and have had Bible studies in my home, I had never led anyone to accept Jesus Christ as Savior. On week 15 of FAITH visitation as I asked an 85-year-old woman the Key Question, went through the outline, and asked her if she wanted to ask Christ into her heart; as she smiled and said, "Yes, I do"—I thought I would explode with joy!"

—*Joey Crosnoe*

"I started participating in FAITH training as a new Christian. I learned to share my faith as something very natural and exciting. Throughout the training, I could not help but think of my sister who lives in another part of the country. I knew she did not know the Lord. I also knew I would have a few opportunities to actually visit with her. When I completed my first semester of FAITH training, I was asked to reenlist as a Team Leader. I really did not think I could do it.

"But it was as though the Lord placed my sister on my mind, and God encouraged me to be prepared for the time when I could share the gospel with her in person. I reenlisted and have been a Team Leader for several semesters since. The training has helped me grow in a boldness and confidence in the gospel. I also continue taking the training realizing God is preparing me for many people who will come into my life who need the gospel."

—*Learner, FBC Daytona Beach, Florida*

FAITH *Tip*

Why I Am in FAITH Training

I grew up as one of 6 children in my family. We were a non-churchgoing, non-Christian family. Actually, we were a pretty dysfunctional family; my father was an alcoholic who quit drinking the last 20 years or so of his life. My mother worked hard to keep our family together.

The only childhood memories of church and God I have were the few times I attended church with school friends. Easter meant that the Easter Bunny came and Christmas meant a decorated tree and presents—the birth of Jesus was an afterthought.

Randy and I have been married 10 years. While we dated and planned a life together, the subject of attending church and letting God lead our lives never came up. When we had our first child the longing for finding a church home became stronger. After the birth of our second son the longing became even stronger.

But we still never took our children to church nor really discussed how much we needed God in our lives. Because we led a non-Christian life our marriage suffered, our own lives suffered, and our children were being deprived of a spiritual foundation.

In April 1998, after several years of saying "Some day we're going to start going to church," our some day arrived. We chose to visit Lynwood because I had read in the newspaper that Brother Mark was starting a series of sermons called "Focus on the Family."

The first Sunday service I had attended in years was very difficult for me; I cried through most of the service, I cried when I got home and for several days afterward. My 8-year-old son asked me what was wrong. I couldn't answer him because I didn't know myself.

On Tuesday of that week a FAITH Team came to our home. The house was a wreck, the baby was crying and ready to go to bed; it was a terrible time for a visit. The FAITH Team could see that and said they would come back on Sunday afternoon. After they left I kept thinking, *I hope they come back and don't forget about us, because I need them and our family needs them.* I since found out that it wasn't them we needed as much as we needed Jesus Christ.

The next Sunday, we attended church again. Again I cried through most of the service and most of the afternoon. Then the FAITH Team arrived—three perfect strangers, yet we felt so comfortable with them. They came to share that there was more to life than what we had—that there was hope for me and my family, that Randy and I could raise our children so that they would know the true meaning of Easter and Christmas and the love of Jesus Christ. They shared the news that God had sent His only begotten Son to die on the cross for all of our sins and that we could have eternal life if we accepted Jesus Christ as our Savior.

That day, May 3, 1998, Randy and I both accepted Christ as our Lord and Savior.

Has our life changed since May 3, 1998? Yes. We have a 20-month-old child who now before dinner each night will clasp his hands together, bow his little head, close his eyes, and say something that only Jesus and his parents could understand. We have an 8-year-old child who knows his mommy and daddy love him with all their hearts but he also knows Jesus loves him even more than that—he thinks that's pretty awesome.

Do we still have times of struggle in our life? Yes. Do we still have times of sorrow? Yes. But the difficult times are made easier with the knowledge that Jesus Christ is in our hearts and is guiding us through life now. Another wonderful thing is that my 13-year-old niece has accepted Jesus Christ as her Savior.

I thank God every day for sending the FAITH Team to our home and for Lynwood Baptist Church. I wonder how my life might have been different if a FAITH Team had visited my home when I was a child.

—Lisa Smith, Lynwood Baptist Church, Cape Giradeau, MO

Notes

For the Team Leader

This weekly feature suggests actions the Team Leader can take to support Team members, prepare for Team Time, and consider ways to improve visits. This work becomes part of the Team Leader's Home Study Assignments. Add any actions suggested by your church's FAITH strategy.

Support Team Members
   ❏ Contact Team members during the week. Remind them you are praying for them. Discuss prayer concerns and answers to prayer.
   ❏ Record specific needs and concerns of Team members in the space provided.

_____

_____

_____

_____

   ❏ Find specific ways to encourage Team members as they prepare for their written and verbal reviews.

_____

_____

_____

_____

_____

Prepare for Session 16
   ❏ Review Home Study Assignments of Team members.
   ❏ Review instructions for Session 16.
   ❏ Be prepared to take your final verbal and written reviews.

[1]Dietrich Bonhoeffer, *The Cost of Discipleship* (New York: MacMillan Publishing Co., 1949), 99.

Prepare to Lead Visits
   ❏ Review the FAITH Visit Outline.
   ❏ Make sure a Team member is ready to take the lead during the visits.

Build Bridges to Sunday School
   ❏ Use information in "An Important Bridge" (p. 238) to share about FAITH during this week's Sunday School leadership team meeting.

SESSION 16

Celebrating Building Bridges: *Final Checkup*

In this session you will

    CHECK IT: take verbal/written reviews to evaluate your learning over the past 16 weeks;

    DO IT: visit according to the plans of your church;

    SHARE IT: celebrate accomplishments or announce plans for a FAITH Festival in which such celebration will occur.

Notes

Leading Team Time

All Team members participate in Team Time. They are primarily responsible for reciting the assigned portion of the FAITH Visit Outline and for discussing other Home Study Assignments.

As you direct this important time of CHECK IT activities with your Team, keep in mind how Learners also look to you as role model; motivator; mentor; and friend. Team Time activities can continue in the car, as the Team travels to and from visits.

Lead CHECK IT Activities

✓ FAITH Visit Outline

❏ Listen while each Learner recites any designated portion of the FAITH Visit Outline. It may be best to ask Learners to recite the segment they seem to have the most difficulty in sharing during a visit.

✓Practice

❏ A brief time of practice can help Team members confidently approach the verbal review.

✓Session 15 (Building Bridges for a Stronger FAITH Strategy) debriefing/FAITH testimony due

❏ Emphasize the importance of each Team member's being available to serve as a Team Leader during future semesters. Review the potential results of choosing not to continue participating in FAITH training.

❏ Ask for the Home Study Assignment "What FAITH Has Meant to Me" testimonies. Turn them in to the FAITH director.

✓ Help for strengthening a visit

❏ Discuss some of the things that have been learned by making evangelistic prospect, ministry, and Opinion Poll visits. Make sure Team members know who will be responsible for taking the lead in making the visits after the written and oral reviews.

Notes

_____

_____

_____

_____

_____

_____

Actions I Need to Take with Learners During the Week

• Write thank-you notes. Include a note of congratulations for their accomplishments. Indicate your continued support.

_____

_____

_____

_____

Notes

Notes

A Quick Review

As a Team Leader, you are concerned about enlisting two people for your own future Team. You are also involved in helping your present Team members to identify persons who would be on their team, particularly if they will be Team Leaders. It is significant for you to model reenlistment and to help Team members identify persons they could enlist for the next semester of training.

The Person God Uses

The person God uses continues to grow as a
Great Commission Christian.

What have you learned about faith during the past several months? The word *faith* describes the trust a person has in God; it identifies confidence in God even when we cannot tell what will happen next.

We began our Orientation session in FAITH Basic by reviewing some of the heroes and heroines of faith as recorded in Hebrews 11. As you reread this significant passage, look once again for characteristics of people of faith.

Look at the example of Abraham. People of faith take God at His word and are led by God to places we have never been and to people we have never seen (vv. 8-9). People of faith believe God's promises and are filled with a growing awareness of His promises (vv. 17-19). People of faith make themselves available to God and allow themselves to be used in extraordinary ways (vv. 23-29).

Faith is no longer merely a word we use in church. *Faith* is no longer just a religious term that refers to our belief. Neither is *faith* merely an acronym that reminds us of a simple, yet powerful, gospel presentation.

You have experienced ways to grow in faith. You have seen what personal Bible study, prayer, witnessing, and ministry does for you as a believer. You have experienced benefits of God's direct impact on your life as you seek His leadership. You have learned to depend on Him in ways you perhaps have never done before. You have realized that ". . . without faith, it is impossible to please God, for he who comes to him must believe that he exists, and that He rewards those who earnestly seek Him" (Heb. 11:6, NIV).

Lord, help me to grow in my faith, and to trust You more because You are God!

Congratulations! You have accomplished another 16 weeks of faithful participation in FAITH Sunday School evangelism training. Hopefully, you will continue to see results in your life and in the life of our church.

FAITH Advanced Written Review

My Score: _____
(Highest Possible Score: 60)
The only way you can fail this test is not to take it!

(Sessions 1-15, point value: 8)

1. Match the following list of words or phrases with the most appropriate definition.

C Divine appointment

e Baptism testimony

f Follow-up visits

a Assimilation

d Sunday School leadership team meetings

g Your Journey Continues

b My Next Step of Faith— Baptism

h Enroll persons in Sunday School

a. Taking the actions needed to help a new member fit into and become part of the class/church

b. Resource used when helping a person consider understanding/ making a commitment to believer's baptism

c. Evidence that God has been at work preparing a person to hear/ respond to the gospel

d. Scheduled time when FAITH Team Leader shares reports with other age-group workers of persons being cultivated and reached

e. Shared during a visit to help explain your experience after accepting Christ as Savior.

f. Visit by Team to deal with baptism, enrollment, or assimilation

g. Building Bridges record for responding to weekly Bible study and for writing your journal notes

h. Can be attempted any time: during initial visit, follow-up visit, or Opinion Poll visit, and in daily life

Notes

*(Course content esp.
Sessions 2-4;
point value: 8)*

2. Place in correct sequence the following eight actions that might occur in a visit:

_____ Use *A Step of Faith*

_____ Return baptism commitment card to the pastor

_____ Conduct a follow-up visit

_____ Ask the Key Question

_____ Share baptism testimony

_____ Explain *My Next Step of Faith—Baptism*

_____ Share the gospel presentation

_____ After visit complete information on FAITH Visit Assignment Card

*(Session 1 content,
Session 2 quiz;
point value: 1)*

_____ 3. Choose the best response: FAITH Advanced is designed to help build bridges between the FAITH Team and which of the following persons or groups?

a. the unchurched

b. Sunday School members

c. persons who make a commitment during a visit

d. all of the above.

*(Session 2 content,
Session 3 quiz;
point value: 1)*

_____ 4. True or False: A FAITH visit is completed once a person makes a profession of faith.

*(Session 2 content,
Session 3 quiz;
point value: 1)*

_____ 5. True or False: Part of the FAITH Team's responsibility in follow-up is to engage other Sunday School class members in assimilation.

*(Session 3 content,
Session 4 quiz;
point value: 1)*

_____ 6. Indicate the correct response: Use *My Next Step of Faith—Baptism* when—

a. making a follow-up visit for someone who enrolled in Sunday School during a FAITH visit;

b. making a follow-up visit for someone who has a ministry need as discovered during a FAITH visit;

c. making a follow-up visit for someone who accepted Christ;

d. a FAITH Team member has completed sharing the FAITH gospel presentation.

(Session 3 content,
Session 4 quiz;
point value: 1)

_____ **7. Three words—*AFTER, NEXT, ALTHOUGH*—help you remember an appropriate format for—**

a. elaboration of your evangelism testimony;

b. baptism testimony;

c. details of your Sunday School testimony.

(Session 3 content,
tract, Session 4 quiz;
point value: 3)

8. List three requirements for a person to be baptized, as identified in *My Next Step of Faith—Baptism*.

_____

_____

_____

_____

(Session 4 content,
Session 5 quiz;
point value: 1)

_____ **9. *True or False:* A different FAITH Team makes the follow-up visit on a prospect who makes a profession of faith.**

(Session 4 content,
Session 5 quiz;
point value: 4)

_____ **10. Choose the best response(s): Which of the following are opportunities to take when making follow-up visits?**

a. to answer questions about the decision

b. uncover needs in the home

c. discuss making the profession of faith public

d. describe opportunities for growth through Bible study/worship.

(Session 5 content,
Session 6 quiz;
point value: 1)

_____ **11. Which of the following statements is *false* about use of the Opinion Poll?**

a. Use the Opinion Poll when your FAITH ministry is needing more prospects to visit.

b. Ask the Opinion Poll questions if you discover a person is already a Christian or church member.

c. A Team can ask Opinion Poll questions while standing at the door, rather than entering the house.

d. Even if a person chooses not to answer the questions, try to get basic information about the person to help (begin) building bridges between him, the FAITH Team and the Sunday School class/department.

Notes

(Session 5 content, Session 6 quiz; point value: 1)

12. What is the purpose for using the Opinion Poll you would share with the person being visited?

_____

_____

_____

(Session 5 content, Session 6 quiz; point value: 2)

_____ **13. Choose the best response(s): What should you do if a person answers the last question on the Opinion Poll with a faith answer?**

  a. Celebrate/affirm the person's response, ask that briefly share what Jesus means to them, and ask them to pray for the ministry of your church.

  b. Try to enroll him/her in the appropriate Sunday School class/department if not participating in any ongoing Bible study group.

  c. Respond with a loud Amen and jump up and down in celebration.

(Session 5 content, Session 6 quiz; point value: 1)

_____ **14. Choose the best response: What should you do if a person answers the last question on the Opinion Poll with a works answer?**

  a. Record the response, thank him, and move on to the next house.

  b. Tell him he is going to hell without Jesus, invite him to Sunday School, and leave.

  c. Ask for permission to share what the Bible says about answering that question, then share the FAITH gospel presentation and use *A Step of Faith* to ask the person if he is willing to accept God's forgiveness.

(Session 6 content, Session 7 quiz; point value: 1)

_____ **15. Choose the best response: To understand forgiveness it is important to understand the meaning of redemption. The word *redemption* refers to—**

  a. using trading stamps at a store;

  b. buying back something;

  c. becoming perfect.

(Session 6 content,   **16. What does universalism mean?**
Session 7 quiz;
point value: 1)

_____

_____

_____

_____

(Session 7 content,   ____ **17. Choose the best response: Why is it**
Session 8 quiz;   **important to understand that God cannot**
point value: 1)   **allow sin into heaven because He is holy?**

   a. God's holiness and justice are seen as synonymous in many ways.

   b. When a person realizes God is holy he responds with anguish over his sins: " . . . I am ruined! For I am a man of unclean lips" (Isa. 6:5, NIV).

   c. When a person realizes God is holy he responds with commitment: "Here I am. Send me!" (Isa. 6:8, NIV).

   d. Sin is totally foreign and against the nature of God, and God will not tolerate anything in His presence not made holy.

   e. All of the above.

(Session 7 content,   ____ **18.** *True or False:* **God is not merciful.**
Session 8 quiz;
point value: 1)

(Session 7 content,   ____ **19.** *True or False:* **God's judgment**
Session 8 quiz;   **against sin is merciful.**
point value: 1)

(Session 7 content,   ____ **20. The best way of understanding the**
Session 8 quiz;   **meaning of** *repent* **is to—**
point value: 1)

   a. change directions in a car;

   b. change your attitude and actions, from sin to God;

   c. change your clothes;

   d. turn or burn.

Notes

Notes

(Session 8 content,
Session 9 quiz;
point value: 1)

_____ **21. HEAVEN HERE is important to share because—**

a. it is a good *H* phrase;

b. it reminds us of the abundant life Jesus provides now;

c. it reminds us of that real Christians do not sin any more;

d. all of the above.

(Session 8 content,
Session 9 quiz;
point value: 1)

_____ **22. HEAVEN HEREAFTER is important to share because—**

a. it is a good *H* phrase;

b. it gives opportunity during the gospel presentation to dispel misconceptions people have about heaven;

c. it gives opportunity to emphasize the fact that believers will spend eternity in God's presence;

d. all of the above.

(Session 9 content,
Session 10 quiz;
point value: 1)

_____ **23.** *True or False:* **When making a ministry (or Sunday School) visit to members, use a different visit outline than when making an evangelistic visit.**

(Session 9 content,
Session 10 quiz;
point value: 2)

_____ **24. Which of the following are valid ways a Team will know to make a ministry visit?**

a. The Visit Assignment Form will indicate a ministry visit.

b. The Opinion Poll will indicate ministry visitation assignments to be made that week.

c. A FAITH Team might learn of the need of a member at the last minute and determine to visit.

d. Door-to-door visitation will reveal persons who need a Sunday School/ministry visit.

(Session 9 content,
Session 10 quiz
point value: 2)

25. Why would a Team want to share the FAITH gospel presentation to a class member during a ministry visit?

_____

_____

(Session 10 content, Session 11 quiz; point value: 4) _____ **26. Choose the best response(s): Which of the following actions can a FAITH Team do with family members in the home?**

a. Ask to enroll the person(s) if they are not participating in a Sunday School.

b. Engage the person in conversation and include the person(s) in the ministry or evangelism visit as appropriate to their age or situation.

c. Have a Team member work with the person one on one particularly if the person is young while the other Team members focus on the older member(s). of the family.

d. Gather information on the person(s) and be prepared to share it through the FAITH Visit Assignment Form for the appropriate Sunday School department.

(Session 11 content, Session 13 quiz; point value: 1) ____ **27. *True or False:* Divine appointments always result in the gospel being shared and accepted.**

(Session 11 content, Session 13 quiz; point value: 1) ____ **28. *True or False:* Planned, assigned visits hold as much potential for divine encounters as do spontaneous, daily-life visits.**

(Session 11 content, Session 13 quiz; point value: 1) ____ **29. Choose the best response: If a person you visit does not respond the way you have learned the FAITH Visit Outline, your best response is to—**

a. pull out your Journal and show the person how he is to respond;

b. realize that you may be experiencing a difficulty; stop the visit to pray;

c. realize that you may be experiencing a difficulty; look for ways to build bridges so the person will remain open to responding to the gospel or ministry.

(Session 11 content, Session 13 quiz; point value: 1) ____ **30. *True or False:* No matter what happens, you have not had a successful visit unless you share the FAITH gospel presentation and the person makes a commitment.**

Notes

*(Session 14 content,
Session 15 quiz)
point value: 1)*

_____ **31. Choose the best response: If a person asks a question while you are sharing the gospel presentation, it is generally best to—**

a. tell the person his question is not appropriate at this time;
b. postpone answering the question unless it is to clarify your response or briefly supplement the presentation with information about the message of the gospel;
c. show him an example of a FAITH Tip;
d. have a Team member distract him while the others figure out what to say.

*(Session 15 content,
point value: 1)*

32. Describe the impact made if only one Team Leader chooses to drop out of active participation in FAITH training.

_____

_____

_____

_____

*(Session 15 content,
point value: 1)*

33. If you fail to ask a person to prayerfully consider God's leadership in participating in FAITH training, then in effect you have said _____ for him or her.

*(Session 15 content,
point value: 1)*

34. Fill in the blank with the correct words: Although you can pre-enlist a potential Team member any time, it is best to officially enroll a person on a FAITH Team _____ _____ before the first session of the next semester.

a. three days
b. three weeks
c. three months

Verbal Review

My Score: _____
(Highest Possible Score: 67)

FAITH VISIT OUTLINE

____ *Preparation*

____ **INTRODUCTION**

____ **INTERESTS**

____ **INVOLVEMENT**

    ____ **Church Experience/Background**

        ____ Ask about the person's church background.

        ____ Listen for clues about the person's spiritual involvement.

    ____ **Sunday School Testimony**

        ____ Tell general benefits of Sunday School.

        ____ Tell a current personal experience.

    ____ **Evangelistic Testimony**

        ____ Tell a little of your pre-conversion experience.

        ____ Say: "I had a life-changing experience."

        ____ Tell recent benefits of your conversion.

____ **INQUIRY**

____ **Key Question:** In your personal opinion, what do you understand it takes for a person to go to heaven?

    ____ Possible answers: Faith, works, unclear, no opinion

____ **Transition Statement:** I'd like to share with you how the Bible answers this question, if it is all right. There is a word that can be used to answer this question: FAITH *(spell out on fingers).*

____ *Presentation*

____ **F is for Forgiveness.**

____ We cannot have eternal life and heaven without God's forgiveness.

    ____ *"In Him [meaning Jesus] we have redemption through His blood, the forgiveness of sins"—Ephesians 1:7a, NKJV.*

Notes

_____ A is for AVAILABLE.

_____ Forgiveness is available. It is—

_____ AVAILABLE FOR ALL

_____ *"For God so loved the world that He gave His only begotten Son, that whoever believes in Him should not perish but have everlasting life"—John 3:16, NKJV.*

_____ BUT NOT AUTOMATIC

_____ *"Not everyone who says to Me, 'Lord, Lord,' shall enter the kingdom of heaven"—Matthew 7:21a, NKJV.*

_____ I is for IMPOSSIBLE.

_____ It is impossible for God to allow sin into heaven.

_____ GOD IS—

_____ • LOVE

_____ *John 3:16, NKJV*

_____ • JUST

_____ *"For judgment is without mercy"—James 2:13a, NKJV.*

_____ MAN IS SINFUL

_____ *"For all have sinned and fall short of the glory of God"— Romans 3:23, NKJV.*

_____ Question: But how can a sinful person enter heaven, where God allows no sin?

_____ T is for TURN.

_____ Question: If you were driving down the road and someone asked you to turn, what would he or she be asking you to do? *(change direction)*

_____ *Turn* means repent.

_____ TURN from something—sin and self

_____ *"But unless you repent you will all likewise perish"— Luke 13:3b, NKJV.*

_____ TURN to Someone; trust Christ only

_____ (The Bible tells us that) *"Christ died for our sins according to the Scriptures, and that He was buried, and that He rose again the third day according to the Scriptures"— 1 Corinthians 15:3b-4, NKJV.*

_____ *"If you confess with your mouth the Lord Jesus and believe in your heart that God has raised Him from the dead, you will be saved"—Romans 10:9, NKJV.*

____ **H is for HEAVEN.**
____ Heaven is eternal life.
____ **HERE**
    ____ *"I have come that they may have life, and that they may have it more abundantly"—John 10:10b, NKJV.*
____ **HEREAFTER**
    ____ *"And if I go and prepare a place for you, I will come again and receive you to Myself; that where I am, there you may be also"—John 14:3, NKJV.*
____ **HOW**
    ____ How can a person have God's forgiveness, heaven and eternal life, and Jesus as personal Savior and Lord?
    ____ Explain based on leaflet picture, F.A.I.T.H. (Forsaking All I Trust Him), Romans 10:9.

____ *Invitation*

____ **INQUIRE**
____ Understanding what we have shared, would you like to receive this forgiveness by trusting in Christ as your personal Savior and Lord?
____ **INVITE**
    ____ Pray to accept Christ.
    ____ Pray for commitment/recommitment.
    ____ Invite to join Sunday School.
____ **INSURE**
____ Use *A Step of Faith* to insure decision.
    ____ **Personal Acceptance**
    ____ **Sunday School Enrollment**
    ____ **Public Confession**

Notes

Notes

Visitation Time
DO IT

As you go . . .

Your visitation schedule may be adjusted somewhat tonight. Allow for the schedule changes, but encourage Teams to return for Celebration Time. This sharing time should be a special time of closure and reports.

Celebration Time
SHARE IT

As you return to share . . .

- Other reports and testimonies
- Session 16 Evaluation Card
- Participation Card
- Visitation forms updated with results of visits

Home Study Assignments

Home Study Assignments reinforce this session and prepare you for the next session. "Journaling" experiences in Your Journey Continues are an important part of your development as a Great Commission Christian through FAITH training. Other assignments may include additional reading that enhances your experience.

Selected features in this section highlight opportunities the Team Leader has to build bridges to his or her Team, class/department (especially through weekly Sunday School leadership team meetings) and church, and community. They can assist you in accomplishing your important responsibilities.

Your Journey Continues

Read Hebrews 11:1. What does this verse mean to you now that you have completed this semester of training?

_____

_____

_____

_____

_____

What are some things you would want a potential FAITH Team member to know about FAITH based on what you have learned?

_____

_____

_____

_____

_____

Describe the most memorable experience(s) you have had as a Team Leader.

_____

_____

_____

Notes

Read Jude 20-25. Rewrite these verses in your own words.

_____
_____
_____
_____
_____

Prayer Concerns   ### Answers to Prayer

_____   _____
_____   _____
_____   _____
_____   _____
_____   _____
_____   _____
_____   _____
_____   _____
_____   _____
_____   _____
_____   _____
_____   _____

An Important Bridge:
Your Weekly Sunday School Leadership Team Meeting

Notes

Use this space to record ways your FAITH Team impacts the work of your Sunday School department or class. Use the information to report during weekly Sunday School leadership team meetings. Identify actions that need to be taken through Sunday School as a result of prayer concerns, needs identified, visits made by the Team, and decisions made by the persons being visited.

Highlight needs/reports affecting your class/department or age group.

_____

_____

_____

Pray now for this important meeting.

_____

_____

What are ways the department/class can celebrate the work of the Holy Spirit through members who have participated in FAITH training?

_____

_____

What actions can be taken to encourage members and leaders to prepare for the next semester of FAITH training?

_____

_____

How does preparation for Sunday need to consider persons who might attend because they received a witness by members during the week?

_____

_____

Use these pages as needed throughout Building Bridges Through FAITH: The Journey Continues. Possibilities are to read (1) *before a specific training session* (2) *for your own information;* (3) *to better equip your Team in a certain area;* or (4) *to be prepared for a particular situation. In some cases, to read one of these articles will be a Home Study Assignment.*

CONTENTS

Building Bridges Though FAITH: Supplement

How to Build Mentoring Relationships

It has been said that by teaching, someone learns yet again. A mentoring relationship is at the heart of being an effective FAITH Team Leader.

A mentor is not someone who has "arrived" or who knows it all; in contrast, such an individual, often a mature believer, reflects a continuing openness to learn and to be taught. A mentor walks alongside those he or she coaches, instructs, develops, and helps to learn specific skills. The goal ought to be for such a relationship to end, as the student outgrows the teacher, and to establish a new one. Think about the mathematics in an *ongoing process* of one person being trained and committed to train two more people as a means of multiplying the FAITH ministry.

A meaningful mentoring relationship is characterized by patience with one another and with the process; emotional maturity; and mutual trust and commitment. The latter characteristics develop as people spend time together; as you commit to spend time beyond the training sessions with your Team Learners, that relationship will solidify. A feature of FAITH is the provision of enough time (16 weeks) for three people to become a team and for Learners to see their Team Leader respond in a variety of different visit situations.

As a Team Leader or other Team member already trained in FAITH, you have an opportunity to intentionally pattern your relationships. As you do, recognize the biblical basis, most notably in Jesus' relationship with the 12 disciples.

Generally, a process similar to the following is associated with mentoring. Notice the similarity to 2 Timothy 2:1-2—principles that continue to guide FAITH.

1. I tell you.
Instruct the learner with basic facts and information regarding the skill.

2. You watch me.
Demonstrate for the learner what the skill actually looks like when it is being used.

3. We do it together.
Involve the learner in actually doing the skill.

4. I watch you.
Assist the learner to become proficient in the skill.[1]

As a Team Leader likely enlisted for your leadership potential, you already know the basic facts and skills of FAITH and are able to help new Learners. A team relationship is supported by 16 weeks of training and experiences—long enough for your Learners to watch you handle many different situations. Your Learners are watching you in other areas—hopefully seeing characteristics they would like to develop in their lives.

Here are some actions to consider taking to develop mentoring relationships with your Team:

• Pray together.

• Spend time together beyond the FAITH sessions. The "For the Team Leader" feature suggests actions to take each week between sessions.

• Recognize that your life is a major part of the lesson. Ask God to help you match your words and your actions. Because Team members are watching you being faithful in Sunday School, arriving on time for Team Team, returning for Celebration Time, and other actions are so important. If your words and your example are inconsistent, Learners get conflicting messages regarding which behavior to incorporate in their own lives.

• Review God's Word for positive examples of mentoring. It could be a rewarding study to look at the Old Testament models of Jethro, Moses, and Joshua; Eli and Samuel; and Elijah and Elisha, among others. In the New Testament, especially give attention to how Jesus related to His disciples and to Paul's relationship with Timothy.

• Make a commitment to one another and to the process. As you spend time together and invest in one another, that commitment should increase. Recognize that the commitment is to your church, as together you help obey the Great Commission.

• Your relationship should point people to God and to strengthening their relationship with Him, not to yourself.

• Numerous books and articles are available on mentoring and coaching. Draw the best principles from business and education to use in your ministry. The *Follow Christ's Example* series addresses how to become a servant leader.

• Receive the benefits of a mentoring relationship yourself.

• Be sensitive to other believers who may be further developed as leaders. Some may be potential new FAITH Learners; share this information with your FAITH director so an individual might be personally contacted for FAITH or some other area of service. Be aware of the results of gift surveys in which someone senses God's calling to evangelism or outreach.

• Your Sunday School class members look to you because of your role in FAITH. Keep before them their role as mentors to one another, and especially to new believers who are becoming a part of the class.

How to Make a Follow-up Visit

**Four Types of
Follow-up Visits**

The person has

- made a public
declaration of faith during
a worship service since
being visited by a FAITH
Team;
- attended Sunday School
but not worship;
- not attended Sunday
School but has attended
the worship service and
has not made a public
declaration of faith;
- not attended either
Sunday School or
worship since making a
commitment during a
FAITH visit.

Every person who, during a FAITH visit, makes a decision to receive Christ or to enroll in Sunday School will need to receive a follow-up visit by the same Team within the next week or two. This is considered the initial follow-up visit. As with other visits, the Team Leader models this visit for Learners.

Follow-up assignments are indicated on FAITH Visit Assignment cards and placed in the appropriate visitation folders. Ideally, cards include updated information that helps ensure meaningful follow-up.

Four Types of Follow-up Visits

- The person has made a public declaration of faith during a worship service since being visited by a FAITH Team;
- The person has attended Sunday School but not a worship service;
- The person has not attended Sunday School but has attended the worship service and has not made a public declaration of faith;
- The person has not attended either Sunday School or worship since making a commitment during a FAITH visit.

It often takes as many as four follow-up visits to help most unchurched persons begin to take actions regarding baptism and initial assimilation into the church. The FAITH Team is essential to beginning the process of assimilation. As has become clear throughout FAITH training, other Sunday School class members (adult class leaders and members, for example) should be activated to help implement additional follow-up actions.

Actions to Take During Initial Follow-up Visits

Initiate relaxed conversation for reacquaintance. Explain the significance of the decision(s) the person made, as recorded on *A Step of Faith;* celebrate together. Talk about the decision(s) and try to answer any questions.

If the person has not yet been baptized, review the information about baptism in *A Step of Faith.* Then use *My Next Step of Faith—Baptism* to explain baptism by immersion as being a wonderful expression of what Christ has done in one's life. Emphasize baptism as an act of obedience to Christ.

Review ways(s) your church recognizes new believers, and encourage the person to attend the worship service to be recognized and affirmed for the decision to accept Jesus as Savior. Indicate again the availability of your Team to stand alongside the new believer.

Although in most cases the new believer will be joining the church, provide any clarification needed about the meaning of being introduced to the church as compared to becoming a church member. (Determine appropriate church polity/procedures for introducing or recognizing new believers, whether or not they join your church.) Indicate that the Sunday School class and any new member class,

among other opportunities, will help the new believer become a contributing church member.

If the person already has attended Bible study/worship, talk about that experience. If not yet attended, discuss personal benefits and encourage the person to participate. Share information about Bible study and other church ministries. If needed, ask for permission to enroll the person/family members in the appropriate Bible study class/department.

Encourage attendance and participation as an ongoing lifestyle. Share specific actions and benefits of actions that help new believers to grow—for example, Bible study, prayer, fellowship with other Christians, and worship.

Review the importance of being obedient to Christ in all areas of life and in learning how to grow as a Christian. As appropriate, share a few examples of actions other new Christians have taken through the church.

Provide Bible study and/or follow-up materials that will be helpful in learning about the Christian faith and your church. Certain materials—such as *Survival Kit for New Christians*—are designed to get a person's journey of faith off to a good start. If a Sunday School class member will work alongside the new believer in a study of basic follow-up information, indicate that relationship. If a new member class is part of your church's assimilation process, indicate the location, date, and times.

Share names and phone numbers of class members who may be contacted. Ask for permission to share the person's name with others in the Sunday School or church who can contact or assist them.

Pray together as you conclude the visit. Once the initial follow-up visit is conducted, other follow-up actions can be assigned as needed. Follow-up visits also are needed when a member has special needs or concerns.

Sometimes Follow-up Is Done by Another Team

On occasion a FAITH Team from one Sunday School class or division makes the initial visit, and follow-up by another class FAITH Team is considered the best approach. For example, a FAITH Team representing workers from a children's department may visit a family in which children are enrolled. During the visit, a parent hears the gospel and prays to receive Christ. The parent has questions about his/her Sunday School class. Follow-up should be done by a FAITH Team from the parent's prospective class.

On occasion, follow-up will be done by a representative of a specific church ministry, such as benevolence, bus outreach, or recreation. It becomes appropriate for members of the person's Sunday School class to be assigned specific follow-up responsibilities. In this way, the person very naturally is assimilated into the life of the class and the church.

How to Help a New Believer Understand Church Membership

Basic principles about church membership can help a new believer begin to understand his new family of faith and his relationship to it. Be careful not to overwhelm someone with truths he now has a lifetime to discover.

"The church keeps Christians focused on the Great Commission as its driving force. . . . The church is the instrument through which God's family takes part in establishing the kingdom of God in the lives of people in our community and world. The church is to bring God's presence into relationships, families, workplaces, and into the marketplace to make a difference in our world. . . .

The church provides a balance of five essential functions for Christians to be effective in fulfilling the Great Commission. These functions are evangelism, discipleship, fellowship, ministry, and worship.

An effective church develops spiritually maturing Christians. . . . The church is committed to provide the functions that will move its members toward spiritual maturity."[2]

Requirements and Expectations of Church Members

"A church member is expected to:

• Be a **believer** in the Lord Jesus Christ. This belief that includes faith and repentance is the spiritual requirement (Acts 2:38).

• Be **baptized** as a symbol of one's spiritual death to sin and one's birth into the rule of God by commemorating the death and resurrection of Jesus through which salvation is made possible.

• Be **faithful** in learning and living revealed truth from God (Acts 2:42).

• Be a **participant** in worship and meetings for mutual building up and encouraging of others' spiritual life (Heb. 10:25).

• Be a **witness** of the saving grace of Jesus Christ to all who are lost (Matt. 28:18-20).

• Be a **servant** for the needs of believers and unbelievers (Gal. 6:10).

• Be a **steward** committed to faithfulness for all that God gives to you.

Some churches have requirements such as completing a new members' class. Others have things that are expected of members, though not required for membership.

The Ordinances of the Church

Ordinance literally means an order or a law. Christ instituted the ordinances of baptism and the Lord's Supper.

Baptism is the symbolic burial and resurrection of believers by immersion in water. It is a testimony of the complete spiritual change in the believer's life from the rule of sin and death to the rule of God bringing eternal life. Baptism provides a commemoration of the death, burial, and resurrection of Jesus Christ that makes salvation possible. . . .

Baptism is . . . the first step of discipleship upon becoming a Christian. We are baptized by immersion. The New Testament writers always used the word *baptizo* (immersion) when speaking of baptism. Immersion is the only way in which baptism portrays the basic facts of the death and resurrection of Jesus and our salvation—bringing death to the old life and a rising up to walk in a newness of life. . . .

During the time of Passover in Jerusalem Jesus and His disciples ate the Passover meal together. Jesus used the occasion to identify Himself as the sacrifice by which believers would be set free from sin and death. . . .

The **Lord's Supper** was established as an ordinance in the church based on such Scriptures as Matthew 26:26-28; Luke 22:19; 1 Corinthians 11:25; 1 Corinthians 10:16-17. These Scriptures teach us to observe the Lord's Supper as:

• *a time to remember the past.*—Jesus' death for our sin reminds us to look back and remember that He is our Savior who died on the cross for our sin. . . .

• *a time to remember our hope for the future.*—. . . His death and resurrection guarantees our hope; we have hope in the ultimate consummation in heaven.

• *a time to remember our unity as God's people united in Him.*

The Leadership of the Church

The word *pastor* comes from the biblical image of God's people as His flock. In Ephesians 4:11, the word *pastor* is closely associated with teaching as a gift of God to the church. The pastor is to establish himself as a leader trustworthy according to the standards established by Jesus.

The word *deacon* comes from the Greek word *diakonos*. This word means *to serve*. Some churches have chosen to establish the office of elder along with *pastor* and *deacon*.

Many of the leadership needs in churches are carried out by lay volunteers."[3] As a new believer becomes aware of his or her spiritual gifts, opportunities for service, and personal interests, service through the church can become especially meaningful.

How to Reclaim Inactive Members

"Remember people don't come to church for friendliness; they come for friends.

"When we say, 'We'll meet you, sit with you, walk with you, sit with you' we've made a friend. It's also so much easier to walk into that class."

—Buddy Appel,
FAITH Coordinator,
Central Baptist Church,
Hixson, Tennessee

In addition to sharing their faith with non-Christians, some FAITH churches are reclaiming inactive members. Consider the experience of Central Baptist Church, Hixson, Tennessee. According to Buddy Appel, FAITH coordinator: "We visit every member who has not attended in a four-week period. We may discover a new member who has yet to come. We have found every possible situation: people upset with the church or at someone's lack of attention to a personal situation.

"Sometime we find people who don't understand Sunday School; all they know is the worship experience. Or they don't realize that they can go to whatever class they're most comfortable in." Hixson has started two Sunday Schools since beginning FAITH in 1997. The first school is traditional, with age-graded classes, and the second school has classes based on topic or interest. So if a person is dissatisfied with an age-graded class, other classes do provide a viable option.

In whatever situation, Appel said, "we try to minister. We have a strong emphasis at our church on spiritual maturity so we highlight that, scripturally, believers should be in Bible study consistently." From this church's experience, some patterns of effectiveness emerge for reclaiming members.

Through good records and consistent assignments to Teams, create the expectancy that FAITH will include ministry visits.—To accommodate the large list of inactive members in their church and to visit everyone who's absent in a four-week period, weekly assignments at Central Hixson almost always include ministry visits.

Assign accountability.—"It is imperative to have a central place for handling and distributing (assignment) information. All of the information comes back to me," said Appel, "and I disseminate it. If you don't have a central point, information will get lost. I know that it gets out and who is accountable for responding."

Also, "we make sure directors or teachers, especially of an open class (if appropriate), get the information. They do a very good job of follow-up on a FAITH Team visit. Sometimes they respond the day they receive a FAITH Team report. With half of our FAITH Teams visiting on Tuesdays and and the other half on Thursdays, the *worst* scenario is to have someone contacted on Sunday and to attend the next Sunday. Usually the contact happens before that first Sunday."Between ministry and evangelistic prospects, "each FAITH Team probably averages at least one good contact a week. We have 50 to 55 Teams and hope to double that number soon."

Prepare classes and departments.—"There is an impact, positive and negative," Appel acknowledged. "If you seriously work to find out about people, you may find that some people have joined another church. But generally, we have shown growth. In our first semester of FAITH, we reclaimed 400 people."

Follow up as needed.—The class reports back that contact was made and when the person comes for the first time; then things are in the hands of the class or department. If a FAITH Team does not represent that class, the name is given to someone else. If within three weeks the church does not hear from the person who was visited, the FAITH Team returns.

How to Use the Opinion Poll

You have access to the Opinion Poll in your visitation folder, and it is the topic for your Session 5 Building Bridges training. Use the cards primarily to gather information from individuals who have had no previous contact with your church or any other church.

Team members generally use this survey in two primary situations: (1) when no other visitation assignment can be made; or (2) when a visit is designated to an area of the community in which nonmembers with no prior contact with the church can be discovered. In the second case, Team members likely will be making contact with people from any age or affinity group.

Use the Opinion Poll card and process to list basic information about persons who are discovered in making visits where no previous information is available. Use the process to assess community/individual openness to ministries by the church, and share comments with leaders to try to become more responsive.

In some cases, the Holy Spirit will grant opportunity through the Opinion Poll for Team members to share a Sunday School testimony, share the gospel presentation, and/or enroll a person in Sunday School. Once information about prospects is gathered, Team Leaders submit that information during Celebration Time. This information is used to prepare the assignment to a specific FAITH Team and/or Sunday School department for follow-up.

Always be prepared to use the Opinion Poll to discover individuals or families who are not participating in any ongoing Bible study or worship or who might be willing to share their opinion about church ministries or hear the FAITH gospel presentation.

Keep in Mind Certain Guidelines

1. On the surface, the Opinion Poll looks relatively easy. Actually, asking the questions is easy, but proper follow-through in many situations can be challenging. For this reason, the Team Leader should model use of the Opinion Poll. Learners need to see this done several times before they lead in such a visit themselves.

2. Be careful not to look too obvious as you move from house to house. Many people resist answering the door if they think a religious group (fearing they might represent a cult) might be canvassing the neighborhood. All the person has to do is go to the back of the house and not answer the knock at the door. In an apartment complex the manager may ask your Team to leave if you are suspected of engaging in solicitation.

3. It generally is best not to enter a home if you are invited in, except to share what the Bible says about the Key Question. You are not there to debate; by staying in one home too long, you easily could miss going to a home where someone needs to hear the gospel and *is* willing to listen.

4. It is best not to approach children unless they are accompanied by an adult. People can easily misunderstand your intentions.

How to Build Bridges to People of Different Belief Systems

Consider the basic belief systems of some of the most visible religions found in many communities. Pages 270-277 are not an attempt to represent the belief of every person who embraces these religions or to suggest that these are the only groups needing the gospel. Neither do these pages attempt to provide the only information you would need to begin to understand these belief systems.

Instead, you are seeking to be prepared to share the simple gospel of our faith with people as God opens doors and gives you opportunity to build bridges. Your objective is to build bridges with people and to earn the right to share how the Bible answers the Key Question. No matter what a person believes about the Bible, God's Word can stand

Building Bridges to Someone of Jewish Belief

Judaism usually is classified in three denominations: Orthodox, Conservative, and Reform. Of the 72 percent who are affiliated with a synagogue, fewer than 10 percent attend synagogue on a regular basis. In the midst of great diversity, it is almost impossible to generalize. The best way to understand the beliefs of any particular person is to speak with him or her directly.

What They Believe

Although Orthodox Jews have a high view of the inspiration of the Hebrew Scriptures, Judaism maintains that a greater authority is to be accorded to Oral Traditions. Judaism teaches that even if a voice from heaven contradicts the consensus of the sages, it (the heavenly voice) is to be rejected.

Judaism offers a lofty humanism, which is essentially idealistic and optimistic. The alienation between God and man is overcome by man as he reaches toward God.

Judaism believes God's will is primarily found in the Mosaic Law (the first five books of the Old Testament), as it has been elaborated and applied to changing circumstances through the centuries. Judaism is optimistic about one's ability to do God's will, and sin generally is not a major concern.

Since the destruction of the Temple in Jerusalem, at least three positions have developed within Judaism regarding atonement for sin. The most common view is that repentance, prayer, and good deeds provide atonement. Jesus is viewed as a humble Jewish reformer and teacher, not the Messiah.

There is no concept of a need for regeneration. If someone has strayed from God, it is only necessary for him to "return" (the Hebrew meaning of *repentance*) and to walk in God's ways.

Actions to Take When Sharing with Someone of Jewish Belief

• Most people of Jewish belief view Christianity as a Gentile religion that has no relevance to them. It is important to communicate that our desire is not that someone would become a Gentile, but that as a Jew he or she would find atonement for sin and a personal relationship with the God of Abraham, Isaac, and Jacob.

• Humility, prayer, and genuine compassion must characterize the Christian witness. Far too often, Jewish impressions of Christianity have been characterized by arrogance, superiority, and a disregard for Jewish culture.

    • Use terminology that emphasizes the Jewishness of our faith. For example, instead of *Christ,* which is based on the Greek word for the "Anointed One," use *Messiah,* which is based on the Hebrew. Instead of saying the *Old Testament,* refer to the *Hebrew Scriptures.*[4]

Building Bridges to a Roman Catholic Friend

What They Believe

    Roman Catholics accept three sources of authority: the Bible, Tradition, and the teaching ministry of the Catholic Church. They are encouraged to read the Bible. Catholics believe that their bishops have been given the task of authentically interpreting both the Bible and Tradition.

    Mary is viewed as a co-mediator of God's grace and as a collaborator with the salvation of Jesus, her Son.

    There are two types of sin: mortal (which destroys the sanctifying grace of God within the individual and necessitates forgiveness through a sacrament of reconciliation) and venial (one that either is not serious or grave or does not involve full knowledge or complete consent.)

    The seven sacraments of the Catholic Church are baptism, confirmation, Eucharist, penance, anointing of the sick, holy orders, and matrimony. The sacraments are the signs and instruments by which the Holy Spirit spreads the grace of Christ, the head, throughout the Church, which is his Body. Baptism is necessary for salvation. Catholics baptize their children shortly after birth.

    Protestants and Catholics affirm the same beliefs about the nature of God and about Jesus—His nature and His death, burial, and resurrection.

Actions to Take When Sharing with Catholics

    • Remember and communicate that salvation does not depend on church membership, but comes through faith in Jesus Christ (Eph. 2:8-9).

    • Pray and trust in the Holy Spirit to use the gospel message to reach the hearts and minds of those who are lost.

    • Share a testimony of your personal faith in Christ as your Savior. Your testimony of what Jesus has accomplished in your life can have great impact.

    • Share the assurance of salvation that God's grace gives you. Make sure you communicate that your assurance is derived from trusting Jesus and not from your own works or your ability to remain faithful.

    • Give the person a New Testament. Catholics now are encouraged to read the Bible. Point out texts in the FAITH gospel presentation.

    • Avoid getting bogged down with secondary issues unrelated to salvation.

    • Keep your presentation Christ-centered.[5]

on its own and the Holy Spirit desires to work in the life of every individual. Although the gospel presentation does not change depending on the person with whom you share, it helps to understand how a person of another belief system might relate to the message of FAITH.

    Consider prayerfully how God might choose to use you and your Team members to build bridges to and share the gospel with individuals of Jewish, Catholic, Mormon, Jehovah's Witness, Islamic, or Hindu beliefs.

Building Bridges to Someone of Mormon Belief
(Also known as The Church of Jesus Christ of Latter-Day Saints)

What They Believe

God (Heavenly Father) is a physical man of flesh and bone who once lived in a world like our own. Through righteous living, obedience to his Heavenly Father, and Celestial Marriage, he progressed to become the god of our universe.

Jesus is one of the Heavenly Father's spirit children who has attained godhood. The Holy Spirit is another of the gods of other worlds. The goal of all good Mormons is to progress to the Celestial Kingdom (the highest level of heavenly glory).

The Bible, in its current, standard form, is a flawed record of God's Word. *The Book of Mormon* (a revision of the King James Version of the Bible with hundreds of additions and changes) is "the most correct of any book on earth, and the keystone of our religion" *(Teaching of the Prophet Joseph Smith,* p. 194). Latter-Day Saints also recognize *The Doctrine and Covenants* as Scripture and *The Pearl of the Great Price* as inspired.

Jesus' atonement (death and resurrection) provides immortality for all people regardless of their faith. Exaltation (godhood) is available only to Mormons through obedience to Latter-Day Saint teachings: faith, baptism, endowments, celestial marriage, and tithing. Baptism for the dead provides post-mortem salvation for non-Mormons and is "by immersion performed by a living person for one who is dead" *(Gospel Principles,* by Joseph Smith, Jr., 375).

Godhood is available only to Mormons who believe and practice the teachings of *The Book of Mormon.* Since people are the preexisted spiritual offspring of the Heavenly Father and Mother, they are born basically good and are "gods in embryo" *(Gospel Principles,* by Joseph Smith, Jr., 11).

There are three levels of glory: (1) exaltation in the Celestial Kingdom for faithful Mormons, where people may become gods or angels; (2) Terrestrial Kingdom, for righteous non-Mormons; (3) Telestial Kingdom, for the wicked and ungodly (not hell) *(The Doctrine and Covenants).*

Mormons regard Joseph Smith, Jr., the founder of their faith, as an inspired prophet. Documented evidence, however, conclusively ties Smith to occult practices, bank fraud, polygamy, and other biblically condemned acts *(A Closer Look at The Book of Mormon,* by Tal Davis, 12).

Latter-Day Saint Terms Similar to Christian Terms But with Different Meanings

Faith for the Mormon is seemingly never spoken of as directed toward the deity of Christ and His full atonement on the cross for the sins of the world. They use this word as a synonym to "belief." They also attest to "faith" and commitment

to the teachings of the (Latter-Day) Church as being more important than "faith" or relationship to Jesus.

For the Mormon, *repentance* involves confessing and abandoning sins as well as restoring all damage done by one's sin. Repentance is a prelude to the process of acquiring salvation by obedience to The Church of Jesus Christ of Latter-Day Saints. Little is said about repentance leading to Jesus Christ.

Baptism (by immersion) must be through a priest in the Aaronic priesthood of the church.

Receiving the Holy Ghost comes through *laying on of hands* by a member of the Melchizedek Priesthood. Such an experience is not a result of faith and belief, but comes mechanically when a baptized Mormon is prayed for by a member of that priestly class.

Other Common Words/Phrases with Different Connotations

- Bible (King James Version)
- Priesthood
- Gospel
- Virgin birth
- Missionaries
- God, Jesus Christ, Holy Spirit

Each devout Saint is now working hard to pay off his or her debt to the church. Their gospel (good news) is no gospel. It is not the gospel of freedom through Christ; it is a gospel of servitude and obligation to a religious organization.

Actions to Take When Sharing with Mormons

- Define the use of your terms.
- Seek to understand the historical and spiritual reliability of the Scriptures as God's Word.
- Be willing to take the time to befriend and build bridges to Mormons.[6]

Building Bridges to a Jehovah's Witness
(Also known as Watchtower Bible and Tract Society)

What They Believe

Jesus was the first created being of Jehovah God (rather than eternally pre-existent as God the Son with the Father). Jesus preexisted as Michael, the archangel, who disappeared from heaven and was conceived miraculously by (the Virgin) Mary.

Jesus provided atonement for sins, but He is primarily spirit.

Jesus was executed on a torture stake instead of the cross.

Jesus was not Messiah until His baptism at age 30. Jehovah's Witnesses deny the full divinity of Jesus.

Jehovah's Witnesses maintain that the Lord's resurrection was purely spiritual and only appeared to be physical.

They show a clear anti-trinitarian bias.

The Bible has been translated by a supposedly inspired committee of interpreters who claim to have the final word about all theological issues. (In fact, their "Bible" has many significant mistranslations which alter and influence their theology.)

144,000 is the number of the elect/faithful.

Salvation comes by baptism.

There is no assurance of salvation, only hope.

Actions to Take When Sharing with a Jehovah's Witness

• Have a clear understanding of your faith and the true message of the Scriptures.

• Acquire a basic knowledge of Jehovah's Witnesses beliefs and practices.

• Establish a friendly, courteous, and sincere relationship with the Jehovah's Witness.

• Define your terms clearly and ask your Jehovah's Witness friend to do so.

• Focus the discussion on the primary issue of the person and work of Christ. Stress the need for a personal relationship with Him.[7]

Building Bridges to Someone of Islamic Belief

Islam claims to be the restoration of original monotheism (one God) and truth and thus to supersede both Judaism and Christianity. It stresses submission to Allah, the Arabic name for God and conformity to the "five pillars" or disciples of that religion as essential for salvation. From its inception, Islam has been an aggressively missionary-oriented religion. Within one century of its formation, and often using military force, Islam spread across the Middle East, most of North Africa, and as far east as India.

While God is, in the understanding of most Muslims, unknowable personally, His will is believed to be perfectly revealed in the holy book, the Qur'an. The Qur'an is to be followed completely, and its teachings form a complete guide for life and society.

The five pillars, the framework for the Muslim's life and discipline, are:

• *The confession of Faith (Shahada):* It is the declaration that there is no god but Allah and Muhammad is his prophet. Repudiation of the Shahada nullifies hope for salvation.

• *Prayer of Salat:* This prayer is an expression of submission to the will of Allah and is done five times a day, preceded by ceremonial washing and facing Mecca.

• *Almsgiving (Zakat):* By giving the required 2 percent of one's capital wealth to the poor and/or for the propagation of Islam, the Muslim's remaining wealth is purified.

• *The Fast (Sawm):* During the course of the lunar month of Ramadan, a fast is to be observed by every Muslim from sunrise to sunset. After sunset, feasting and other celebrations often occur. The daylight hours are set aside for self-purification.

• *Pilgrimage (Hajj):* All Muslims who are economically and physically able are required to journey to Mecca at least once in their lifetime.

What They Believe

God is numerically and absolutely one. God is beyond the understanding of man so that only his will may be revealed and known.

The most serious sin that can be ascribed to people is that of considering God as more than one. Humankind is considered weak and forgetful but not fallen.

The world will be judged at the end of time by Allah. The good deeds and obedience of all people to the five pillars and the Qur'an will serve as the basis of judgment.

Salvation is determined by faith, as defined by Islam, as well as by compiling good deeds primarily in conformity to the five pillars.

The term *jihad* or "struggle" is often considered as both external and internal, both a physical and a spiritual struggle. The enemies of Islam, or "idolaters," state the Qur'an may be slain "wherever you find them" (Surah:5). Paradise is promised for those who die fighting in the cause of Islam. Moderate Muslims emphasize the spiritual dimension of Jihad and not its political element.

Actions to Take When Sharing with Muslims

• Be courteous and loving.

• Reflect interest in their beliefs. Allow them time to articulate their views.

• Become acquainted with their basic beliefs.

• Be willing to examine passages of the Qur'an concerning their beliefs.

• Stick to the cardinal doctrines of the Christian faith, but take time to respond to all sincere questions.

• Point out the centrality of the person and work of Jesus Christ for salvation.

• Stress that because of Jesus, because of His death on the cross and His resurrection, one may have the full assurance of salvation, both now and for eternity.

• Share the FAITH gospel presentation. Point out that salvation is a gift and not to be earned.

• Pray for the fullness of the Holy Spirit. Trust Him to provide wisdom and grace.

• Be willing to become a friend.[8]

Building Bridges to Someone of Hindu Belief

Hinduism has no single creed and recognizes no final truth. It is the most diverse of all major world religions. At its core, Hinduism has pagan background, in which the forces of nature and human heroes are personified as gods and goddesses. They are worshiped with prayers and offerings.

What They Believe

God (Brahman) is the one impersonal, ultimate, but unknowable, spiritual Reality. Most Hindus worship two mythical incarnations: Krishna and Rama. On special occasions, Hindus may worship other gods, as well as family and individual deities. Hindus claim that there are 330 million gods.

Hindus accept various forms of pantheism (everything is god) and reject the Christian doctrine of creation. According to Hinduism, Brahman alone exists; everything is ultimately an illusion (maya). There is no beginning or conclusion to creation, only endless repetitions or cycles of creation and destruction.

The eternal soul (atman) of man is a manifestation or "spark" of Brahman mysteriously trapped in the physical body. Samsara, repeated lives or reincarnations, are required before the soul can be liberated from the body. An individual's present life is determined by the law of karma (actions, words, and thoughts in previous lifetimes). The physical body is ultimately an illusion with little inherent or permanent worth. Bodies generally are cremated, and the eternal soul goes to an intermediate state of punishment or reward before rebirth in another body. Rebirths are experienced until karma has been removed to allow the soul's absorption in to Brahman.

Hindus have no concept of rebellion against a Holy God. Ignorance of unity with Brahman, desire, and violation of dharma, (one's social duty) are humanity's problems.

There is no clear concept of salvation in Hinduism. Moksha (freedom from infinite being and selfhood and final realization of the truth), is the goal of existence. Yoga and meditation, the way of works, the way of knowledge or the way of love and devotion are valid paths for moksha.

Actions to Take When Encountering/Seeking to Witness to Hindus

- Stress the uniqueness of Jesus Christ as God's revelation of Himself.
- Emphasize the necessity of following Jesus to the exclusion of all other deities.
- Give a copy of the New Testament. If a Hindu desires to study the Bible, suggest that he or she begin with the Gospel of John. Point out passages that explain salvation (such as those highlighted in the FAITH gospel presentation.)[9]

As a Team Leader, you will lead your Team to visit persons who have intersected their lives in some way with your church. You will have opportunity to encounter people from a great variety of belief systems by conducting Opinion Poll visits and by being available for divine appointments. You certainly will encounter individuals from a host of religious (and nonreligious) backgrounds as you increase in sensitivity to those whom God intersects with your life.

In general, consider these actions when encountering or seeking to witness to some from another belief system:

- Pray and trust the Holy Spirit to use the gospel message to reach the hearts and minds of these individuals.
- Share your evangelistic testimony as learned in FAITH training. If not given the opportunity to share the FAITH gospel presentation, be prepared to share your testimony of coming to and growing in personal faith in Jesus Christ as your Lord and Savior. A non-Christian cannot discount your personal experience and testimony, even though he or she may not believe the Bible or in God.
- Use words and concepts that are simple and clear; do not use "churchy" words.
- Share the assurance of salvation that God's grace gives you. Indicate your hope in the resurrection. Make sure you communicate that your assurance is derived from God's grace and not from your good works or your ability to be spiritual.
- Emphasize the message of the cover picture on *A Step of Faith,* and indicate how you identify with its message. Encourage the person to share what he understands about and how she relates to the message of the picture.
- Be willing to develop relationships with and build bridges to people. Seek to enroll the individual or family members in Sunday School and to provide ongoing ministry to them.
- Keep the focus of the gospel message Christ-centered.
- Do not try to engage the person in an argument about theology. Seek to share the simple message of good news of salvation that is available only through faith in Jesus Christ.

[1] From "Developing Leaders," *Associational Handbook,* Tab 5-3, © Copyright 1998 LifeWay Christian Resources of the Southern Baptist Convention. All rights reserved.

[2] From Ralph W Hodge, *Taking the Next Step: a Guide for New Church Members* (Nashville: Convention Press, 1996), 13.

[3] Ibid., 22-28.

[4] From the "Belief Bulletin: Judaism," published by the North American Mission Board of the Southern Baptist Convention. Reprinted with permission.

[5] From the "Belief Bulletin: Roman Catholicism," published by the North American Mission Board of the Southern Baptist Convention. Reprinted with permission.

[6] Adapted from the "Belief Bulletins: The Mormon Puzzle Comparison Chart: Mormonism vs. Christianity"; "A Closer Look at the Book of Mormon"; and "A Closer Look at the Mormon Plan of Salvation," all published by the North American Mission Board of the Southern Baptist Convention. Reprinted with permission.

[7] Adapted from the "Belief Bulletins: "Jehovah's Witnesses" and "A Closer Look at Jehovah's Witnesses View of Christ," both published by the North American Mission Board of the Southern Baptist Convention. Reprinted with permission.

[8] From the "Belief Bulletin: Islam," published by the North American Mission Board of the Southern Baptist Convention. Reprinted with permission.

[9] From the "Belief Bulletin: Hinduism," published by the North American Mission Board of the Southern Baptist Convention. Reprinted with permission.

Contributors

David Apple, manager, Sunday School/FAITH Training Section, Sunday School/FAITH Ministry Department, leads the section that provides FAITH Training Clinics, along with other Sunday School leadership training events. With consultants and FAITH church leaders, David helps shape the experiences participants receive at a clinic. He also continues to shape FAITH through his writing.

Bobby Welch, senior pastor, First Baptist Church, Daytona Beach, Florida, devotes a significant amount of time to helping other churches discover the benefits of FAITH. He especially enjoys the time he spends teaching FAITH Basic to first-time Learners in his own church—and to seeing Learners become confident and capable of sharing their faith.

Doug Williams, national consultant for the FAITH Sunday School Evangelism Strategy, lives in Oneonta, Alabama. Often accompanied by his wife, Rachel, Doug travels extensively as he teaches FAITH Training Clinics. When he is home, he and Rachel participate in FAITH alongside their son, Bruce, who directs the FAITH strategy at First Baptist Church, Oneonta.

CHRISTIAN GROWTH STUDY PLAN

Preparing Christians to Serve

In the **Christian Growth Study Plan (formerly Church Study Course),** this book **Building Bridges Through FAITH: The Journey Continues Journal** is a resource for course credit in **three** Leadership and Skill Development diploma plans. To receive credit, read the book, complete the learning activities, show your work to your pastor, a staff member or church leader, then complete the following information. This page may be duplicated. Send the completed page to:

**Christian Growth Study Plan
127 Ninth Avenue, North, MSN 117
Nashville, TN 37234-0117
FAX: (615)251-5067**

For information about the Christian Growth Study Plan, refer to the current Christian Growth Study Plan Catalog. Your church office may have a copy. If not, request a free copy from the Christian Growth Study Plan office (615/251-2525).

COURSE CREDIT INFORMATION

Please check the appropriate box indicating the diploma you want to apply this credit. You may check more than one.

❑ **Adult Leadership—The Adult Leader's Role in Ministry, Witnessing, and Reaching People (LS-0037, Sunday School)**
❑ **General Church Leadership—Developing the Ministry and Evangelism Skills of the General Church Leader (LS-0050, Sunday School)**
❑ **Adult Leadership—Developing Ministry and Evangelism Skills (LS-0054, Sunday School)**

PARTICIPANT INFORMATION

Social Security Number (USA Only)	Personal CGSP Number*		Date of Birth (Mo., Day, Yr.)

Name (First, MI, Last)		Home Phone
❑Mr. ❑Miss ❑Mrs. ❑		

Address (Street, Route, or P.O. Box)	City, State, or Province	Zip/Postal Code

CHURCH INFORMATION

Church Name

Address (Street, Route, or P.O. Box)	City, State, or Province	Zip/Postal Code

CHANGE REQUEST ONLY

❑Former Name

❑Former Address	City, State, or Province	Zip/Postal Code

❑Former Church	City, State, or Province	Zip/Postal Code

Signature of Pastor, Conference Leader, or Other Church Leader	Date

*New participants are requested but not required to give SS# and date of birth. Existing participants, please give CGSP# when using SS# for the first time. Thereafter, only one ID# is required. *Mail To:* Christian Growth Study Plan, 127 Ninth Ave., North, MSN 117, Nashville, TN 37234-0117. Fax: (615)251-5067